AMERICAN SON

RICHARD BLOW

AMERICAN SON

A PORTRAIT OF
John F. Kennedy, Jr.

HENRY HOLT AND COMPANY · NEW YORK

Henry Holt and Company, LLC
Publishers since 1866
115 West 18th Street
New York, New York 10011

Henry Holt® is a registered trademark of
Henry Holt and Company, LLC.

Library of Congress Cataloging-in-Publication Data
Blow, Richard.
American son : a portrait of John F. Kennedy, Jr. / Richard Blow.—1st ed.
p. cm.
ISBN 0-8050-7051-6 (hb)
1. Kennedy, John F. (John Fitzgerald), 1960–1999
2. Children of presidents—United States—Biography.
3. Celebrities—United States—Biography. I. Title.

E843.K42 B58 2002
973.922'092—dc21   2002017229
[B]

Henry Holt books are available for special promotions
and premiums. For details contact: Director, Special Markets.

First Edition 2002

Designed by Victoria Hartman

Printed in the United States of America
3   5   7   9   10   8   6   4   2

For my parents

AMERICAN SON

PROLOGUE

Certain places always bring back memories of certain people. Most Manhattanites associate Tribeca, the downtown neighborhood just below SoHo, with the artists, actors, and financiers who call the place their home. But inevitably, I associate the area with John F. Kennedy, Jr., and when I go there a part of me still expects to see him around every corner. I think of him riding his bike over the cobblestone streets or walking on sunny weekend mornings with his wife, Carolyn, and their dog, Friday. I picture him in sunglasses, backpack slung over his shoulders, rollerblading down lower Broadway on his way home from work in the evening, weaving his way through the busy traffic as the streetlights glow overhead.

One morning not long ago I made a point of paying a visit to North Moore Street, the two-block-long passage in Tribeca where John and Carolyn lived in a loft apartment. On one corner of their block, construction workers hammered and sawed as they converted an old warehouse into luxury apartments. Down the street, Bubby's, a popular local hangout, was bustling with a brunch crowd of happy new couples and forty-something parents with their young children.

I hadn't walked down North Moore since an unhappy afternoon in late July 1999, just a few days after John and Carolyn died. The street had looked very different then. A procession of taxis and limos and cars with out-of-state license plates had nudged and honked its way down the block. Mourners were placing flowers and notes in front of 20 North Moore, John's building. One of them had left a front page from the *New York Post* of November 23, 1963, the day after John's father had been assassinated. Camera crews and television reporters had set up positions along the block like guardposts.

Now they were gone. The mourning was over, along with the optimistic days when John and Carolyn walked along, laughing through these streets, planning their future even as they did their best to ignore the inevitable stares of passersby and the constant intrusions of photographers. Everything looked the same, but felt different.

I decided to walk to the river. John's apartment was just a couple of blocks from the Hudson, and he stored a kayak at a nearby boathouse. He loved to take it out after sunset, when he was nearly invisible on the black water. John told me that it was peaceful darting across the Hudson under cover of night, the lights of Manhattan twinkling to the east, the shadowy New Jersey waterfront to the west, the chugging of boats and the faint roar of planes blanketing him as he skimmed over the surface. He loved the solitude, the calm of it. True, kayaking at night wasn't exactly safe. It could get tricky when a boat pilot didn't see John or he was paddling home and the tide turned against him. But he didn't mind. He thought that invisibility, no matter how fleeting, was worth a little risk.

John described his fondness for kayaking to me one night in June 1995, soon after I began working as an editor at *George*, the political magazine he was starting. Sharing details of our hobbies and interests, all of us at *George* were just beginning to get to know one another. But understanding John required far more than simply learning his likes and dislikes.

Over the time I worked at *George,* from May 1995 until a few months after John died on July 16, 1999, I slowly came to see that he was far more complex than the public realized—more complex, certainly, than I had suspected when I first started working at the magazine. He was one of the most photographed people in the world, and his image was ubiquitous. Perhaps because of that we all believed we knew him. But those countless pictures never explained him; the things that explained John were not visible in photographs.

I had the opportunity to observe John from a different vantage point: professional proximity. I wasn't his best friend or favorite employee. John did not confess to me his darkest secrets or most painful revelations. In truth, much of our early relationship was marked by stark disagreements and mutual skepticism. But we spent four years working closely together, in the confines of an intimate office where the pressures of publishing a magazine merged with those of being employed by one of the most famous people in the world. During that time I came to be fascinated by John Kennedy and, what is more, to admire and respect him. I saw him struggle, torn between creating a life for himself and trying to fulfill the world's expectations. Many people would judge John by what he did not accomplish. I was increasingly impressed by what he did.

John's four years at *George* challenged him and forced him to grow. His mother, Jacqueline Kennedy Onassis, died in May 1994, and with her passing the Kennedy-watching public narrowed its attention to John. He left a secure and prestigious trade, the law, to join the media, a profession whose practitioners had hounded him since he was a child. And he was editing a magazine that broke new editorial ground but struggled critically and commercially.

His decision to become a magazine editor was neither widely understood nor widely applauded. According to, well, almost everybody, John F. Kennedy, Jr., should never have founded a magazine, certainly not one that put movie stars on its cover. Editing *George* was said to trivialize John. He was supposed to go into politics. Many Americans wanted him to be president one day, and any lesser achievement would disappoint. Besides, what did he know about journalism?

But it wasn't only the task of running *George* that changed John's life during those years. About a year after starting the magazine, he got married. His bride was a glamorous beauty named Carolyn Bessette, an intense and emotional woman who, despite John's near-desperate attempts to protect her, was shaken by the close scrutiny her marriage provoked. John's relationship with Carolyn was far from simple, but he struggled to make it work. Born into a clan that left little room for self-determination, he longed for a family he could truly call his own.

A new business, a new visibility, and a new marriage—these things precipitated a coming of age for John, a time when he was putting his youth behind him and preparing for what I believe would have been a remarkable future. These were not easy years for him, and so working for him was not always easy. Sometimes I longed to quit *George*. Other times I was certain I would be fired. But I survived long enough to find it hard to imagine life without John Kennedy—only to face that absence far sooner than I had ever expected.

Down in Tribeca during that recent visit, I couldn't help but think of all the things that might have been. But that was a pointless exercise, and so I forced myself to think of something more true to the man he was: I imagined John on the river, setting out at nightfall, dipping his blades into the black water, dodging the tugboats and moving, always in motion, moving forward.

One

For four years, whenever I told someone that I worked at *George* magazine, the response invariably came back, "Oh, did you know John before?"—as if to get a job there you had to be a Kennedy acolyte. At first, I found the question slightly insulting. Before signing on at *George,* I'd never met John Kennedy, nor even wanted to.

In the winter of 1995, I was thirty years old and happily editing a Washington magazine called *Regardie's.* A freewheeling monthly with an underdog's attitude, *Regardie's* covered everything from mayors to murders. (Back then, Washington was saddled with a mayor who wouldn't go away, the crack-smoking Marion Barry, and, not coincidentally, a whole lot of murders.) Owner Bill Regardie was a D.C. businessman who felt so neglected in his politics-obsessed hometown that he started a magazine and named it after himself. Malcolm Forbes had done it, right?

A pleasantly plump man with an owlish face and a smile that suggested mischief, Regardie was never afraid of publicity; he once called the *Washington Post* to leak the news that he'd had liposuction. (The *Post* ran with it.) He had a reputation for being eccentric. Once, in the 1980s, he smashed an art director's entire office to pieces with a baseball bat. But he was also loyal and generous. When one of his editors was weighing a job offer from another magazine, Regardie bought the man a Porsche. Of course, that was the '80s. By the end of the decade, a recession had hit Washington hard, and Regardie temporarily closed his magazine.

I helped him restart it, coming on board not long after Bill Clinton took the oath of office in January 1993. It was a fortuitous time to edit a Washington magazine. Twelve years of Republican rule had left the capital listless, stocked with the same well-stuffed white men who had rolled into town with Ronald Reagan in 1980. The Clintonites were younger, more diverse, and more idealistic, and the city perked up with their arrival as a plant stretches toward the sun. It's hard to imagine now, given the disappointments that followed, but in the beginning Bill Clinton changed Washington for the better. He gave the city a sense of purpose.

Regardie's was a small magazine with a staff you could fit comfortably into a VW Bug. We were young and hungry and produced a magazine that oscillated between the amateurish and the unexpectedly noteworthy. Our competition was the *Washington Post,* which covered local news almost as an afterthought, and *Washingtonian* magazine, which seemed to consider D.C. a vast food court for suburban housewives. Editorially speaking, *Regardie's* had room to maneuver.

Washington is teeming with great stories, gripping tales of power, ego, ambition, idealism, sex, greed, envy, and corruption. Those were the kinds of narratives we tried to publish, and by mid-1994, *Regardie's* was attracting some attention. One evening Clinton aide George Stephanopoulos cornered me at the gym where we were both members. *Regardie's* had published an item about a bank loan Stephanopoulos had received on suspiciously generous terms, and the young political celebrity was anxious to rebut it. "I can't believe your fucking magazine printed that crap," Stephanopoulos fumed, jabbing a finger toward my chest. As sweaty Stairmaster devotees looked on in surprise, Stephanopoulos spent the next five minutes trashing me and my magazine. I couldn't have been happier. To a young journalist, a strong reaction—even a hostile one—from a person in power is the highest praise.

As life at *Regardie's* heated up, so did my personal life: I had fallen in love with a kind and beautiful woman named Nyssa Tussing. We met at a party in November 1993. I found her smart and funny, with a gentle streak that drew me toward her. And it didn't hurt that we'd grown up one town apart in southern Connecticut. Before long, we began spending all our spare time together.

But just when life seemed to have settled into a comfortable groove, angry rumbles from the heartland began to shake Washington. On November 8, 1994, American voters dispatched a bilious horde of Clinton-hating crusaders to storm the capital. With Newt Gingrich as standard bearer, these hard-right conservatives took office in January 1995 and quickly locked the Clintonites in a mutually destructive death grip. Suddenly, the optimistic vigor of the city flagged. These outsiders did not want to use the government to help the country. They wanted to shut it down.

Nyssa and I felt the aftershocks almost at once. She worked for Democratic Party chair David Wilhelm, a well-meaning man widely blamed by inside-the-Beltway types for the Democrats' losses. Bill Clinton's modest tax increase and Hillary Clinton's health care fiasco were the more likely culprits, but the White House needed a scapegoat. In short order Wilhelm was packing his bags. And before he was long gone, Nyssa lost her job as well.

As if that weren't enough, the city of Washington was beginning to take its toll on us. One morning in February 1995 I walked out of my apartment building to find my car propped up on cement blocks. A week later a tenant in my building was greeted in the lobby by four men with guns. They forced him back to his apartment, where his girl-friend was showering. Two of the intruders escorted the tenant to a nearby ATM, while the other two waited in the apartment for a beeper message signaling that the job was successful. The robbery chilled me: Nyssa and I had walked through that lobby not half an hour earlier.

Then, in the first week of March 1995, Bill Regardie came into my office, plopped his gentle bulk down in a chair, wheezed an apologetic sigh, and announced that he was pulling the plug on *Regardie's*. The magazine was hemorrhaging cash, he explained. We couldn't get enough advertising. He was rich, but not rich enough.

Newt Gingrich running amok, *Regardie's* down the tubes—I was unemployed and uninspired. Several weeks of job-hunting yielded no exciting prospects. Not until early April, during my weekly basketball game with a group of fellow writers, did I catch wind of something intriguing. "Have you heard about this new political magazine JFK Jr. is starting in New York?" one player asked me as we were shooting warm-up baskets.

"Nope," I admitted.

"It's going to be called *George* or something," he said. "Might be worth checking out."

A political magazine based in New York? Edited by John F. Kennedy, Jr.? It sounded a little improbable. And what kind of a name was *George* anyway?

On the other hand, I thought, it would get me out of Washington.

• • •

The first step seemed to be contacting John F. Kennedy, Jr. But how? *George* wasn't listed in the phone book. Nor, not surprisingly, was JFK Jr. What then? I didn't play football with any Kennedys who could serve as back channels. Once I had gone on a date with a woman who later married one of John's cousins, but, well, she later married one of John's cousins. I didn't even know where she lived anymore.

I turned to my basketball friend for help. He knew the man John had hired as *George's* editor, a magazine veteran named Eric Etheridge. I'd heard of Etheridge. As an editor at *Harper's, Rolling Stone,* and the *New York Observer,* he had developed a reputation among magazine types as smart and literary, the kind of editor writers appreciate. That was encouraging, so I called to introduce myself. Etheridge said he was going to be in Washington the very next week. Why didn't we meet for breakfast at the Hay-Adams?

On April 4, I walked into the dining room of that august hotel, about three blocks from the White House, and immediately saw someone who didn't look like he came from Washington. Dressed in a casual tan suit cut more fashionably than anything worn on Capitol Hill, Eric was tall and thin, with floppy brown hair and opaque glasses. I joined him and ordered coffee, pancakes, and eggs, which is the kind of thing you do when you're unemployed and someone else is picking up the tab.

Stabbing vigorously at a bowl of fresh strawberries, Eric couldn't contain his enthusiasm as he talked about this new project. It would be, he said, a political magazine for Americans turned off by political magazines—the kind of readers most Washingtonians consider huckle-berries. *George* would be the country's first mass-market political journal. He needed someone who knew Washington, but was not of Washington.

The concept struck a chord with me. My father had been an editor, too, at *Reader's Digest,* a lucrative but middlebrow publication that cultural elitists loved to mock. Remember the jokes when *Reader's Digest* published a condensed version of the Bible? I do.

So even though I attended Yale and spent three years studying American history in a Harvard doctoral program, I had always felt a kinship with outsiders and the less-than-powerful. And that part of me relished the idea of a political magazine that Washington might scorn but ordinary Americans would want to pick up.

I didn't much care that John F. Kennedy, Jr., would be *George*'s editor-in-chief. Born in 1964, I was too young to have been transformed by President Kennedy; Woodward and Bernstein were my heroes. Nor did I ever pay particular attention to Jacqueline Kennedy Onassis, probably because I only knew her as the world's most famous widow. In general, I just wasn't that interested in celebrities.

If anything, the little I knew of John made me wary. He was strikingly handsome, dated gorgeous women, and reputedly wasn't the sharpest knife in the drawer. He'd gone to Brown, which, although it had recently acquired cachet among the rich and trendy, wasn't known for its academic rigor. (If you failed a class at Brown, you could simply excise it from your transcript.) Most worrisome, Kennedy had no experience as a journalist. He hadn't even had a job in a year or so.

Then again, I was collecting unemployment checks from the D.C. government. I was hardly in a position to judge.

At breakfast, Eric asked me to send him a list of ten or twelve possible story ideas for *George*. I typed up every one I could think of, then did what any self-respecting journalist would do—asked my writer friends for theirs. (If I get the job, I assured them, you'll get the story assignments.) In mid-April, I faxed Eric forty-six story ideas for the as yet nonexistent *George* magazine.

About a week later, Eric called from New York. John Kennedy wanted to meet me.

· · ·

On the morning of April 24, I put on a blue suit and hopped on an 8:00 Metroliner to New York. With sunlight pouring in from the east, the train rolled through the frazzled industrial gauntlet of Baltimore, Wilmington, Philadelphia, and Trenton, New Jersey. Close to New York, a fire was raging in the Meadowlands, the grossly polluted but strangely majestic swamps of northern New Jersey. As the swamp grass burned, preternaturally orange flames leapt hungrily toward the sky and inky black smoke rolled over the train, obscuring the view from my window until we plunged underground to travel below the Hudson River and into Penn Station.

After Eric's call, I had done some research on my prospective employer to prepare myself. Reviewing it during the train ride, I realized that I was more than a little nervous. While it was convenient to call this man a celebrity, the label was reductive and not particularly accurate; he was an iconic part of American political and cultural history, and his life was truly unusual.

John F. Kennedy, Jr., was born on November 25, 1960, less than three weeks after his father had defeated Richard Nixon in a very close presidential election. Son of the world's most glamorous parents, the first baby ever born to a president-elect, John was famous from the moment of his birth. As an infant in the White House, he was rambunctious and adorable, a mop-headed little boy introduced to the nation through charming black-and-white pictures that portrayed him peering out from under the Oval Office desk, rushing into his father's arms, and sitting contemplatively in a rowboat on a sandy beach. There appeared to be more pictures of baby John with his father than with his mother, perhaps because JFK appreciated the political value of a beautiful child, while Jacqueline Bouvier Kennedy preferred to preserve more privacy for her children.

John's blissful White House life came to an end on November 22, 1963, just three days before his third birthday, when President Kennedy was assassinated. At his father's funeral, the little boy had raised his right hand to his forehead to salute the president's casket. Among the thousands of pictures of John F. Kennedy, Jr., this one would become and forever remain the most famous. Father and son had become eternally connected in the world's memory and imagination.

Upon leaving the White House, Jackie Kennedy took John and his older sister, Caroline, to New York City, where they lived in an apartment at 1040 Fifth Avenue, across the street from Central Park. John grew up there, remaining in his mother's book-lined home even during the years from 1968 to 1975, when she was married to Greek shipping magnate Aristotle Onassis. When school was in session, Jackie stayed in New York to watch Caroline and John, who continued to be an irrepressible, energetic, and friendly child. As Jackie said in a 1967 newspaper interview, "Caroline is more withdrawn. John, well, he's something else. John makes friends with everybody. Immediately." Young John also fell in love with the outdoors and with all modes of transportation. From skis to horses, planes to boats, and motorcycles to helicopters, he was addicted to motion.

In 1975, after graduating from Collegiate, a private boys' school on the Upper West Side, John headed to Phillips Andover Academy, a Massachusetts prep school. Whipcord thin, he had curly brown hair and eyes that, in pictures, looked almost sullen. Throughout his adolescence, his mother—who did not want John to grow up feeling entitled—encouraged him to partake of "real" experiences. During high school summers, he helped rebuild a Guatemalan village devastated by an earthquake and dug fence holes on the Wyoming ranch of Grateful Dead lyricist John Perry Barlow, a friend of a friend of Jackie's. He was not, however, a diligent student. After failing a final exam at Andover, he was compelled to stay an extra year before heading to Brown.

The Providence, Rhode Island, college was an unexpected choice for John—the Kennedys were a Harvard family—and he made unusual choices there. (Unusual, at least, for a Kennedy whose primary interest was expected to be politics.) John's main extracurricular activity was theater, where he was said to be gifted but, again, not particularly driven. He lived in a house off-campus and joined the fraternity Phi Kappa Psi. Throughout his Brown years he was reputed to be the object of continuing female obsession. One magazine claimed that women slept in the hallways outside his dorm room. But judging by a string of long-term relationships, he seemed more interested in monogamy than in exploiting the easy availability of beautiful women.

John graduated from Brown in 1983 and spent the following year alternating between adventure and public service, wreck-diving off the coast of New England and volunteering for Mother Teresa in India. Back in New York in 1984, he took a low-level planning job at New York City's Office of Business Development. He also appeared in the occasional Off-Broadway play. It was reported that he wanted to be an actor, but that his mother disapproved and pressured him to get a law degree. In September 1986, he enrolled at New York University Law School—an excellent school, but again, an untraditional choice for a man who could have attended any law school he desired. His undergraduate grades might have been unimpressive, but what law school would have said no to the son of John and Jackie Kennedy?

As he neared thirty, John matured into an extraordinarily handsome man. Losing some of its youthfulness, his face acquired a leaner, more chiseled look. He cut his hair and shed the slightly sloppy mass of curls he'd had as a teenager. He appeared more self-confident— and self-aware—about his good looks than in the past. (How could he not? In 1988, after all, *People* magazine named him "The Sexiest Man Alive.") Though he was regularly photographed shirtless in Central Park, playing frisbee or touch football, he also began dressing up for work, and looked comfortable and elegant in a suit.

Perhaps not surprisingly, his girlfriends grew steadily more high-profile. He was rumored to have had flings with a voluptuous blond model named Ashley Richardson, the actress Sarah Jessica Parker, and Madonna. (The veracity of these gossip-page reports was hard to determine; John never gave interviews about his personal life, or anything else, for that matter.) In 1988, he began a six-year on-again, off-again relationship with actress Daryl Hannah. For a while they lived together in her Upper West Side apartment.

After graduating from NYU in 1989, John joined the office of Manhattan district attorney Robert Morgenthau. He struggled, however, to pass the New York bar exam. Many would-be lawyers fail the first time they take the test, but John failed twice—and applicants who fail three times are compelled to resign from the D.A.'s office. The second setback came in February 1990 and prompted the infamous *New York Post* headline THE HUNK FLUNKS. Making the best of an embarrassing situation, John admitted, "I'm clearly not a major legal genius." But he saved himself from even deeper mortification by passing the bar in July 1990.

Over four years at Morgenthau's office, John prosecuted six criminal cases and won them all. It was whispered that Morgenthau assigned him cases that not even the most inept prosecutor could bungle. Yet no one denied that John seemed to have a way with juries. They found him modest, sincere, and believable.

In July 1993, John mysteriously quit the D.A.'s office. His next public moment did not come until the morning of May 20, 1994, when he stood outside his mother's apartment to inform reporters that Jacqueline Kennedy Onassis had died of non-Hodgkin's lymphoma. "Last night at around 10:15 my mother passed on," he said quietly. "She was surrounded by her friends and her family and her books and the people and the things that she loved. She did it in her own way and in her own terms, and we all feel lucky for that, and now she's in God's hands."

John's short statement had a profound impact on his life. That he, and not his sister Caroline, had delivered the sad news suggested to many observers that John was to be the visible Kennedy, the heir will-ing to step into the public eye. With his mother gone, Kennedy-watchers suggested, it was time for John to grow up, to figure out what he wanted to do with his life. Maybe, they said, he was ready for poli-tics: John had spoken with a gentle, somber eloquence that hinted at a previously unseen seriousness within this young man.

After that painful moment, however, John dropped out of sight for a while. In the autumn of 1994, he reappeared to campaign for his Uncle Ted's reelection in Massachusetts. At about the same time, there were scattered whispers that he had a new girlfriend, another willowy blonde, though no one was certain of her identity. And then, in the spring of 1995, came the first rumors that he was starting a political magazine.

Preparing to meet this icon, I was unsure what to make of his résumé. John was clearly very different from his sister. Caroline had gone to law school at Columbia and passed the bar on her first try, but never actually practiced law. After marrying architect and museum designer Edwin Schlossberg in 1986, she had given birth to three chil-dren. Caroline consistently kept an extremely low public profile.

John seemed to have a more ambivalent relationship toward the press, sometimes resenting its intrusions, other times providing pho-tographers with ample opportunities to take his picture. Was he a public or private man? John couldn't seem to make up his mind.

He also seemed conflicted about his relationship to the sprawling Kennedy clan. It was said that his mother had disapproved of the Kennedy family's influence on her son, and pictures of him cavorting with his rambunctious cousins were rare. Even so, John showed up in court at the 1991 rape trial of William Kennedy Smith to show sup-port for his cousin, who was acquitted.

John did promote his father's legacy through, for example, the Pro-files in Courage Awards, given out annually by the Kennedy School of

Government at Harvard. But although he was constantly asked, he displayed no desire to go into politics. In the summer of 1987, he'd worked in the Justice Department's Civil Rights Division—but this was the Reagan Justice Department, and the head of the division, William Bradford Reynolds, was hardly a liberal in the Kennedy mode. In August 1988, John gave a brief but worshipfully received speech at the Democratic convention in Atlanta. But all in all, his political involvement had been limited, if not perfunctory. He spent more time on the boards of nonprofit organizations that took a decidedly nonpolitical bent, such as the Robin Hood Foundation, which sponsored antipoverty programs, and Naked Angels, a theater group.

John F. Kennedy, Jr., would turn thirty-five in 1995. He was still a young man but middle age was looming. His course in life seemed uncertain and pointed in no specific direction—certainly not toward the media.

Why then was he joining it?

. . .

From grimy, claustrophobic Penn Station I took a cab to 1633 Broadway, the home of Hachette Filipacchi Magazines, the media company that would be publishing *George*. Hachette's building, an ominous black and silver skyscraper, seemed to have sucked the light out of the surrounding neighborhood. Fiftieth and 51st streets to the south and north were dark, grungy blocks dotted with hole-in-the-wall donut joints and neon-lit sex shops with names like "Bare Elegance." Even the Winter Garden theater across Broadway—presenting *Cats* for the umpteenth year—looked sad and forlorn.

On the forty-first floor, the elevator opened onto a small, austere lobby decorated with generic gray carpet and cheaply framed photographs from Hachette magazines. There were models in bathing suits (from *Elle*), home interiors (*Metropolitan Home*), and soaring planes (*Flying*). Flanking a receptionist's desk were four white doors, each with a black digital keypad about waist-high.

Summoned by the receptionist, Eric Etheridge punched in a code on one of the keypads and ushered me through the door facing west, which led to a long corridor. A massive *George* logo, banana-yellow letters against an orange-soda background, occupied one entire wall. The corridor opened onto a hallway tracing the building's perimeter, flanked by offices on the window side and cubicles toward the interior. It felt like one of those old Habitrail tunnels for gerbils and other small rodents.

Overflowing with magazines and newspapers, Eric's office was down the hall toward the north side of the building. A small television was tuned to C-Span, and the voice of some congressional orator droned like a white-noise machine. Through the window behind Eric's desk, I could see across the Hudson to Giants Stadium in the Meadowlands, underneath which Bobby Kennedy's old foe, Jimmy Hoffa, may be gradually decomposing. Planes bound for Newark, La Guardia, and JFK airports crisscrossed the sky. To the north was the graceful span of the George Washington Bridge. South was the Statue of Liberty.

Eric and I were sitting chatting when I heard a knock on the door and John Kennedy stuck his head in.

I jumped to my feet.

"Hi," he said, pushing the door open and extending his hand. "I'm John."

"I know," I said, quickly standing up and shaking his hand. His grip was firm, but not self-consciously so. "I mean . . . nice to meet you."

I'll admit, I was a little taken aback. Flattering as they were, photographs did not do the man justice. He was about six feet tall, with broad shoulders and a V-shaped torso tapering into a slender waist.

He wore a crisp white shirt, a simple beige tie, and a charcoal suit that fit as if he had been the designer's mannequin. He had strong thick hands and big stubby fingers, like a rugby player or a carpenter.

Almost automatically, I cross-referenced his parents. His build clearly came from his father. The hawkish nose, however, reminded me of Jackie Onassis. That thick Irish hair, practically stitched into his scalp—definitely JFK. But its warm chestnut color was his mother's, as were his brown eyes. His body exuded a masculine strength, but there was something warm and feminine in his eyes. On balance, I decided, he looked slightly more like his mother than his father. The center of his face—eyes, nose—was dominated by her features. But he seemed to have inherited the best of both his parents, so that he was more attractive than either.

I had feared that meeting John F. Kennedy, Jr., would leave me tongue-tied. After all, it's easy to consider yourself a celebrity skeptic when you've never actually met one. But that "Hi, I'm John" calmed me. It was appealingly understated, as if we'd met at a beach barbecue and he'd handed me a beer. It helped that his body language was relaxed and casual. He seems normal enough, I thought.

We shifted to his corner office, whose two wall-length, waist-to-ceiling picture windows looked west toward the Hudson and north toward Central Park. I could see where the park began about ten blocks away, a long green rectangle racing toward Harlem, interrupted by the steel blue oval of a reservoir—the Jacqueline Kennedy Onassis Reservoir, as I later discovered. The office was furnished with two mostly empty bookshelves, a bare desk, a black leather desk chair, and a round table of yellow wood with a couple of chairs. It was the office of a man who didn't want to get too comfortable there. "Have a seat," John said, and we both did.

Cup of coffee? John asked. Soda?

I shook my head no. Why risk spillage?

Where are you from? John continued. What do you think of Washington? How would you feel about moving to New York?

I told him about the demise of *Regardie's*, about Washington's eat-its-own-young mood, and about Nyssa, who'd been feeling politically disillusioned since the ouster of her boss and, like me, was ready to flee D.C. I wouldn't normally talk about my girlfriend in a job interview, but something about his manner suggested that such informality was perfectly acceptable.

Not surprisingly, John also had some strong opinions about Washington. He believed in its potential, but he was frustrated with its insularity, self-importance, and partisanship. He confessed that he never liked visiting the city—it made him claustrophobic. "I hope this magazine gets read in Washington," John said. "But I'd prefer it get read everywhere else."

His voice was of medium tenor, with none of the broad Massachusetts accent of his father, nor his mother's fabled whisper. He chuckled a lot. In fact, throughout the interview he often seemed wryly amused about one thing or another. He also kept shifting in his chair, turning to stare toward the park. I couldn't tell if I was boring him or if he just found it hard to stay seated. And though our talk felt more like a conversation than an interview, the directness of John's questions unnerved me, because really, why would he be interested in me? I liked my life just fine, but as I spoke of it, it suddenly seemed merely adequate—compared to his, anyway.

I was relieved when the conversation turned to the magazine. *George* was inspired by a new political reality, John explained—the first of many times I would hear him make this argument. Thanks to Vietnam and Watergate–inspired disillusionment, as well as the growing power of the entertainment business, most Americans paid little attention to politics except when it came wrapped in popular culture—in music by Bruce Springsteen, or on TV, in a show like *Roseanne,* or in the movies. Especially the movies. In peacetime, Hollywood captivated Americans far more than Washington did, a truth that politicians had long resisted but were finally conceding. Grasping for relevance like drowning men fighting for life preservers, they were hastily adopting more cinematic styles of dressing, speaking, and posing. And they were jumping on the bandwagons of pop culture: MTV, talk radio, late-night TV shows. Those forums could be risky. They could backfire, making politicians look silly and uncool. But pop culture had helped Bill Clinton win the 1992 election, while the inability to speak America's common language had made George Bush look feeble and out of touch.

Yet even as Washington gazed admiringly west, John said, the stars in Los Angeles were turning to the nation's capital for inspiration. From Barbra Streisand on the left to the ultra-conservative Charlton Heston, celebrities were speaking out on issues, forming political action committees, hosting fund-raisers, and testifying on Capitol Hill. Whether they truly cared about politics or simply enjoyed the appearance of substance was sometimes questionable, but the power of celebrity activism was not. When stars spoke, Americans listened. Many people seemed to trust these marquee names at least as much as they did politicians, and sometimes more.

That reality, however, was not acknowledged by the political press. The existing handful of small, partisan political journals—mouthpieces of elite culture such as *The New Republic* and *National Review*— either ignored this dialectic between politics and pop culture or growled at it like a dog before a mailman. As a result, only a minuscule audience of political junkies read those magazines. Which meant, John said, that there was a need for a political publication that put civic-minded celebrities on the cover, wrote about the human side of politicians, and was beautifully designed, like *Vanity Fair* or *Rolling Stone*. *George* would entertain readers, but it would also encourage them to reconnect with politics, to get involved in civic life. Reflecting John's respect for the people who entered public service and named after George Washington, the magazine would signify an intimate appreciation of American politicians, whom we respected but still called by their first names—as if they were family members.

John's explanation left some important questions unanswered. Would *George* publish negative stories about politicians? Scandalous stories? And if *George* wasn't at least slightly salacious, would people really want to read it?

I probably should have asked those questions, but I didn't; I wanted this job more than I had half an hour before. Despite my skepticism, I found myself intrigued by my potential boss. Maybe I'd had low expectations, but John didn't come across as a playboy or a dumb jock. He twisted his grammar from time to time, and his attention continued to wander toward the window. But there was something compelling about his presence. I couldn't quite pin it down, but I felt it.

One thing I knew I liked: John Kennedy wasn't starting this magazine because he had discovered an untapped consumer demographic he could pitch to advertisers. Unlike virtually all new magazines, *George* was being founded upon an *idea*. Better still, a radical idea. Shunning insiders to reach regular Americans, John was proposing a sneak attack on the fortress of elitist political journalism. Celebrity— his own and that of others—would serve as his Trojan horse. *George* wouldn't be partisan, but it would be profoundly democratic.

It was starting to sound like a very interesting place to work.

The interview over, I stood to leave. From the corner of my eye I spied a framed picture of John and his father. Dressed in plaid overalls, white socks, and tiny shoes, John was playing on a patio while his dad watched over him. Both were smiling. A handsome father, an adorable toddler, they did not look like a president and his heir, but simply a man and his son.

"That's a wonderful picture," I blurted out.

For just a second—or was I imagining it?—John hesitated. "Thanks," he said. Was there an edge to his voice? Or was I imagining that, too?

Nice work, I thought as I rode the elevator. Now he thinks you're a groupie.

But my slip couldn't have done too much damage, because Eric called a few days later. John enjoyed talking with you, he said. Come work for *George*.

I thought about it for four or five seconds. "When do I start?"

.   .   .

Right away, it turned out. Eric offered me the job on Thursday, April 27, 1995. I began on Monday, May first. That didn't give me much time to move to New York, so I had to commute by Metroliner, heading north on Monday mornings, then back to D.C. on Friday nights.

Until I could find an apartment in Manhattan, John put me up at the New York Athletic Club on Central Park South. He was a member, and he'd lived there himself for a time after moving out of Daryl Hannah's apartment in 1994. I would learn that he loved places that felt like old New York—the city of Walter Winchell, Damon Runyon, Joseph Mitchell, and Joe DiMaggio—and the NYAC oozed tradition. Stocked with mahogany reading tables and green leather chairs, the club felt as if it hadn't opened its windows since Teddy Roosevelt's day. You could still find dusty, canvas-covered medicine balls in its sixth-floor gym, next to the stationary bikes and rowing machines.

I bunked in a tiny room on the fourteenth floor, surrounded by the sounds of a new city. When I woke up in the morning and before I fell asleep at night, I could hear the grinding of garbage trucks, the swishing of street cleaners, and the *whoo-whoo-whoo-whoo* of car alarms drifting up from the street. But the atmosphere at the club was a little snooty for my taste. Even after I'd stayed there for weeks, the doormen still gave me suspicious looks every time I entered; I looked about half a century younger than the average member, and I had a problem with one of the rules. You couldn't even walk in the front door without a jacket and tie. The Manhattan summer of 1995 was suffocatingly hot, and on those nights when I'd been working late, I couldn't bear the thought of such constriction. So I'd stumble in the back entrance, past the club's pungent dumpsters, to ride up the gray steel freight elevator and crumple into bed.

That Nyssa was moving to New York with me made the club more palatable. She set up an office in our little warren, mailing résumés and setting up interviews. Before long she found a job at Burson-Marsteller, a giant public relations firm that could use someone with her political experience.

John put us in touch with a high-powered real estate agent named Kathy Sloane. A few months before, Sloane had helped sell his mother's apartment. (Five years later, she would help Bill and Hillary Clinton buy a house in Chappaqua, New York.)

"I don't think she's going to make much of a commission off us," I warned John.

"I'll call her," he said matter-of-factly. "She'll help you."

She did. But it was the beginning of Manhattan's 1990s real estate boom, so finding an apartment wasn't easy—especially one with anything near the space and light we'd enjoyed in our Washington homes. Not until the middle of June did we discover a small but cozy one-bedroom on Manhattan's Upper West Side, just four blocks from Central Park. Soon the moving trucks arrived.

I never really got to say good-bye to my friends in Washington. *George* was off and running, and I was running with it.

Two

G*eorge* didn't have an office until the spring of 1995, but the magazine was conceived by John Kennedy and his partner, Michael Berman, more than two years earlier. The two men first met late in 1983. John, twenty-three at the time, was working in New York's Office of Business Development. Michael, twenty-six, had founded a public relations firm called PRNY and was consulting for the same department where John was assigned. As they later recalled, John enjoyed Michael's quick mind and dry humor, and Michael found John warm and funny and surprisingly creative.

Over time Michael became not just John's friend but also an informal adviser. In June 1990 he urged John to take his third try at the bar exam at an alternate location for people with special needs. John had an unusual challenge: photographers. The main testing site was New York's Jacob Javits Center, a sterile, soulless building with exterior walls made almost entirely of glass. The place was perfect for paparazzi, whose flashes were bound to unnerve the famous would-be attorney. John heeded Michael's advice, got permission to take the bar elsewhere, and passed it.

John took pride in his work in the district attorney's office, and he enjoyed talking about the different trials he had won. But he told Michael that he longed for something more entepreneurial, more adventurous. He admitted he had a short attention span, that he often thought of his future in five-year chunks and it was nearly time for something new.

So he and Michael created a holding company, Random Ventures, whose very name conceded a certain lack of direction. They considered mass-producing handmade kayaks; John had found one he loved, and he thought they could make and sell the same model. Soon enough they discovered that this particular craft was impossible to mass-produce.

In early 1993 they came up with the idea for *George*. Politics seemed to be seeping into every other arena of popular culture—why not magazines? Just as he had helped provide a spark for *Regardie's*, Bill Clinton also inspired John and Michael—not so much with his politics, but with his youth, his energy, and his use of pop culture venues such as MTV and Arsenio Hall's talk show to engage young people. John and Michael could relate. Michael understood marketing, John had an insider's view of politics. Michael worked in pop culture, John was pop culture. There was, as John would say later, a "synergy."

After hashing out the idea in the months after Clinton's inauguration, John attended a two-day seminar on magazine production, and they both financed market research asking whether people would buy such a product. The answer, in numbers larger than they had expected, was yes—especially if John's name were attached, but not exclusively. Unlike the kayaks, *George*—John came up with the name—sounded viable.

Next they had to find a backer with deep pockets. Starting in mid-1993, John and Michael began shopping *George* to publishers and private investors, but the money men were unimpressed. Politics isn't popular, they said. No one wants to read about politicians—except geeks and insiders.

Time and again John and Michael heard that the best they could hope for was a circulation of 100,000, and that it would take five years to reach even that underwhelming plateau. Other political magazines all had audiences of about that size, and none made a dime. They were underwritten by politically sympathetic good samaritans.

With such a small circulation, John and Michael's product could never attract mainstream advertisers—no profit-generating fashion, liquor, or car ads. Like a Sunday morning public affairs show, *George* would be stuck with dreary advertisements from oil companies and lobbying groups. They're called "tombstone ads," because that's what they look like, and for *George* that was also what they would signify.

Thankfully, not every media heavy was dismissive. After reading a gossip item about John and Michael in *New York* magazine in March 1995, David Pecker, the CEO of Hachette Filipacchi Magazines, picked up the phone and called Michael. Your project sounds interesting, he said. Let's talk.

Virtually invisible in New York media circles, Hachette was a division of a mammoth French conglomerate called the Lagardere Group. In addition to *Elle,* the American version of the lucrative French fashion magazine, Hachette published profitable yet humdrum titles such as *Road & Track, Woman's Day,* and *Flying*. In a magazine community dominated by the more glamorous publishers Condé Nast and Hearst, most people couldn't even pronounce the company's name, twisting ha-*shet* filla-*pocky* into *hatchet filly-packy*. Pecker, a mustachioed, slick-haired Bronx native, was an ambitious man who yearned to raise his company's profile—and his own. What faster way than by signing up JFK Jr.?

Within weeks of meeting Michael and John, Pecker agreed to invest $20 million over five years. That wasn't a lot of money—the *Talk* magazine start-up in 1999 was reported to have burned through $20 million in one year alone—but it was a start. Suddenly John and Michael had their magazine. Or at least the funding for it, along with some office space at Hachette's headquarters.

What they didn't have was anything to put on its pages. As of May, when I joined, *George* was all the high concept $20 million could buy, and time was scarce: The inaugural issue had to be shipped to the printer by the beginning of August. We had a mere three months to create *George*. Ninety days in which to figure out what stories to assign and who to assign them to. Ninety days to have those stories reported and written and edited and fact-checked and libel-proofed and photographed and designed. Ninety days to get everything right, or at least mostly right. First issues attract a lot more interest than second ones do, so they need to make a good first impression.

Moreover, this challenge was to be undertaken by a staff with a mean age of about twenty-seven. A staff stocked with editors who, by and large, knew next to nothing about politics, because, for the most part, John and Eric wanted editors who weren't politically savvy. The theory was that if a politically illiterate editor found a story interesting, so would other readers who were interested in politics but weren't junkies.

There were about a dozen of us at *George* that summer. Roughly half that number were already working when I showed up on the first of May, and the rest arrived over the next month. Crammed into cubicles on the northwest corner of the forty-first floor, we were idealistic, naive, and utterly unprepared for what we were getting into. This was true of John, too—in some important ways, especially John.

He, of course, was the editor-in-chief. How that role would be defined over the long term was unclear, but early on John did a bit of everything, from meeting with car advertisers in Detroit to generating story ideas to writing a mission statement for new hires. And he would be a presence in the magazine itself: Every month, John would write the editor's letter to introduce that issue, and he would also conduct a question-and-answer interview with a political personality. The latter was something he had agreed to reluctantly—he didn't want people to think he was claiming journalism experience that he didn't have. But Eric and Michael both agreed that it made no sense to have an asset like John Kennedy and not use him for more than a single page in *George*.

John would not actually be editing stories, however; he would not be reading first drafts, suggesting changes to the writers, or re-writing copy line by line. That was usual—line-editing is labor intensive and an inefficient use of an editor-in-chief's time. It's also a labor of love. Editors spend hours poring over sentences, hunting for the perfect word, always pushing to say something better, smarter, and faster. John had never shown a predilection for such sedentary labor.

Besides, that was why he had hired Eric Etheridge. Eric, who had the nuts-and-bolts experience John lacked, would be choosing writers, assigning stories, and supervising all the line-editing. There was bound to be some overlap in responsibilities, but it was assumed that things would iron themselves out once the magazine was rolling.

Michael, meanwhile, would run the business end of the magazine, and he was an imposing presence in his own right. A tall man with curly brown hair, he had a lean, intense face that could morph quickly from a beatific smile into a Grinchian scowl. He was smart, confident, and charming, qualities critical to the task of selling ads and marketing *George*. But he could also be curt and calculating, especially when he thought John needed someone to play the role of heavy.

Michael's number two was Elinore Carmody, a tough-talking, chain-smoking blonde who could guide him through the wilds of New York publishing. Just as Eric brought industry experience to the editorial side, Elinore, the former advertising director at the women's magazines *Mademoiselle* and *Mirabella,* would do the same for Michael.

After the editor-in-chief and publisher, the third most important job at any glossy magazine is usually that of creative director, the person who designs the magazine and selects its photographers. *George's* creative director was a wise-cracking Matt Dillon look-alike named Matt Berman. (Or, as he sometimes put it, "Matt no-relation-to-Michael Berman.") Matt took a perverse delight in proclaiming that he had never read a single book from start to finish. But he could pick up a pen and draw wonderful, graceful, and sometimes wicked caricatures without a moment's thought. Before *George,* he had worked in fashion and "shelter" magazines. He couldn't have cared less about politics, which was exactly what John and Michael wanted—someone who would bring an eye for beauty to a traditionally unglamorous arena.

Three senior editors would be editing the longer articles, the features, in the magazine. My mandate was to land big stories from inside Washington. Working with me was Gary Ginsberg, a lawyer friend of John's from Brown who'd spent time in the Clinton administration. Gary was a type that every magazine needs. He seemed to know everyone in New York and Washington, and he had a gift for getting people to tell him things, juicy tidbits that made stories racier. If a writer was having trouble getting access, Gary always knew just who to call.

Last on board as senior editor was Elizabeth "Biz" Mitchell, a quiet, waiflike blonde from the music magazine *Spin.* Biz, who lived in Brooklyn with her musician husband, was smart and funny in a dark way, like a character in a Charles Addams cartoon. Her beat was the politics of culture. It was her job to discover the rapper releasing a controversial album or the performance artist who was infuriating cultural watchdogs like Jesse Helms and Bill Bennett.

Working on the shorter pieces—the fluffy appetizers that magazine people call "the front of the book"—were three associate editors named Rachel Clark, Manny Howard, and Hugo Lindgren who came, respectively, from *Esquire, New York,* and *Metropolis,* a design magazine. Elaine Marotta, formerly of *Mademoiselle,* was the managing editor, the person who organizes the flow of copy and artwork. Finally, John and Michael shared a secretary, a fearless young woman named Rosemarie Terenzio, whom Michael had brought over from his PR company.

We were a motley but enthusiastic crew, considerably smaller in number than the staffs of a typical glossy start-up. But from the beginning, we all got along, and that was important, because we had too much to do to waste time sparring.

.   .   .

My first weeks were alternately calm and anxious—calm because we didn't have any stories to work on, anxious for the same reason. Every morning during that May and June, Eric would meet with Biz, Gary, and me to hash out the day's news. We'd sit in his office with C-Span on in the background, as if we could absorb the intricacies of Capitol Hill through osmosis. Drinking our morning coffee and eating bagels—or, in Eric's case, fresh strawberries—we'd debate how to assign stories in June that would make good reading in September. Gary and I enjoyed the meetings, because we loved talking politics and now we were actually getting paid to do just that. At Hachette, we didn't get paid very much—salaries there were far lower than industry norms. But there was nothing I would rather have been doing.

Biz disliked those meetings, though. She was used to the less collegial atmosphere at *Spin*. The competition to get stories in that magazine had been so intense, she admitted, she would hide her stories from the other editors until the last possible moment, when the articles had progressed too far for her masthead peers to question their merits. Having everyone know what she was working on unnerved her.

We needed all the articles we could get, though, because for every story we assigned that panned out, two would fizzle. The writer would suddenly develop writer's block of unprecedented severity or decide to enter the heroin phase of her career, like the journalist I couldn't get on the phone because she was in drug rehab and wasn't supposed to receive phone calls. "But she's on deadline!" I yelled. The hospital took a message.

It wasn't only writers who made life complicated. Since *George* hadn't published its first issue, the subjects of our stories had their doubts about our intentions. Could they trust us? Should they cooperate with our reporters? Many were starting to hear bits and pieces about the magazine, and their first reactions were the same as my own—they were skeptical. Especially the politicians. Elected officials are a conservative bunch when it comes to the press. If they agonized over talking to the eminently uncontroversial *New York Times,* why would they grant an interview to a flaky magazine they'd never even seen?

I had to admit that, for political journalists, we were posing some oddball questions. I'd wager that the *Washington Post* never sent the 1996 presidential candidates questionnaires inquiring about their favorite candy bar, vegetable, and band. The candidates didn't know quite how to respond. "None," answered Tennessee governor Lamar Alexander to that last question. Bob Dole's staff faxed this response: "The best king of the jungle? *George!* Everyone's favorite Jefferson? *George!* The magazine that's taking up way too much of this campaign's time? *George!*" After all that effort, the least they could have done was to fill out the questionnaire.

Even the stories that worked didn't come easy. Following negotiations with a literary agent so prolonged you'd think we were hammering out a peace treaty in Yugoslavia, best-selling novelist Caleb Carr, author of *The Alienist,* agreed to write an introductory essay. Carr was also a historian, and the combination of thriller writer and history buff felt very *George,* as we liked to say. But when deadline time arrived in mid-July, Carr simply disappeared.

After days of frantic phone-calling, Eric finally located Carr, who was ill with an ailment whose nature we could never quite ascertain. At first Eric was gentle. "I'm so sorry. By the way, are you done yet?" After sympathy failed, he got tough: "Look, how sick are you, *really?*" Carr wound up turning in an elegant essay, but the experience was bad for our blood pressure.

We had even worse luck with Gore Vidal. In early June John asked Vidal to write a piece on George Washington's image in American culture, and Vidal agreed. Thanks to my unfinished (all right, unstarted) Ph.D., I was *George's* expert on colonial America, so John handed the task of editing the crotchety genius to me. I was delighted. Thirty years old, and I was editing Gore Vidal!

My euphoria lasted until Vidal, writing from his comfortable Italian villa, faxed in his essay. As I read its opening lines, my heart sank.

He had first encountered Washington, Vidal sneered, in grade school, when compelled to read a biography of the first president—"a standard hagiography of the sort that every nation inflicts upon its young in order to make them so patriotic that they will go fight in wars not of their choosing while paying taxes for the privilege."

Following this were about four thousand equally bilious words.

Though I didn't know John well at the time, I did know that defaming a dead president was not his style. Especially the one our magazine was named after. So I faxed Vidal a delicately scripted note suggesting a few teensy-weensy changes, which I hoped might "flesh out" the piece. Within minutes, Vidal was on the phone. "People don't edit my work," he declared in a voice dry as dust. "They either use it— or they don't."

I gulped. *Regardie's* writers had never made such pronouncements. "Well, yes, Mr. Vidal, but . . ."

Vidal continued as if I weren't speaking. "You seem to know a lot about Washington—why don't *you* write the piece?"

The connection was crackly, but the sarcasm in his voice came through loud and clear.

So we killed the great man's essay. ("Killed"—that's the charming term editors use when they decide not to run an article.) Vidal later published it in a collection and recounted its origins in typically self-aggrandizing fashion. "An amiable young man who identified himself as the son of an old friend, John F. Kennedy, rang to ask me if I would write a light piece for the first issue of a nonpolitical political magazine he was starting," Vidal sniffed. "I obliged, but when asked would I add this or subtract that, I said, 'Think of this as a birthday present. You can always turn it in for something else.' He did."

I had to laugh when I read that. Even then I was sure that John would never have referred to himself as "the son of an old friend." Vidal merely wanted to remind the world that he had known John's father.

As for me, I didn't mind being erased from Vidal's account. I had quickly learned that those who had some interaction with John, no matter how small, usually deleted the go-between. It just didn't sound as impressive to say, "One of John Kennedy's editors called me. . . ."

Throughout June, John watched our work closely but rarely imposed his judgments. In editorial meetings, he often looked like he was on the verge of saying something, but then cut himself off. Telling us what to do apparently didn't feel right to him. He was confident in his vision, but uncomfortable calling himself a journalist or an editor. Though opinionated and clearly well versed in public affairs, John was smart enough to know what he didn't know—the workings of a magazine. And, I think, he knew we would resent it if he appeared to presume that he could learn in weeks the skills we had acquired over years. Maybe most important, I'm not sure John *wanted* to call himself a journalist. He'd frowned on the profession his whole life. He couldn't switch sides that quickly.

. . .

In late June, John flew to Alabama to interview former governor George Wallace, the bitter foe of Jack and Bobby Kennedy during the fight for civil rights. It was a choice with provocative subtexts: Wallace was a JFK contemporary who, in 1972, had been shot and nearly killed while running for president. He would never walk again. Why had John picked Wallace for his first interview? You couldn't call this a commercial choice; though Wallace had renounced his old beliefs, he was still best known as a practitioner of ugly racial politics. Anyway, most young people didn't have a clue who George Wallace was.

Having never conducted an interview, John brought Gary to Alabama to help. Gary had never interviewed anyone either, but he was an ideal traveling companion, smart and unobtrusive and good with logistics, which John was not. (Every day he chained his key ring to a belt loop; he admitted he'd lose it if he didn't.) Gary was a details guy. During his tenure in politics, he was the kind of staffer who operated in the background, standing behind the speaker at a press conference or whispering in a committee chairman's ear.

The two visited Wallace at his modest ranch-style home in Montgomery. Seventy-four years old, bedridden, suffering constant pain from the shooting twenty-three years earlier, the once-rabid segregationist could barely hear or speak. John and Gary were forced to write their questions on posterboard with a magic marker. John would hold up the sign and Gary would shout the question, just in case. Then the two would wait while Wallace churned out barely audible answers. A single sentence could consume a minute, slow and inexorable, like a caterpillar grinding up a leaf.

Back in New York, we dispatched the interview tapes to a transcription service. The prognosis was grim. On tape Wallace was even less intelligible than in person; we didn't have enough material to print an interview. Someone would have to return to Alabama.

John had a scheduling conflict, so this time I flew with Gary to Montgomery. We found Wallace propped up in bed watching a black-and-white television, his side table crammed with photos of himself and other politicians, including a conspicuously prominent one of him and JFK. He wore a pair of starched white pajamas. On his lap was a round, white ceramic ashtray holding seven stumpy cigar butts, one of which was still emitting a lazy trail of smoke. From time to time, Wallace would extend his right arm and clutch the ragged cigar in his thick, clumsy fingers, like one of those arcade claws that fall upon stuffed animals. Then he'd push the cigar between his pink, withered lips and inhale slowly, so slowly that the gray ash at its end never even flickered red. Though he barely moved his head, he tracked us with his eyes; Wallace's spirit lived in those smoldering eyes. *I've stared down a lot tougher than you boys,* they seemed to say. And though he braced himself before every answer, he was determined to talk no matter how much pain the effort incited. Not many people asked George Wallace for interviews anymore.

Gary and I did what we could to extract more material, but the experience felt ghoulish, as if we were pilfering loose change from beneath a pauper's mattress. Still, I was determined to ask hard questions. After being a bigot for so long, could a man truly change? On white legal-size paper I scribbled, "Do you think there will be blacks in heaven?"

A fire surged into Wallace's eyes and I involuntarily took a step back. "Of course there will," he said, his voice suddenly strong. "Of course there will."

John cut that question from the interview. He said it was confrontational and that he would never have asked it. I thought the question was fair, but I didn't argue. John might not have been an experienced journalist, but *George* was his magazine, and he was laying down a marker: He had to be comfortable with all it contained.

. . .

About once a week John would convene an editorial meeting in his office. Sitting around his table or perched on the radiator that ran along the window, drinking coffee and Diet Cokes, we'd update him on stories in progress and propose new ones. Sipping a cup of coffee, or reaching out and sipping from one of ours, John mostly listened. Often as not, he let Eric guide discussions. At times I got the impression that he was feeling us out, taking the measure of people he had surrounded himself with but did not yet trust. Other times he just seemed uncomfortable at the prospect of revealing what he thought or felt. Editorial meetings can be intimate; whether through a heated disagreement or a hesitantly proposed idea, they can expose your instincts, your passions, and your deepest beliefs. John didn't seem ready for that.

Inevitably, though, he remained the center of gravity. If John cleared his throat, all heads pivoted in his direction. If we were debating an idea, everyone would monitor John's expression. Was he frowning or nodding in agreement? When he did weigh in, he couldn't help but emphasize the distance between him and us. No matter what we might teach him about the practice of journalism, he knew more about the realities of power and politics than we ever could. He seemed to have met everyone, experienced everything. In one meeting we started discussing Richard Nixon and someone made a disparaging remark about Nixon's character.

"Actually," John said, "I always liked Nixon."

We gave him a collective you-must-be-kidding look.

"He and my father got along well after the election," John explained. "Not many people can relate to life at that level of politics. Those who do feel a bond, regardless of what party they belong to.

"After my father's death," John continued, "Nixon was very kind to my mother. He invited us to the White House once, and my mother and sister were convinced that I would spill my milk, because I always did. So we sat down to dinner and after maybe ten minutes I knocked my glass of milk all over the table."

"Was Nixon pissed?" someone asked.

John smiled and shook his head. "Nah, not at all. He helped wipe it up."

We laughed and sat for a moment, imagining towheaded John Kennedy, Jr., and doleful Dick Nixon bonding over spilled milk. But then the moment stretched out and became awkward. None of the rest of us had such good Nixon stories to tell. None of us had *any* Nixon stories to tell.

John would sense that unease and try to alleviate it, usually with humor. From time to time, he'd slip into his affectionate imitation of cousin-in-law Arnold Schwarzenegger. We'd laugh, because our boss was a great mimic; his Schwarzenegger was dead-on. And the fact that he was joking about a relative in our presence made us feel he'd taken us into his confidence.

Though John might laugh about his famous family, the rest of us lived in fear of committing a Kennedy-related faux pas. Walking into one editorial meeting, Josh Cohen, Eric's twenty-something assistant, cracked a joke with a Lee Harvey Oswald punch line. As he realized what he'd done, the color drained from his face.

But if John heard Josh's quip, he said nothing. We all breathed a sigh of relief, knowing that it could easily have been any of us. Who hasn't cracked a Kennedy joke?

After our edit meetings, we'd return to our cubicles to work the phones, calling writers like telemarketers pitching new customers. *Hello, Mr. Jones? Yes, sir, how are you today? Well, I'm calling because I represent a new magazine, and I thought you might be interested in* . . .

Eric and Michael would push John to solicit big names, literary celebrities who wouldn't ordinarily write for a new magazine but might be swayed by a phone call from John Kennedy. He'd usually make the call, but not happily. He seemed to feel he was exploiting himself, asking a personal favor, rather than making a business proposition—and he wasn't entirely wrong. If the writer said no, John felt he'd cheapened himself for naught.

Several times he asked historian Doris Kearns Goodwin to contribute, but she kept turning him down. It reached the point where he would wince if someone even mentioned her name. In another effort to score a writer, he had dinner with Harvard professor and *New Yorker* contributor Henry Louis Gates. But when I asked how it went, John snorted in disgust. "He's not going to write for us. He just wanted to have dinner with me." After the screenwriter Nora Ephron declined his request to write, John joked, "I must be losing my juice."

Gradually, however, John became a more involved and confident editor. Much as we reporters and editors like to pretend otherwise, journalism isn't rocket science. It requires curiosity, a point of view, and the ability to sniff out a compelling narrative. If you have those qualities—and John did—you can usually pick up the nitty-gritty fast.

By July, as writers started to turn in drafts of their articles, John was asserting himself more regularly. In one meeting, he didn't like a story on how Colin Powell could win the presidency. It vanished. A piece on Mexican politics bored him. Poof, it was gone.

Eric, the enthusiastic patron of both those articles, did not respond well. Even though the decisions were John's, Eric would have to deliver the bad news to the writers. Not only was that a difficult task, it was embarrassing. It represented an acknowledgment that John Kennedy, journalistic novice, and not Eric Etheridge, magazine maestro, was calling the shots at *George*.

As it happened, John was right more often than not. Perhaps because he hadn't spent his career in journalism, he had an intuition about what made good reading for regular people, readers who did not share the obsessions of the New York media elite. The Mexican politics piece, for example, didn't; it was too esoteric. But John's involvement was frustrating for Eric, who had waited years for the opportunity to run his own magazine.

Smart as he was, Eric had miscalculated. He gave every impression of thinking—and perhaps hoping—that John would be an absentee editor, popping his head into the office every few weeks to confirm that we were happily typing away. It was an understandable mistake. John was a celebrity, and celebrities don't normally hold day jobs. Particularly not one whom the press had portrayed as something akin to a golden retriever, lovable and handsome but none too bright.

Yet John had too much at stake to be laissez-faire about *George*. He knew full well that if his magazine flopped, the press would beat him like a drum. And the stakes were constantly being raised. Though John and Michael had originally expected something like forty pages of ads in our first issue, we could tell already that this number was far too conservative; *George* was shaping up to be the hot magazine for ad buyers that fall. Elinore Carmody joked that selling ads for the first issue was simply a matter of picking up the phone. (She made sure, though, that any advertiser who wanted to be in our first issue was required to buy an ad in our second.) The only downside was that the more ad pages we had—and we would finish with a record total of 186—the more stories we needed to put between them.

With our July 31 deadline looking like the edge of a cliff, the pressure started to get to John. He began to suffer the effects of Graves' disease, a thyroid disorder that sapped his energy and made him cranky. By midafternoon on many days, he would be slumping in his chair, looking mystified by his body's betrayal. To treat the condition, he would drink an iodine concoction washed down with seltzer, grimacing as he did.

As the month went on, John admitted that he was waking up at five in the morning, so taut with anxiety he could not fall back asleep. In a very real way, *George*'s debut was John's debut, and he knew it. Sometimes, in the lonely hours before the dawn, that scared him.

Three

We may have had an insanely small amount of time to create a magazine from scratch, but at least I knew how to assign and edit articles. The hardest part of my job was learning a skill I'd never anticipated needing: protecting John Kennedy. I learned how to do it the hard way—by screwing up.

In late July my old colleague Andrew Sullivan, then editor of *The New Republic,* called from Washington to say he was coming to New York.

"Great," I said. "Drop by, I'll introduce you to John." When I was twenty-two and fresh out of college, I had interned at *The New Republic* for nine months. Though I'd never felt at home there—owner Marty Peretz used to joke that I was *TNR*'s token WASP—I still had great respect for the magazine.

Sullivan did visit, and I introduced the two men, leaving them to chat in John's office. It seemed like a win-win situation. The new magazine could learn from the old, and vice versa. Besides, two editors of political magazines should know each other—or so I thought.

But I was naive; I didn't realize that even intellectual journalists can't resist writing about celebrity. A week or so later, I picked up *The New Republic* to discover that Sullivan had chronicled the encounter. "The content of *George*," Sullivan proclaimed, "is almost irrelevant." The magazine would be a "user-friendly version of celebrity-hood" for John, because "his early attempts—constantly taking his shirt off in Central Park for the benefit of strangers—were somewhat inefficient."

John wasn't giving interviews to anyone that summer. *Newsweek*, *Esquire*, and *New York* were all preparing cover stories about him, yet he refused to speak to their reporters—an awkward position for an editor whose staff was busily asking other people for interviews. But over the course of thirty-five years, John had constructed a formidable wall of privacy, and he wasn't about to dismantle it all at once. Now Sullivan had landed a valuable little scoop—thanks to me.

I e-mailed Sullivan. You've put me in a tight spot, I said. You didn't visit as a reporter. You were my guest.

"If you or John-John cannot see the point or amusement of my piece," he shot back, "then you have truly become as brain-dead as he is."

That went well, I thought, and carried the magazine into John's office to confess the bad news. He nodded when he saw me; he had already read Sullivan's article.

"I'm sorry," I said. "I had no idea he would do that. He never told me he was going to write something."

"I don't want him in this office again," John replied, and his voice had a chill I'd never heard in it before. "He's not welcome here."

Shaken, I walked out determined to keep my head down, stay out of trouble, and do my work. I had never guessed that I would have to shield John from other members of my own profession, even my old friends. But now I knew.

. . .

Such seriousness was still the exception at *George*, however, because John believed that work should be fun. Some weekends he would hide his new puppy Friday (named after the day John got him) in a duffel bag and sneak him past the building guards. With Friday slung under one arm, John would stroll into the office wearing shorts, a T-shirt, wrap-around sunglasses, and, when he was in a particularly good mood, a pair of bright red high-top Nikes. A cheerful, slightly hyperactive black-and-white Canaan, Friday would race around our corridors while John made cooing noises or wrestled him to the ground. Or John would play keepaway with a tennis ball, chucking it back and forth with one of us while Friday dashed madly to and fro trying to intercept our tosses.

John's idea of fun usually required physical activity, but there was only so much we could do amid computers and cubicles. So one balmy afternoon John decided that it was too nice to stay indoors. He dispatched an intern to buy a football, and we abandoned our desks to walk the ten blocks north to Central Park. Finding a clear patch of ground just south of the Sheep's Meadow, we divided into teams of five and played two-handed touch. John was aggressive and competitive, clearly trying to win. Josh Cohen, Eric's assistant, and associate editor Hugo Lindgren were naturally athletic. But most of us were a few notches below John's usual competition, and he didn't exactly look winded at the end of the game. Besides, it was a little distracting to play with him, since passersby kept taking pictures.

My colleagues and I were spending so much time together we could not help but blur our personal and professional lives. Occasionally when I was working late or on a weekend, Nyssa would come visit, although not too often—Hachette didn't like paying for after-hours air-conditioning, and after about ten minutes in that forty-first-floor oven, you felt like a potato in tin foil.

But our days were so long it sometimes seemed that if our significant others wanted to see us when we were actually conscious, they had to come to *George*. So I met Gary's wife, Susannah, a soft-spoken but savvy producer at NBC News, and Biz's husband, Matt, a talented guitar player in a jazz band called The Flying Neutrinos. And, before too long, I met Carolyn Bessette.

I was joining Nyssa for dinner after work one day when John offered me a ride downtown. "Carolyn's picking me up," he said. Though I'd never spoken with Carolyn, I knew she was John's girlfriend; back in May, John had recommended that Nyssa talk to Carolyn about jobs in the public relations business because Carolyn had been a publicist for Calvin Klein. They spoke over the phone, and Carolyn suggested that Nyssa not seek employment at Calvin Klein. The office atmosphere was so oppressive, Carolyn said, that when she'd put a picture of John on her desk, she'd been asked to remove it—the photo apparently didn't fit with the mandatory minimalist decor.

John and I walked out of the building lobby toward Broadway. A forest green Saab was idling in the middle of the block. As we approached, the driver's door opened and Carolyn Bessette stepped out.

The first thing that I noticed about her was her hair—blond, spaghetti-straight, plunging to the middle of her back. No professional, shoulder-length bob for this woman. And she was tall—probably six feet without heels, I guessed. She was wearing sunglasses, blue jeans, a black sleeveless top, and sandals, and her arms were long and slender and tanned.

"Carolyn, this is Rich," John said. "Rich, Carolyn."

She said hello and looked right at me and smiled. It was quite a smile.

"Nice to meet you," I said, stammering a little as I got in the car. So much for my attempt to act blasé.

In July, John threw a dinner party for the staff, a sign that he was beginning to feel more comfortable with us. From work we took the #1 subway line south to Franklin Street and trooped around the corner to 20 North Moore, riding the industrial elevator to the top floor, where it opened onto John's loft, a long, rectangular space. Occupying the entire floor, John's apartment was big enough to throw a football in. It felt palatial, though not in a gaudy way—as if its owner liked to live well, but inconspicuously.

His open kitchen was modern and spotless, separated from a wooden dining room table by a long counter. The refrigerator was overflowing with fresh fruits and vegetables. His handyman, Ephigenio Pinheiro, a middle-aged native of Portugal with a soothing demeanor and quiet, observant eyes, bustled around setting out bowls of food. John was a gracious host, making sure to spend a few minutes chatting with each of us. Another famous person might have been nervous letting a group of new coworkers into his home; John seemed to realize that we might be nervous being let in.

He had majored in American history at Brown, and his bookshelves were crammed with history, biography, and the New Journalism of the '60s and '70s, works by Hunter Thompson and Norman Mailer and Tom Wolfe—but I saw nothing by or about any Kennedys. In the front of the apartment lay a pile of athletic equipment: bike, rollerblades, frisbee. Of his artwork, one photograph stood out, a stark black-and-white image, probably from the '40s or '50s, of African-American convicts in the Deep South. Penned in by high walls, they were dancing in a dusty prison courtyard. The picture had a gritty, *Cool Hand Luke* feel to it.

John's bedroom was at the far end of the apartment. It gave no hints of wild nights; it was just a pleasant, tidy room dominated by a queen-size bed. Like the entire apartment, the bedroom looked expensive but not ostentatious—and it too was free of Kennedy iconography. I saw no busts of his father, no portraits of his mother, no plaques or commendations or trophies—nothing to suggest that the occupant of this apartment was anyone other than an affluent young man with excellent taste.

· · ·

One unexpected challenge of working at *George* was maintaining concentration. John attracted so much press that sometimes it seemed as if instead of editing *George,* we could spend all day reading about it.

New York City has two dominant tabloid newspapers, the New York *Daily News* and the *New York Post.* The *Daily News* positions itself as a responsible paper for the city's middle class, with a little gossip thrown in to sweeten the pot. The *Post,* on the other hand, is deliriously sensational. Celebrities run amok on its page one, and gossip columns dominate the front of the paper. Foremost among them is the notorious Page Six, the meanest—and most avidly read—gossip sheet in New York.

That summer, the *News* and the *Post* teemed with items about John. They fell into three categories. The first group consisted of tidbits on our rush to publish, such as the report in the *Daily News* on July 10 that we had asked the comedienne Roseanne Barr to write for us. We had, but Barr's sour essay was barely comprehensible and she refused to rewrite, so we spiked the story.

The second genre detailed stories of the prince amid the hacks. In early August Page Six declared that "staffers at *George* have erected a wall to separate themselves from the other magazines at the Hachette offices on Broadway. One disenfranchised wag scrawled on the barrier, 'Ich Bin Ein Berliner.' "

What wall? What graffiti? Like many of the gossip items, this one couldn't properly be called wrong—that would imply there were facts to get right. The item was complete fiction, yet hard to shrug off. We were editors, not celebrities. We'd never experienced tabloid journalism from the subject's perspective.

John had a different attitude toward gossip columns, a sort of bemused fascination, as if they were covering a stranger who happened to share his name. This composite character was an irresponsible, oversexed, intellectually challenged doppelgänger who made great copy. When the tabloids arrived in our office mail—we subscribed to all of them, even the *Star* and *National Enquirer*—John would riffle through the stack of mail on Rose's desk and pluck them out. If they contained a story about him, he'd sit at his round table—he almost never sat behind his desk—put his feet up, and plunge in. He'd learn that he had shared a night of "wild passion" with Sharon Stone on Martha's Vineyard. Or that his mother had secretly feared he was gay. Or that he was calling Elle Macpherson to confess how much he appreciated her "nice buns."

John would kick back and laugh. Part of him admired the tabloids' creativity, and part of him was flattered by the attention. All those Hollywood types who whined and moaned about the tabloids seemed silly by comparison. John endured more scrutiny than anyone except Madonna and Princess Diana, yet he almost always responded with grace and good humor, and if the tabloids were reasonable in their pursuit of him, he generally let them go about their business. (He also never resorted to the bodyguards often hired by high-profile celebrities. Hachette had at one point hired a bodyguard to stand watch near the lobby receptionist, and for about a week the man sat on a sofa and read *Elle*. On his way in and out of the office, John would walk by the bodyguard and nod, growing more embarrassed with each passing day. Ultimately John thanked the man and said that he didn't really need a bodyguard after all.)

But not all of the gossip items were wrong, and in the middle of the summer a few started appearing on Page Six that felt unnervingly accurate. Suspicion quickly fell upon a temporary secretary, and in short order the woman was let go.

The incident set off shock waves around the office. At Michael's urging, John had Gary draw up a confidentiality agreement stipulating that employees could not talk to the press about the magazine or John or Michael's personal or professional lives. No one wanted to sign it— it felt odd for journalists to self-restrict their own speech—yet we did, as it was clear we had little choice. Anyway, Gary assured us that the document was designed to help create an office environment in which John could relax, and that was something we all wanted. As it turned out, in the months following John grew so comfortable around us that new employees weren't even required to sign the agreement.

The gossip items that did bother John were the ones that dragged Carolyn into the picture. He knew he was fair game; he'd been born famous. But she wasn't a celebrity, and she certainly wasn't flaunting her relationship with John. Couldn't they leave her alone? Was it really necessary for the papers to provide the world its first glimpse of Carolyn when she was on a boat with John, wearing a tiny bikini?—and shot from behind?

Yet Carolyn's relative anonymity only seemed to make the tabloids more curious. "Who's That Girl?" asked the *Post* on July 31 after John, Carolyn, and his cousin Anthony Radziwill attended a party in East Hampton, New York.

My coworkers and I could gauge the veracity of items about *George*. But we couldn't verify what was printed about John and

Carolyn. So shooting e-mails back and forth, we speculated. (It was a nice respite from editing.) Was it true, as the *Post* claimed toward the end of the summer, that "John-John Proposes—But pals say live-in love is stringing him along"?

We would never have asked, because that was part of the deal— we didn't ask John the questions that the outside world wanted to know. He heard those questions enough already. Besides, if you didn't know something about John, you could never be suspected of having leaked it should that detail find its way into print.

But we hoped that Carolyn wasn't stringing John along, because he was ecstatic in her company. When she visited, he could not work. He would gaze upon her as if he couldn't completely believe what his eyes were taking in. He could not stop touching her, running his fingers through her hair, stroking her arms. Carolyn accepted his attentions but rarely reciprocated. At least in public, John was the more openly affectionate of the two.

Often that summer Carolyn would drop by, lounging on the couch in Matt Berman's office. She didn't know much about journalism, but having worked in fashion, she was fluent in the vernacular of style and design. Carolyn could spend hours with Matt talking about the trendiest models and photographers—she seemed to know them all. If you wandered into Matt's office while she was there, you never wanted to leave; she was a more vivid creature than any of the models in *George*'s advertisements.

If the men in the office found excuses to spend time around Carolyn, the women were entranced by John, sometimes going so far as to debate his physical attributes. Of course, it wasn't just the women in the office who fawned over John. Once he asked me to join him at lunch with a top literary agent representing a secret, anonymously written book about the Clintons. From what we'd heard, it sounded perfect for a *George* excerpt. John was willing to do the lunch, but he wanted me along as insurance. If the agent made him uncomfortable, he could up and leave, explaining that he had another appointment, and it wouldn't feel as though he was walking out on someone. He never wanted to be impolite, but he couldn't stand to feel trapped.

We met at an expense-account place on the East Side, and the agent was a paragon of professionalism. If she was excited to be having lunch with John Kennedy, she gave no hint. She wouldn't tell us a thing about the book—not even its title. After John asked for the bill, he excused himself to use the men's room. I picked up the conversation where he had left off, but after about three seconds I noticed that the woman wasn't listening. Instead, she was staring at John's backside, watching with a look of rapture on her face as my boss walked away.

Then there was the time John and Gary and Eric and I were headed to lunch at the Judson Grill, a 52nd Street restaurant that was something of a cafeteria for Hachette editors. As we neared the restaurant door, a striking blonde woman approaching from the other side began rushing toward us. I felt as much as saw John brace himself.

But then the woman gave me a big hug and I realized she was Kate Bohner, a Victoria's Secret model-turned-television commentator who'd been married to the writer Michael Lewis, one of my basketball teammates in Washington. "It's so good to see you," she gushed. "I heard you'd come to New York!"

I introduced Kate around, and after we entered Judson Grill, John gave me an amused "Who knew?" kind of look.

The next day Bohner called me at the office. "I'm sorry if I embarrassed you," she said. "I was just so excited to see John Kennedy!"

I should have been annoyed, I suppose, but I wasn't—if I were a woman, I expect I'd have done the same. I wasn't even upset when Nyssa confessed that she too found John gorgeous. Besides, John was always a gentleman with Nyssa. He'd regularly ask after her, and when she visited *George,* he would make sure to say hello and inquire about her new job. She would invariably respond that it was fine, but that wasn't really true; Burson-Marsteller was proving to be a consulting sweatshop. Nyssa was working the same long hours I was, but with none of my enthusiasm.

One summer evening she and I accompanied John and Carolyn to an Off-Broadway musical produced by Eric's girlfriend, a playwright and performance artist. Afterward Carolyn asked us to join them for dinner at Bowery Bar, a downtown nightspot that was hot at the time. Carolyn, Nyssa, and I shared a cab while John, who had ridden his bike to the theater, pedaled off, arriving at the restaurant just minutes after we did.

Bowery Bar had been the choice of one of our dinner companions, John Perry Barlow, the Grateful Dead lyricist on whose ranch John had worked as a teenager. Carolyn knew the bartender and chatted with him while we waited for John, but Bowery Bar would not have been John's pick. The restaurant was crowded and cacophonous, filled with light-headed fashionistas who flitted like butterflies from table to table. Everyone was air-kissing and ordering flavored vodkas. It was, in a word John used to describe superficial events he dreaded, "a clusterfuck." Plus, Barlow had brought along some friends, women John didn't know, and he looked taken aback by that.

You'd think that going out to dinner with John Kennedy and Carolyn Bessette at a trendy restaurant would be glamorous and exciting. You'd think so, but it wasn't—not once the initial rush wore off. Instead, it was draining. Even after we sat down at a table in the courtyard, Nyssa and I felt out of place. We looked more D.C. than New York, more Banana Republic than Gucci, and everyone at this bar looked like they worked only to pay for their designer clothing. Worse, all eyes were on our table, sometimes furtively, sometimes not. Though John and Carolyn didn't seem to notice, the eavesdropping made me self-conscious. The simplest tasks, like putting a forkful of food into your mouth, become considerably more difficult when a hundred or so people keep glancing your way.

Just making conversation was stressful. As in those old E. F. Hutton ads, when John or Carolyn spoke, everyone listened—however commonplace their words. Meanwhile, we felt that everything we said had to be witty and scintillating. Otherwise, why should John and Carolyn talk to us, when they could be talking to anyone? It was easier to say as little as possible. When the bill finally came, I realized I was relieved.

As Nyssa and I stepped out the restaurant door with John and Carolyn, we saw—no, *felt*—a sudden blur of movement, a herd of men sprinting toward us shouting and pointing their cameras, the flashes causing us to blink and backpedal.

Carolyn practically dove into a waiting car, but John had his bike to worry about. As the photographers shouted "John! Over here, John! Look over here!" he dropped to one knee to undo the bike's combination lock. Nyssa and I stood frozen, not knowing what to do but not wanting to abandon John. I instinctively grabbed Nyssa's hand, then, torn between protecting her and defending John, let go and tried to block the photographers. They glared at me as if I had just committed a faux pas of unspeakable gravity. "Hey, you! Get out of the way!" they shouted, their wheedling tones suddenly indignant.

After a furious left-right-left spin of the lock, John hopped onto his bike and zoomed off. It was as if someone had yelled "Cut!" The photographers put down their equipment and drifted away like a pack of scavengers who have finished their nighttime feeding. Quickly as it had been lit up, the night faded back to black.

Maybe thirty seconds had passed.

Nyssa and I fumbled for each other's hand and walked west down the block. "You okay?" I asked her.

"I think so," she said slowly, as if she were checking herself for broken bones. "That was so . . . *weird*."

As we neared the corner, we saw a dark figure just ahead. "Not another one," I said. It took us a second to realize that it was John, standing over his bike, slightly out of breath.

"You all right?" he asked. "You looked a little freaked back there."

We nodded. "They don't chase you?" I asked.

"Nah." John smiled. "They can't run that fast."

We nodded again.

"Well . . . good night then," John said. He hopped back on his bike and pedaled away, growing smaller under the streetlights until he was just a shadow, then gone.

Four

I don't remember exactly when I learned that John and Michael wanted Cindy Crawford dressed as George Washington for the cover of our first issue, but I definitely remember my reaction: *Uh-oh*.

I wasn't alone in that sentiment. Several of my colleagues also wondered how we could put a model on the cover of our first issue. True, *George* would focus on the intersection of pop culture and politics, but what did Cindy Crawford have to do with politics? We'd get laughed right out of the starting gate.

John, however, loved the idea, and he had a rationale for Crawford that he fiercely advocated. He wanted to tell the world that *George* was not your typical political magazine. *George* would be all-American, gorgeous, and unapologetically commercial. We'd respect history, but we'd tweak it from time to time. Who represented those aspirations better than Cindy Crawford dressed as Washington? The image was playful and subversive, exactly what John wanted.

In any event, John and Michael weren't about to put their decision up for a vote. This wasn't a democracy. They did agree, however, that we needed to find some reason to put Crawford inside the magazine as well. It would be too weird to have her on the cover and nowhere else.

So we decided that Crawford and fashion designer Isaac Mizrahi should comment on the clothing of politicians and their spouses. (Mizrahi was the star of *Unzipped,* a documentary about the fashion world that Hachette had recently coproduced.) The model and the designer sat in Michael's office and watched a slide show, while associate editor Rachel Clark guided the conversation. It worked pretty well, actually. The resulting article effectively tweaked the bland homogeneity of the political dress code.

If you were an oh-so-serious pundit like George Will or Nina Totenburg, you'd hate this kind of stuff (which, it turned out, they did). This was small-*d* democratic punditry; Crawford and Mizrahi were like those puppet characters from *Mystery Science Theater* who fired off acerbic comments about the movies they were watching. If I had finished graduate school, I would have said that their commentary offered an ironic, post-postmodern deconstruction of punditry that undermined the validity of the entire enterprise. But since I hadn't, I just thought it was funny.

. . .

Our July 31 deadline fell on a Monday and getting the issue put to bed came right down to the wire. We worked feverishly that night, giving stories one last read, typing photo captions into computer layouts, changing a word here or there in a headline. Late in the evening, Carolyn was in Matt Berman's office, debating what color the cover should be. John and Michael were wandering the hallways like nervous parents before a baptism.

I left at about one in the morning, utterly exhausted. Finishing that first issue had been incredibly hard work, but God, it was fun. In fact, I felt a little sad that it was done. Even then, I knew that everything was about to change.

·   ·   ·

Over the next few weeks we began work on our second issue, which would come out two months after the first. But it was difficult not to get distracted by our coming unveiling. Finally, like a hot new stock, *George* went public on the morning of September 7, 1995.

Shortly after nine o'clock that Thursday, some 250 reporters began staking out seats inside Federal Hall, a granite and marble temple near Wall Street where, in 1789, George Washington first took the oath of the presidency. Thirty television crews hastily snapped together their equipment like overgrown kids composing Lego sculptures. Decked out in double-breasted suits, rented musclemen with wires jammed into their ears and brawny hands tucked behind their backs cast unflinching stares into the crowd.

The prime seats were saved for the press, so much of the staff wouldn't get to sit. While Elinore Carmody, Eric Etheridge, Matt Berman, and Gary Ginsberg had chairs up front—Elinore, Eric, and Matt because they were department heads, Gary because he always managed to land near the action—Biz and I and the associate editors stood on the balcony overlooking the stage, pacing back and forth nervously. For three months we had labored intensely—and secretly—to create this magazine. We'd learned to cope with a level of scrutiny without precedent for a new magazine. Now, at last, we were introducing *George* to a media mob that had desperately been trying to discover something, anything, about what our magazine would look like, what it would contain, and just what JFK Jr. was up to.

John was anxious about this press conference; he'd never done anything like it. Up to that point, almost certainly the largest assemblage of reporters he'd ever had to address had come the morning after his mother's death, and no one would have thought of asking him a tough question on that day. Now there was no reason for the press to hold back. Here was an opportunity hundreds of reporters had been waiting for—the chance to ask John F. Kennedy, Jr., questions about his personal life. Our nightmare scenario was that no one would ask a single question about *George*.

To prepare, John had gotten coaching from image consultant Michael Sheehan, who had worked with Bill Clinton, and Paul Begala, a Clinton spin doctor who'd also advised John's uncle Ted. Sheehan and Begala had spent hours drilling John on potentially embarrassing questions. "Why did you fail the bar exam—are you stupid, or just lazy?" "Is it true about you and Sharon Stone?" "Who's your new girlfriend, anyway?" "Madonna has an article in your first issue—did you have to sleep with her to get her to write it?"

Together they cooked up some answers. The night before, John practiced his speech behind a makeshift podium in his apartment while Gary and Carolyn listened and offered their advice. Even so, John was nervous. Tossing and turning in bed, he hadn't been able to fall asleep till well past midnight.

Not that John wasn't skilled with the press. On a bad day, he dealt with more reporters than most people face in their lifetimes—a lot more, if you count photographers. But in the past he had always hidden behind an assumed identity, a public facade that sheltered his true self. On the stage at Brown, he inhabited other people's characters. In 1988, when he kicked off the Democratic National Convention, he symbolized party mythology. Standing before juries as a prosecutor, he played a role that his mother had apparently wanted for him more than he had.

This day was different. Both his parents were gone, and no one could say he was starting this magazine because JFK or Jackie O. wanted him to. In fact, a lot of people were whispering just the opposite—that *George,* rumored to be the *People* of politics, would have made John's parents cringe. John was on his own now, and that made this day a watershed moment on the Kennedy time line. Or a pivotal scene in the JFK Jr. movie.

Because the Kennedys, with their generational saga of triumphs and tragedies, starred in America's most-watched family drama. Collectively and individually, their stories constituted what cultural critic Neal Gabler has called a "life movie." Americans are so enamored of the movies, Gabler has argued, that we want to see real life packaged like a two-hour film, with all the heroes and villains, the dramatic highs and lows, of a good flick. And in the second half of the twentieth century—a period coinciding with Hollywood's rise to cultural dominance—the Kennedys had provided ample fodder for such a production.

Few life movies had a more devoted audience than John Kennedy's. For thirty-five years its images had unscrolled before a nation's fascinated and often doting eyes. Now he was adding a new scene. The sex symbol who zealously guarded his privacy and hated the press was actually joining that sinister guild. The reporters' curiosity was understandable. Just what in God's name *was* he doing?

Shortly after ten o'clock John and two supporting actors strode on the stage and sat on metal folding chairs. On John's right was David Pecker, his black hair slicked back, his bushy mustache looking walrus-like. Next to David was Michael Berman, wearing a dark suit and a gold tie of the monotone style in fashion then. Michael usually looked powerful and even intimidating in a suit, but now he sat crossing and uncrossing his legs, appearing decidedly ill at ease. This press conference had been his idea, and everyone else—Hachette executives,

John—had vigorously opposed it. What if it degenerated into a feeding frenzy on John's personal life? But Michael, who was torn between protecting John and using him to *George*'s advantage, had insisted. Finally John had relented. Public relations is what you do, he said to Michael, so if you think a press conference is a good idea, I'll do it. But everything I know tells me not to.

Little wonder that Michael was starting to sweat.

David and Michael spoke first, but I don't recall a thing they said. Pecker probably tried to explain the correct pronunciation of Hachette Filipacchi. Michael—well, I do remember one thing Michael said. "Being John Kennedy's partner," he said, "is a little like being Dolly Parton's feet. I'm sure they're perfectly nice, but they tend to get overshadowed."

Then, to a long round of applause and a string of flashbulbs, John rose from his chair and strolled to the microphone. He was dressed in a navy suit with a white shirt, a dark blue tie, and a white pocket square, an accoutrement he always wore on important occasions. The day before he'd gotten a haircut so severe that we teased him and dubbed it his Eddie Munster look.

John grasped the podium with both hands and surveyed the crowd. "Ladies and gentlemen," he said, "meet *George*."

He swung around a mounted display to reveal the cover of our first issue: Cindy Crawford decked out in a white wig and Revolutionary garb—or at least Matt Berman's version of Revolutionary garb. Her long blue jacket was unbuttoned to reveal a lacy white bustier and a smooth, flat stomach. She wore mustard-colored spandex leggings tucked into knee-high black boots, and her powdered face was spiced up with fire-engine red lipstick.

The reporters burst into applause.

"I don't think I've seen as many of you gathered in one place since they announced the results of my first bar exam," John quipped.

The line sounded scripted, which it was, but its self-deprecation was disarming. The reporters laughed, and John seemed to stand a little taller at the podium.

"Politics isn't dull," John said. "Why should a magazine covering it be? Politics is a drive. It's about trial and loss, the pursuit of power, and the price of ambition for its own sake . . . a stage on which the mighty stumble."

As John spoke, flashbulbs illuminated the room in such a constant stream that it appeared someone had turned on a strobe light. After he finished his prepared speech, he opened the floor to questions—but not before he volunteered a few responses in advance. "Yes. No," he said. "We're only good friends. None of your business. Honest, she's my cousin from Rhode Island. I've worn both. Maybe someday, but not in New Jersey."

Again the scribes laughed. They probably had planned to inquire, among other things, about the nature of John's relationship with Madonna, or if Carolyn and he were getting married, or whether he wore boxers or briefs, or about the published report that he planned to run for the Senate from New Jersey. They didn't know what to expect this morning, and John was putting them at ease—and in the process, making it harder for them to be rude. It was smart strategy. The reporters would write about how modest and self-effacing John was, when his real intention was to discourage invasive questions. The tactic was transparently manipulative, but charming nonetheless.

One reporter asked how *George* could be nonpartisan given its editor's family ties.

"My uncle Ted said, 'If I'm still talking to you by Thanksgiving, then you're not doing your job,'" John quipped. Paul Begala had helped come up with that line, and the crowd loved it; John looked more confident with every passing moment.

"How do you feel about joining the media that has made your life hell?" another reporter called out.

John smiled and shook his head. "You didn't make my life hell." Sure, sometimes he was annoyed by the attention. But it was "part of the bargain" of being him.

"What would your mother say if she could see *George*?"

John paused for a second and said quietly, "My mother would be mildly amused to see me up here, and very proud."

Something happened then. Even from where I stood, way up on the balcony, I could feel it, that powerful, unexpected blurring of the iconic and the actual, the life movie and real life, just like I'd experienced after seeing that photo in John's office. There was a collective intake of breath, as if everyone in the room suddenly took a step back. For half a heartbeat, the reporters stopped seeing John as a commodity and connected with him as a person, an orphan who, rich and famous though he may have been, had to make his way in the world like all the rest of us.

Then someone else raised his hand and the moment was gone.

.   .   .

Within days of its appearance, the first 500,000-copy print run of *George* was sold out. We were astonished. No one, not even John, had any idea that so many people would be curious about *George*. We went back to press and printed 100,000 more—and they too sold out. In Times Square, grassroots entrepreneurs were hawking copies for two and three times the $2.95 cover price.

During the following weeks, it seemed that every political journalist, magazine reviewer, and op-ed columnist in the country weighed in on our magazine. Perhaps that was a testament to the originality of

John and Michael's idea, or perhaps the pundits knew that if they wrote about John Kennedy, more people would read their columns than if they didn't.

Which didn't mean they liked *George*. For the most part, they did not—as if in order to justify the guilty pleasure of writing about its editor they felt compelled to criticize both him and his magazine. Older writers proclaimed *George* the end of the world as we read it. *Too many pictures!* Washington insiders sniffed that *George* wasn't really political. *Too many celebrities!* Ideologues charged that *George* lacked a point of view. *Too nonpartisan!* And reporters who had covered John's father doubted that John was living up to expectations. "I wish him all the best, but still I am skeptical," declared writer David Halberstam.

We'd worked so long in a cocoon and were so proud of what we had created that we were a little blindsided by the criticism. But as the days went on, the chorus of naysayers only heightened our sense of camaraderie, of distance from the outside world. Besides, with Michael's help, John had initiated a plan to bypass the elite media.

On September 18, he made a cameo appearance on the television show *Murphy Brown*. In the scene, he gave Murphy a birthday present—a free one-year subscription to *George*. John was on for only about a minute, but he came across as warm and funny. In a review, though, the *Daily News* sniped that his entrance prompted "shrieks and squeals" from the studio audience. "Not exactly the same response his father got when he debated Richard Nixon in 1960."

Okay, so he wasn't running for president—yet. But wasn't there a larger point to make? The celebrity journalist and president's son was appearing on a TV show whose star, a fictional journalist, had been attacked by a vice president, Dan Quayle, who had once been lampooned for comparing himself to JFK. Try parsing that. It was a

moment when culture and politics were woven together in an inseparable dialectic. What more justification of *George* did our critics require? They might not like that politics and pop culture had become
so intertwined, but how could they deny the reality?

The criticism that most angered me came from *New York Times*
columnist Maureen Dowd. Slicing through the magazine like a morti-
cian on speed, Dowd wrote that *George* would "drain politics of its
gravity and moral force." She mocked John for having attended a magazine seminar and quoted her friend Leon Wieseltier, literary editor of
The New Republic, who said, "Politics . . . has the sizzle of seriousness.
But the message of *George* is, don't take it seriously."

I read the column in disbelief. Who wrote more frequently about
politics and pop culture than Maureen Dowd? That's why her column
was so popular—because she made politics entertaining. Was she a
hypocrite, a monopolist, or both?

Before I could think better of it, I took to my keyboard to bang out
an angry retort. "Yes, of course in starting *George* John had certain
advantages," I wrote Dowd. "But he also had wolves lunging at his
heels—people like you, for example, who love a chance to lambaste a
celebrity who dares to venture onto your turf."

I dropped the letter in the mail. Dowd replied within days. "Don't
be mad at me," she wrote in loopy letters on stiff *Times* stationery.
"I'm paid to be a baby curmudgeon, and it's no fun. I'd go back to
reporting in a minute. I've subscribed and I promise only plugs from
now on."

Two days after the *Murphy Brown* episode appeared, we gathered
in Eric's office to watch our boss appear on *Larry King Live.* Though
it was nine o'clock at night, we were still at work, eating Thai food and
sweating. Our first issue might be flying off the stands, but Hachette
still didn't want to pay for after-hours air-conditioning.

The show started. Almost immediately, King asked John what his mother would think of *George*.

John paused, then answered, "When we first talked about the idea, she said, 'John, you're not going to do the *Mad* magazine of politics?' And I said, 'Well, no . . .'" He smiled a little at the memory. "She had a sense of humor, and I don't think that she was a slave to conventional wisdom. There's a certain irony in the whole enterprise that she would have appreciated."

Next King asked how John remembered his father.

"I see him in a variety of ways," John said. "I understand that my father is part of the mythology of this country, and he was also a very compelling political figure. And you can certainly"—and here his tone changed, becoming more distant, as if he were reminding himself to stay on message—"certainly he was aware himself of the opportunities for politics to be both fun and serious."

"How does it feel to be the son of a legend?" King asked.

"It's complicated," John said thoughtfully. "And it makes for a rich and complicated life, so . . ."

He paused for a moment, then shrugged, and I could see him torn between his resistance to making himself vulnerable and his antipathy to phoniness. "But that's part of the puzzle to figure out in my life," he said, and waited for the next question.

. . .

Very soon, the puzzle of John's existence began to pose problems for *George,* as we learned that our editor's identity was both our biggest asset and our most treacherous minefield.

Our second issue would hit the stands in November, just before Oliver Stone's film *Nixon* would open. Stone, a mainstream director making a movie about a political legend, was a natural *George* story. Not to mention that he had directed *JFK*, the conspiracy-theory film on the assassination of John's father. Eric wanted John to interview Stone so badly he was practically hopping up and down. For the first time, John would publicly discuss the conspiracy theories swirling around his father's death. What editor wouldn't kill to publish that?

Eric was right, of course. If we printed only that interview along with a few dozen blank pages, people would still rush to buy the magazine. But there was one problem: John didn't want to do it. He had made a conscious decision not to live his life haunted by his father's assassination, trying to answer unanswerable questions. He'd never even seen *JFK*. Oliver Stone, the assassination groupie, made John feel like Captain Kirk being stalked by the world's looniest Trekkie. On the other hand, John recognized that this story was manna from heaven for *George,* and in those early days, he was bending over backwards to try to do what we, the pros, thought he should do. In the end, against his better judgment, he agreed to interview Oliver Stone.

But he refused to do it alone, so he and Michael flew to L.A. The three men met for a get-to-know-you dinner at Rockenwagner, a restaurant in Santa Monica. John and Michael had agreed beforehand that if Stone was making him uneasy, John would excuse himself to use the rest room, and Michael would change the subject.

Things did not go well. John felt awkward asking questions, but Stone didn't hesitate to interrogate him. Michael tried to intervene, but Stone bored in on John. As they started their main course, Stone asked John's opinion of the second gunman theory. What did John think? Lee Harvey Oswald couldn't really have killed John's father alone, could he? Shot him from that far away, then shot him again? There *had* to be a conspiracy.

John excused himself, stood up, and walked away. As planned, Michael changed the subject. After John returned, dinner ended as soon as they could politely bring it to a close.

Back in New York, we met in John's office and tried to come up with a replacement interview in a hurry. John apologized to Eric, who could not mask his disappointment, but he refused to contact Stone again. As he spoke, John's emotions flickered back and forth on his face, a psychological slide show revealing disgust with Stone, guilt over letting us down, and self-recrimination for doing something he hadn't felt comfortable with. He shuddered as he said, "I just couldn't sit across a table from that man for two hours. I just couldn't."

So instead of a cover featuring Anthony Hopkins posing as Richard Nixon, Michael suggested Robin Williams as George Washington, but we couldn't figure out how Williams had even a tenuous connection to politics. Instead, we hastily threw together a cover with Robert De Niro, who was then starring in the film *Casino,* for a feature on gambling and politics. A flimsy piece of work, it withstood only a cursory read. We had fallen from the possibility of a home-run cover to the reality of a ho-hum one.

· · ·

A few weeks after my exchange with Maureen Dowd, John announced that he wanted to interview her. Did Dowd dare to sit down with someone she'd bashed in print? John would like to find out. He hoped she would—but he doubted it.

I hadn't told John about my note to Dowd, and now I confessed to him that Dowd might have reason to be wary of an interview with *George.* Wincing, John suggested that the next time I felt the urge to write such a letter, I resist the temptation. We'd fight back when the time was right, he said. I just nodded; I knew he was right. (John asked Dowd anyway; she said no.)

John did enjoy fighting back, when he could do so on his terms. Not content to leave well enough alone, Andrew Sullivan published a story in a December issue of *The New Republic* headlined "Why *George* Sucks." So John proposed that *George* take out a full-page ad in *TNR*. If they wouldn't accept it, we would leak that tidbit to the *Washington Post*. I don't think we ever did either, but John was tickled pink just considering the mischief we could make.

Truth was, John didn't lose much sleep over the critics as long as they kept writing about us. He would have enjoyed critical praise, but he certainly didn't expect it. The tut-tutting of the Boston-to-Washington corridor only confirmed his view of the elite media as insular and defensive. In any event, he came to believe that after *George*'s initial wave of publicity the press was easing up on him. At lunch one day after our second issue came out, John announced happily that he was fading from the gossip pages. He, Eric, Gary, and I were eating at the Judson Grill.

People never wrote about him anymore, John said with amusement. Everyone had warned him that by starting *George* he was forfeiting his privacy, but he actually had *more* privacy now.

Gary snorted. "Oh, come on, John. You *like* to be in the papers."

Gary, who had known John longer than the rest of us, could get away with such teasing. He used to rib John about his ranking in the Observer 500, the *New York Observer*'s annual list of the most-mentioned names in New York gossip columns. The joke wasn't that John was mentioned so often; it was that he didn't appear *enough*. "You're losing your juice, John," Gary would kid.

That day at lunch, John conceded that sometimes he enjoyed all the attention. "Yeah, I like the press, a little," he said. "But this is great. They can't call me a dilettante anymore, and they can't call me an unemployed lawyer. Now if they want to write about me, they have to mention *George,* and they don't want to do that. So they don't write about me."

But John was mistaking a momentary lull for a meaningful respite. Just a week or so after our lunch, *Crain's New York Business,* a small but respected newspaper, confirmed that John was now a larger target than ever. The journal ran a trade advertisement with the following copy: "Although our ad pages are up 20%, imagine how well we could have done if we had an incredibly handsome, famous and oh-so-eligible son of an ex-president on staff, and then shamelessly trotted him before the national press like a pack of self-serving media harlots."

So much for John staying out of the press.

.   .   .

Although he seemed generally impervious to the gossips and the critics, John did care about the mail we got from readers. Fortunately, it was overwhelmingly positive, which was unusual; most readers only write letters to magazines when they're mad about something. The letters to *George* were written by people of all ages who wanted to be inspired by politics but weren't. They didn't call themselves Republican or Democrat, and they read *George* because it was, in John's word, "postpartisan." Some of the plaudits, of course, came from people who revered John's parents, such as the correspondent who praised the magazine, then wrote, "On a personal note, John, your parents are looking down from the heavens with big smiles on their faces. Keep up the good work. Remember that you and your sister have a very special place in the country's heart. . . ."

One day John photocopied a review from the *Virginian-Pilot,* a Hampton Roads, Virginia, newspaper. "To: All," he wrote on it in his hasty left-handed scrawl. "Re: Wonderful us." The review had been penned by a columnist who, while buying tickets for the movie *The American President,* had found "the woman in the glass booth at the Commodore" reading *George.* And, the writer emphasized, liking it. "I can't remember the last time I saw a ticket-taker reading a magazine about politics."

John proudly bracketed that line with a felt-tip pen, then added an asterisk next to it, and underneath wrote "Yes!"

I couldn't have agreed more. So what if we didn't have the insiders and the elites on our side? We had the people—or at least a lot of them. A million Americans had bought the first two issues of our magazine, instantly making *George* the country's largest political magazine. Wasn't that more important than having the sanction of the intelligentsia?

To John, I think, it was. Though he'd grown up wealthy and privileged, he still felt more comfortable around ordinary Americans than with his moneyed peers. Maybe it was because he empathized with people who had never finished at the top of their classes, or who had failed tests, or who had been constantly underestimated. And maybe it was because, despite all his advantages, sometimes even John didn't feel like a winner.

. . .

There was one question none of us wanted to ask: Were readers buying *George* because they liked the magazine or to get a glimpse of John? It was an important question, because if they were buying it only for a regular dose of JFK Jr., then our work was more or less irrelevant.

It was too soon to know the answer to that question, but it was already clear that many of our readers felt a powerful connection to John and hoped that he would run for office one day. If he ever did,

George would be a useful launching pad. The magazine was attracting tens of thousands of subscribers. They were already giving John money; they would very likely contribute to a campaign. *George's* pages gave John a forum in which to outline his beliefs, and people were intensely curious to know what was on his mind.

The more I saw how ordinary people related to John—the way they waved to him on the street as if he were an old friend, or the fascination with which they stared at him on the subway or photographed him when they thought he wasn't looking—the more I came to believe that if John ever did run for office, Americans would vote for him in droves. They would do so because they thought they knew him but wanted to know him better. Because he was a national common denominator, part of the imagery inside the cultural scrapbook of every American. And because his father and uncle had died before their time, John represented the chance to cap his family's saga of tragedy with a happy ending.

We received a package in the mail one day that epitomized many people's feelings about John. It was wrapped in brown paper and tied with coarse string. In black marker, it was addressed to "John Kennedy, *George* Magazine, New York." It looked like the kind of package you think maybe you shouldn't open.

Inside, however, was a framed, faded black-and-white picture of John's father accompanied by a handwritten note from an elderly African-American woman. She lived somewhere in the Deep South— Louisiana or Alabama or Mississippi, I don't remember exactly where. The woman wrote that this picture of JFK had hung over her family's kitchen table for almost forty years—ever since the 1960 presidential race. Her family had kept it there so that they would never forget all that President Kennedy had done for them.

Now she wanted John to have this picture. She thought it was time.

Five

"Mom and Dad are fighting again," I said to Biz one October day as the sounds of John and Michael screaming at each other ripped through the hallways. I had graduated from the cubicle where I'd resided in May, and we were sitting in my small, boxy office about forty feet down the hall from John's.

"Which one's which?" Biz asked, and we both tried to laugh.

Our two authority figures had taken to shouting at each other. John in particular was shockingly loud. Working at my computer, I'd suddenly hear him hurling obscenities at his partner. Everyone could hear it; John wasn't keeping his voice down. If I was on the phone, I'd have to cover the mouthpiece so the person at the other end wouldn't get an earful. The furious outbursts put us all on edge. When they occurred, doors would shut up and down the hall.

While John screamed, Michael glowered and muttered. Eventually one of the two would storm down the hallway, the other chasing hard on his heels. More hollering would ensue. A door would slam, the din would grow muffled but still audible.

It was unnerving to hear two grown men who sounded as though they wanted to tear each other limb from limb. Two grown men who happened to be your employers in a high-profile, closely watched start-up business. The fights had specific flash points—Would John make a sales call? Why was John running a particular story?—but fundamentally they were about the challenges of two close friends going into business together when one of them was famous. Could Michael handle the fact that, though legally and intellectually John's equal partner, he would never receive equal credit? In September, when the *Washington Post* wanted to run a story about *George*, John had insisted that the paper could photograph him only if Michael and David Pecker were in the picture. But when the first editions of the paper came out, the *Post* had deliberately blurred the other men. David and Michael looked as if they were melting.

The challenge for John was different. Could he promote *George* even when it meant compromising his sense of dignity, his feel for what was appropriate and what wasn't? A case in point: That fall, Michael decided that John should interview Chelsea Clinton. One presidential kid talking to another—a surefire crowd pleaser. But John flatly refused to do the interview. Hillary Clinton had once asked his mother for advice on raising a child in the White House, John explained. His mother's response: Never let Chelsea talk to the press. And now Michael wanted John to defy his mother's wishes? Not a chance.

Which meant another fight in the hallways.

People at other Hachette magazines heard the shouting and word of the fights started getting out. One reporter asked Michael about rumors of "loud noises coming from the offices of *George*." "Screaming?" he responded, laughing.

But before long the fighting stopped being funny and became seriously divisive. When the magazine started, John's office was just three doors down from Michael's on the floor's northwest corner. After a few issues, John moved to the southwest end of the corridor, sacrificing his Central Park panorama for a view of the Statue of Liberty and greater distance from Michael.

Though she had been hired by Michael, Rosemarie Terenzio uprooted and planted herself outside John's office. She could not work for both, and, perhaps inevitably, she chose John. And so John's secretary also became an issue between the two men.

Rose was about thirty years old, with curly dark hair cascading around a pale face and brown-black eyes. She had no discernible interest in journalism, but was fascinated by celebrity. She was a hunt-and-peck typist, but she was street-smart, and she combined that with street language. Rare was the day you wouldn't hear Rose cursing like a longshoreman. Sometimes a particularly colorful string of profanities would be followed by the crash of the telephone receiver hitting its cradle as she dispatched another JFK Jr. supplicant. John wanted a bad cop, and didn't seem to mind if Rose occasionally enforced her duties a little too enthusiastically.

He forgave her draconian measures because he thought her authentic and entertaining. He also knew that, because she was not model-beautiful, the tabloids would never link them. And because he added excitement to her life, she would be eternally loyal. "Rose," one of my colleagues said, "would throw herself in front of a truck for John." She aggressively forged a friendship with Carolyn, who would drop by Rose's apartment late at night to talk about John or pass along the designer clothes she was given that didn't fit. Soon Rose was sporting Prada and Manolo Blahniks at the office. The two women would talk for hours a day on the phone and, for a while, Rose even dyed her hair blond and straightened it to look more like Carolyn's.

Some of my colleagues speculated that Rose stoked the tension between John and Michael to advance her standing with John, and although Michael professed indifference, it was generally believed he felt betrayed by her. He had brought her to *George*. Now she was switching sides?

Rose was not, however, the only person coming between the two men. So was Carolyn Bessette. The night we closed the first issue and Carolyn lingered in the office till past midnight, Michael had left around nine, but not before telling John that Carolyn's presence was distracting the entire staff (which, in fact, it was). What frustrated Michael most was that Carolyn had wanted to change the color of the cover, and had almost succeeded.

Carolyn didn't appreciate Michael's intervention and neither did John. Though she visited less frequently after that, she remained a behind-the-scenes influence; John passed along his girlfriend's advice on photographers and models to use. (She once nixed a cover with model Gabrielle Reece because, she told Matt Berman, Reece was passé.) It was a volatile triangle: John, his business partner and old friend, and Carolyn, who was determined to be involved in every part of her boyfriend's life.

Michael knew which way the wind was blowing, and his sense of the inevitable made him steadily more uneasy.

·   ·   ·

At Christmas, John and Michael gave us small plastic wristwatches with white faces sporting black *George* logos. They didn't cost much, but they captured the heartfelt sincerity that John and Michael communicated so passionately when they weren't fighting with each other. "For the good times ahead! John and Michael," proclaimed the gift cards that came with the watches. John wore his all the time.

There were other, more valuable perks that flowed from John. Fashion houses constantly sent him clothing and shoes, and if they didn't fit, he'd redistribute them. To my dismay, I was too big for the suits. Gary landed them instead—$1,500 Italian suits impossible to afford on an editor's salary.

Even more fun were the basketball tickets. When John couldn't use his two courtside seats to Knicks games, he'd often give them to a staffer who'd been working hard or having a bad week. Now, that was a kick, walking down the steps of Madison Square Garden, closer and closer and closer till you were just behind the endline, maybe ten feet from the Knicks bench, the sports photographers kneeling in front of you, the ingratiating ushers taking your food order, Tom Brokaw to your right, Spike Lee mid-court, Woody Allen and Soon-Yi sitting some fifteen rows up. Back in 1996, the tickets cost $1,000 apiece.

Then there was the time in October 1996 when the Yankees made the play-offs and John decided we could use an afternoon off. So Rose called the office of Yankees owner George Steinbrenner and left a message from John. Steinbrenner himself called back. You couldn't buy tickets to that play-off series against Baltimore, they'd sold out so fast. But Steinbrenner gave us thirty. The game was terrific: that afternoon a twelve-year-old boy named Jeffrey Maier made baseball history when he reached over the right-field fence to catch a lazy fly ball hit by Derek Jeter in the eighth inning. The umpire called it a homer and the Yankees won as a result.

Another time John bought the staff tickets to *1776*, a musical about the writing of the Constitution. It was a little dopey—Ben Franklin and John Adams singing away about the glorious document—but I suspect John thought the civics lesson would be good for us. He confessed that he'd listened to the record of *1776* so much when he was a kid, he could remember all the lyrics. He even broke into song— "We're com-*ing*, to Philadelphia . . ."

Once John got a call from a Navy press aide. The aircraft carrier *John F. Kennedy* was leaving drydock. Would John care to be on board? John couldn't—but, he told the man, some of his staff might. So a Navy jet flew an assistant and a researcher, two of our most junior staffers, out to the *John F. Kennedy,* where they had dinner with the captain in his quarters and spent the night.

And then there were the ties. John sent out a memo one December day to the men on staff: "Re: Fine neckwear. Due to oversupply and under-demand (too many ties and not enough neck), I am parting with some fine neck drapery. If you are interested in acquiring any of said booty, it's hanging in the back hall closet."

It's a little embarrassing to recall, but we quickly made our way to the closet, where John usually stashed his rollerblades and gym clothes, to find dozens of exquisite ties by Versace, Canali, and Zegna. They got snapped up in minutes. Once or twice a year from then on, John would repeat the giveaway.

In time I stopped taking ties because it felt odd to wear my boss's hand-me-downs. Not everyone could afford that luxury, however. Twenty-one-year-old editorial assistants making little more than a living wage would stroll through our office decked out in Gap khakis, Old Navy button-downs, and $200 ties once worn by John Kennedy.

.　.　.

In early January 1996 three feet of snow blanketed New York and essentially shut the city down. With the snow still falling on January 8, only a handful of us made it to work, and John suggested an early lunch. On the way, we retrieved the football from his closet and tossed it around the newly padded streets of an eerily silent city. Slipping and sliding, we lunged for buttonhooks in the middle of a great white Broadway, fired bullets across Seventh Avenue, and cheered our completions as if watched by thousands of fans. Gary hip-checked John into a snowbank, and John returned the favor. Soon snowballs were whizzing through the air. Bundled-up New Yorkers scooting along the sidewalks hastily got out of our way. Thanks to the swirling snow they couldn't see who John was, and for perhaps the first time, I stopped being self-conscious around him. Romping like a kid, I forgot that I was throwing a football around the streets of Manhattan with John F. Kennedy, Jr., substituting in a ritual he usually performed with his famous family. For a moment, he was just John, and I realized that if I liked him when he was famous, I liked him more when he wasn't.

But such moments were fleeting; business had a way of intruding on the fun. About a week later, Rose was on the phone, which was unusual because it was Monday night and I was at home. "John wants to have an early meeting tomorrow," she announced.

The next morning everyone seemed a little tense; Rose had given no hint what this meeting was about. At around 9:30 the art and editorial staffs, perhaps fifteen of us now, convened in John's office. We took seats around the table or on top of the windowsill, our backs to the park. No one said a word. John shut the door behind him and leaned against the edge of his desk. He had a neutral look on his face.

"As some of you may know," he said, "Eric Etheridge and *George* magazine are parting ways."

He must be kidding, I thought. That's crazy. *George* is just starting to gel. We've been publishing for only four months. It's too soon for this.

A pained silence stretched out.

From now on, John told us, he would be running the show. Eric would not be replaced.

· · ·

I should have seen the signs. The tension over Oliver Stone. The painful awkwardness between Eric and John at meetings, like when a couple is fighting and they're hoping that no one can tell but everyone can. And one other thing—probably Eric's biggest mistake.

Early in the summer, Eric had typed up a mailing to all 535 press secretaries on Capitol Hill, something so innocuous I can't even remember exactly what it said. I believe it was a "We're *George*, get to know us" kind of thing.

Eric wanted to affix John's name to the form letter, and though John was out of the office, he did. Off went hundreds of letters to Capitol Hill, all with John Kennedy's name on the bottom. When Rose informed John of what Eric had done, John marched into Eric's office and shut the door. Afterward, Eric looked shaken and wouldn't talk about it. That had been months ago—but the damage, apparently, was permanent.

Eric's ouster shattered the media lull. Because Eric was smart, conventional wisdom held that John now wanted to dumb-down *George*. The political magazine *The Weekly Standard* ran a satire in which John penned a diary entry about Daryl Hannah. "Last night Daryl tried to slog her way through the article on how both Democrats and Republicans love *Baywatch*," the *Standard* wrote. "Finally she threw down the magazine in disgust. 'If I want to read a doctoral thesis,' she said, 'I'll go to grad school.'"

Never mind that John and Hannah hadn't been dating for more than a year—the suggestion that John was creating a magazine for dummies hurt *George*. Especially in tandem with the fact that after our first two issues the number of ad pages in our February/March 1996 issue, with outspoken basketball star Charles Barkley on the cover, had plunged. We had expected that decline because many advertisers who buy into first issues quickly drop out. But suddenly we had a perception problem. "The magic appears to be wearing off for John F. Kennedy Jr.'s magazine venture," warned the *New York Post*.

It didn't help that sales of the Barkley issue fell dramatically from the 500,000-plus average of the Cindy Crawford and Robert De Niro issues to less than 300,000. Barkley had been a last-minute choice. With our third-issue deadlines looming and no interview subject chosen, I had recommended that John speak with Barkley, who was making noises about running for governor of Alabama. Word had it that higher-ups at Hachette weren't pleased with the choice. It was a commonly held belief—not just at Hachette but generally within the glossy magazine business—that African-American cover subjects attracted lower newstand sales. That we sold fewer copies of the Barkley issue no doubt had more to do with an inevitable decrease in curiosity about *George* than with race. But I wished that we could have defied the conventional wisdom and continued selling beyond expectations.

The third-issue drop in advertising and circulation made it abundantly clear that the enormous success of our first two issues had a downside; we could probably never match that success, but we would always be judged by it. Even so, we still had 100 pages of advertising in that third issue, or about 60 more than we'd originally forecast.

With Eric gone, Biz Mitchell and I, now *George*'s most veteran journalists, found ourselves doing the lion's share of editing. It would have been nice if we worked well together, but we didn't. When she wasn't working solo, Biz seemed to prefer interacting only with John. Moreover, she and I had different visions of the magazine. I thought we should reach out to Middle America. Biz, a Brown graduate like John, wanted a more alternative magazine; she proposed a feature on "why kids are ruining America." I thought the story cynical and said so.

But John had some doubts about my judgment; I had allowed Andrew Sullivan to violate his privacy and mishandled the Maureen Dowd situation. And he knew that I was sorry to see Eric go. Despite the missteps Eric had taken, I respected him enormously. He had taught me a great deal about the craft of editing. Besides, I had become convinced that as soon as John was ready to take the helm, he would have ousted whoever sat in Eric's office.

John felt comfortable around Biz, though. Maybe it was because they'd both gone to Brown, or because she hadn't made the kind of gaffes I had, or because she never took an adversarial approach to covering politicians. She let John know that when she was a little girl she'd developed a crush on Gerald Ford. She'd even written the president a mash note. John seemed to like that.

Biz got her piece about kids—Bret Easton Ellis, the author of *American Psycho,* wrote an essay about the tragic flaws of American youth that was published in our June/July 1996 issue, which featured the actress Demi Moore on the cover. It was world-weary stuff. "Sure, not all kids are bad, but collectively they're getting worse. Why should we blame ourselves?"

Still, at any magazine you win some and you lose some, and I was pleased with my contributions. In our third issue, one of my writers, a Washington reporter named Nina Burleigh, had broken the news that feminist author Naomi Wolf was secretly advising Bill Clinton on his reelection campaign. That revelation, picked up in newspapers across the country, prompted a Maureen Dowd column crediting *George,* which Dowd sent me along with another note. It read, "Richard—plug No. 1—as promised! Maureen."

. . .

Some of our pieces drew attention, some didn't. But *George's* most popular feature by far was John's monthly interview. Interviews are usually the easiest form of magazine journalism—you sit down with someone interesting, ask good questions, and edit the results. John's interviews, however, proved an unexpected challenge. We had expected the process to go smoothly. Who would say no to a sit-down with JFK Jr.? Yet every issue, we agonized over it.

The problem wasn't that people would turn him down, but that John had very definite feelings about whom he would interview. In general, celebrities were verboten. "How about Spike Lee, John?" we'd say. "He's political." John would shake his head. "Alec Baldwin?" He'd groan. "Sarah Jessica Parker? She's an activist." (That was a particularly bad idea. The two had gone out once or twice, and John felt Parker had publicized their dates. He'd never let us write about her for anything.) Anyway, we'd yank and tug as if trying to walk a very large and intractable dog, but John wouldn't budge. Celebrity, it became clear, bored him. It separated him from life's everyday pleasures—a quiet walk, an uninterrupted meal—and it certainly wasn't the aspect of *George* he wanted to focus on. The people who fascinated him committed acts of heroism without benefit or expectation of fame.

An example. Some months down the road, I assigned a story on the film *Ghosts of Mississippi* to Willie Morris, the fabled southern writer. Willie had been a consultant on the film and wrote a moving piece for us about the murder of civil rights leader Medgar Evers and the district attorney who, almost thirty years later, convicted white supremacist Byron De La Beckwith. The D.A.'s name was Bobby DeLaughter.

Willie Morris was old school, charming, gracious, and courtly, a natural storyteller who wouldn't let a phone call end without inviting me to come on down to Jackson. I felt fortunate to work with him. But he was on the downslope of his career and deeply sentimental about the past. People said he drank too much, which may have been why it was impossible to reach him before noon. I preferred to think that he was locked in his study with his Smith-Corona and no phone; Willie was the last writer I knew who actually mailed in a typed manuscript.

Working on *Ghosts of Mississippi* invigorated Willie, and one day

he called to announce that he was coming to New York for its premiere. He was organizing a dinner at Elaine's, the East Side watering
hole that established itself as a hangout for hard-drinking writers in
the 1960s. His old friend Bill Styron would be there, he said, as would
Rob Reiner, the movie's director, and Bobby DeLaughter. Would I
come? Would John?

Prevailing upon John to cut into his free time was always a
dilemma. Every day he was besieged by people who wanted him to
attend this luncheon or that black-tie gala. Part of my job was to
reduce that stress, not add to it. But forging relationships with Morris
and Styron could only help *George,* so I did pass the request along,
and somewhat to my surprise, John accepted the invitation.

By the time dinner started that Saturday night, I was certain I'd
made a terrible mistake. William Styron never showed up, but Rob
Reiner and Fred Zollo, the movie's producer, did. I came with Nyssa,
who wasn't overly enthusiastic about joining this testosterone-filled
gathering. John arrived late and visibly on edge. Loud and boisterous,
Elaine's is the kind of restaurant where diners spend more time table-
hopping than eating. We sat in the back; John always sat in the rear of
restaurants, his back to the other diners, so that they would be less
likely to recognize him and, if they did, find it hard to approach him or
take a picture. But still, he looked exposed. The restaurant had that
strange electricity I had come to recognize as the feeling a place had
when all its inhabitants knew John was present but wanted to appear
too blasé to care.

Willie threw back cocktail after cocktail. The more liquor he put
inside him, the more puffery came out. Rob Reiner was a cinematic
genius, he assured John. Fred Zollo? Courage personified, a hero for
making this movie. Reaching over the table to pat my forearm, he
swore to John that I was the best editor he'd ever had. Nyssa said little

but squeezed my leg under the table from time to time, sensing how uncomfortable I was. John was staring at his plate as if he'd never seen pasta before.

Halfway through dinner the actor James Woods, who played the murderous Byron De La Beckwith in the film, burst into the restaurant like a gunman flinging open a saloon door. A blonde perhaps half his age, all platinum and silicone and collagen, dangled from his arm. The movie people fizzed like cheap bubbly at a shotgun wedding.

"Jimmy! Jimmy Woods! Fuckin' Jimmy Woods!" Rob Reiner shouted.

"Rob! Rob Fuckin' Reiner!" Woods hollered back.

Then, while heads turned throughout Elaine's and the blonde stared hungrily at John, everyone hugged. This was not going well.

But then John turned to Bobby DeLaughter. The district attorney had sat quietly through the meal, taking in the hubbub from behind thick glasses. DeLaughter was played by Alec Baldwin in the movie, but in reality he was physically nondescript and, at least in this company, shy. Appearances deceived. DeLaughter had risked his career and his life to resuscitate a just but unpopular prosecution. Fighting the inertia of time and the hiss of bigotry, this man had done something heroic.

Could you tell me how you did it? John said to DeLaughter. How you convicted this killer?

DeLaughter looked uneasy. John Kennedy, who had lost a father to an assassin, was asking him about a similar abomination. But John's tone made clear that he wasn't just being polite.

So DeLaughter started to tell his story. He talked about how he dug up new evidence, reinterviewed old witnesses, and did his best to ignore death threats. He spoke slowly in a thick Mississippi drawl, and as he continued the rest of the table quieted down and began to listen. John sat transfixed. From time to time DeLaughter would lapse into a modest silence, unsure how much detail John really wanted. "Mmm-hmm," John would prod. "And then what happened?"

DeLaughter would nod and pick up where he'd left off.

"That was a good man," John said to me on Monday morning.

• • •

Damn it, I thought, we're going to miss this flight.

It was the last week in January, and I was pacing back and forth at the gate of the US Air shuttle at La Guardia Airport waiting for John. Our plane was due to take off in seven minutes. We were already five hours late for our meeting in Virginia, and he was supposed to meet me here. But John was nowhere in sight, and the gate attendants were checking their watches.

We had an appointment with the National Rifle Asssociation, a group one doesn't want to keep waiting. With deadlines for our April/May 1996 issue looming, we had again lacked an interview subject. So I'd nominated Marion Hammer, a gun-toting grandmother who happened to be the NRA's president. Guns in America—a delicate subject for John. But John liked to beard the lion in its den. It was, I had come to believe, why he wanted to interview Maureen Dowd, why he had worked in the Reagan Justice Department. It was too easy to talk only to people who would tell him what he wanted to hear. So I wasn't surprised when John agreed to do the interview, just pleased that he asked me to accompany him.

We were supposed to leave bright and early, but John didn't show. He'd cocooned himself in the New York University law library to prepare. Rose called Hammer's office to postpone, and I paced around the office, irritated that John had put off his preparation until the last minute. At first we thought we'd be only a couple hours late, but two became three, then four . . . Finally John called Rose to tell her that he was ready and would meet me at the airport.

I glanced at my watch. Three minutes to departure.

"What took you so long?" John said from behind me.

He was wearing a black suit and sunglasses and exuded such calm you'd never know that we were seconds from missing our flight. If I hadn't been so tense, I would have noticed that his arrival had already caused a minor commotion, people whispering, ogling, some pretending not to look while others flat-out stared. Because their gazes took me in—*Nope, never saw him before*—and kept right on going, I could study these looks and the judgment they contained. People scanned John like a bar code and carried their conclusions home like groceries, to be unwrapped and digested later. Was he as good-looking as in pictures? As tall? Was he friendly, or a jerk? Where was that beautiful girlfriend of his?

We walked down the pathway to the US Air 737. Heads swiveled as John stepped onto the plane. We found an open row and John took the window seat. He asked for my thoughts on Hammer, but I felt uneasy talking. Wasn't everyone around us listening to every word we said?

One of my colleagues once told me a story about flying with our boss. The actress Jennifer Aniston also happened to be on the flight. When she saw John, Aniston, who was single at the time, rose from her seat and stretched, lifting her arms slowly over her head, then carefully walked up and down the aisle of the business-class section, like a model on a catwalk.

John ignored her. He rarely gave any sign of noticing how anyone reacted to him, but traveling in public sapped his energy. If someone approached him politely, he was polite in return. It was, I think, the legacy of both his mother, with her emphasis on manners, and of his father, because in every stranger, politicians see a voter. Repeating that act of goodwill many times a day exhausted John, but it sent people away glowing as if they'd been touched by a faith healer.

"He's so *nice*," people would unfailingly say to me after they met him.

Often I was tempted to respond, "What did you expect? You've just told him what a great admirer of his you are, or how much his father meant to you. Or you looked at him with puppy love in your eyes. Why shouldn't he be nice? Just because he's famous?"

But of course I would never say that. I would simply agree: "Yes, he really is nice." I had come to believe that because John was a celebrity, people didn't expect him to be friendly, and that one of the reasons John mattered was because, in a democracy increasingly ruled by fame, he showed that celebrities did not have to act like monarchists.

The flight to Washington was uneventful. Marion Hammer was waiting patiently when at about five o'clock we finally arrived at the NRA's expensive but charmless headquarters in the northern Virginia suburbs. She was a tiny woman, a notch above five feet with a bowl-shaped head of Brillo-gray hair, who gripped my hand in hers and yanked it up and down as if she were pumping water. We sat in her office surrounded by a Frederic Remington sculpture of a horseman, a framed copy of the Bill of Rights, and a rather melodramatic oil painting of an eagle in flight.

While renowned photographer Bruce Davidson snapped pictures, John asked questions about Hammer's love of firearms. Hammer, who had given guns to her preteen grandchildren, answered every inquiry without evasion or apology. She treated John as she would any journalist, and he looked grateful for that, especially because the questions were sometimes uncomfortably personal.

"What do you say to a bereaved family member who has lost a loved one to senseless, gun-related violence?" John asked.

Hammer didn't flinch. "I would say that it's tragic," she answered, "but the reality is: the gun didn't do it, the individual did."

If anything, John was the twitchy one. He kept interrupting his interview to ask Davidson, "Are you about done?" And he would not ask Hammer the kind of personal questions readers expect. Hammer had once scared off rapists in a parking garage by brandishing a gun, but John conspicuously avoided raising the incident. He sounded hesitant, his labyrinthine queries twisting and turning in search of a point.

After an hour or so the other offices went dark and we heard the distant whine of vacuum cleaners as maintenance crews started their shifts. If we didn't wrap things up, we'd miss the last shuttle home. So John thanked Hammer, and she invited him back anytime. As we were leaving, she offered us some peanut butter and chocolate chip cookies that she'd baked for John.

On the flight back, John looked wiped out. "I think that went all right, don't you?" he said, then leaned his head against the window and fell sound asleep.

. . .

Before being published, John's interviews would be edited for clarity. (He'd usually assign the task to a different editor every month, so that no jealousies would develop.) In a way, the editing was a shame, because the cuts drained the interview of John's voice, the revealing speech of a man in transition, and to my mind that was usually more intriguing than the responses to his questions. I don't think he'd ever considered, before starting *George,* how difficult it would be for him to become something he wasn't sure he believed in. Could he be the kind of journalist he would want to write about him? Or, pressured by the public demand for titillation, would he slide into the gutter alongside all those pack rats who sensationalized his every move?

After all, John hated it when strangers asked him personal questions, even if they were phrased as gently as, say, Larry King put them. Now he was the one in the inquisitor's seat. Torn between his new responsibilities and his old instincts, John found interviewing a self-inflicted torture that often led to mutilated syntax and considerable angst.

Even so, the popularity of the interviews was a large part of the magazine's early success, and in August 1996 we upped the publication of *George* from once every two months to monthly. But John disliked the role of interviewer so much he began to skip months. Because advertisers clamored to be positioned near his interviews, John's discomfort cost *George* hundreds of thousands of advertising dollars and probably ten to twenty thousand newsstand sales every time he took a month off.

He also squirmed at the idea of putting his name on the cover to promote the interviews. We wanted to brand the franchise, call it "The John Kennedy Interview." He'd protest, "Can't we just call it 'The *George* Interview'?" No, we couldn't; that would defeat the purpose. So we compromised, constructing catch phrases: "John Kennedy Duels with the NRA's Top Gun." "Cokie Roberts Mouths Off to John Kennedy." That sort of thing. Those slightly hokey coverlines worked well enough, but "The John Kennedy Interview," simple and to the point, would have been better.

Our surveys showed that readers loved our photos of John sitting with his interview subject. In our second issue, Matt Berman had gone so far as to fake a photo of John talking to Robert De Niro by merging two separate images on the Macintosh. John and another celebrity—that was *George*'s money shot.

But the pictures embarrassed him. What other print reporter posed for his magazine? Every month Matt, who knew he could land the world's best photographers if they were offered the opportunity to shoot John, had to plead with him to pose. Again, we compromised. More and more often, the photos of John were shot in shadow or from behind or blurred.

So that no one could suggest that the interviews were not really his work, John eventually stopped having another editor sit in. Without a colleague present, John got increasingly personal in those conversations. Then the interviews started to get really interesting.

From Billy Graham to Gary Hart to, yes, Dan Quayle, John wanted to speak with people who could *teach* him. Again and again, he asked his subjects about the price of public life. What sacrifices—of privacy, of family, of authentic experience—were required from those who ran for office? He posed his queries in myriad ways, but in truth there was only one question: Is it time for me to reject my mother's desire for private life and follow the public path of my father?

Consider his interview with Warren Beatty, which John conducted alone. If John's father had chosen Hollywood over Washington, he would have been Beatty—glamorous, charming, seductive, but with an underlying intelligence and seriousness. Jackie Kennedy had recognized the similarities enough to ask Beatty to play JFK in the movie *PT 109*, the story of JFK's service in World War II. Beatty, who declined the part, had known JFK and did bear a slight resemblance to John's father. But as a younger man, he bore a striking resemblance to John. It was hardly surprising that their conversation turned to family matters.

"I can't resist asking whether you saw *JFK*," Beatty said.

"I didn't," John replied, "though I probably should have."

"Why didn't you?"

"I didn't want to," John said simply. Why not? That, of course, was the real question, but John was not ready to answer it.

At the end of the interview John asked Beatty, "If you had to tell your kids to choose between acting and politics, what would you recommend?"

"I would recommend neither," Beatty said.

"Why not?"

"Because someone has to be compelled to do either of those things. You can't recommend to someone to be a show-off."

Here was the great drama of John's life played out in plain sight, and it wasn't the tabloids who were digging it up. John was self-publishing a psychobiography in semimonthly installments. This authorized chronicle was a stroke of genius: He had found a way to reclaim his life story from its tabloid producers, to seize control of his public narrative. And for once, the person making money off John Kennedy wasn't the *Star* or the *Enquirer*, but John himself.

His most telling interview may have been with Iain Calder, a Brit who had once edited the *National Enquirer*. The *George* hook was the tabloids' increasing coverage of politicians, but John's agenda was personal. The tabs had harassed him for as long as he could remember; he wanted to call them on their behavior. Iain Calder, as it turned out, offered insights into John's life movie that John had never expected. They came when John asked Calder about an incident in which one reporter had tried to blackmail Ted Kennedy.

"When I was at college," John said in the interview, "I once got a call, and it was a British voice on the other end. He said, 'We have information that you're gay, and we have photographs to prove it'— photographs taken in a bar or something. I said, no, it wasn't true. Then they called my uncle Teddy . . . and said, 'We have these photographs of John, but if you pose for some Christmas pictures with your family, we may not run them.' Could that have been the *National Enquirer*?"

Calder replied, "That doesn't sound like something we would do, mainly because it wouldn't work."

But if it would, John said, would you do it?

"No, I wouldn't," Calder said. "I mean, even if we had great pictures of you in a [gay] bar, we would never have used them—even if the pictures were true."

Why not? John asked.

"Because our readers consider you a beloved figure."

"You're too kind," John said. "But wouldn't that be all the more reason?"

"No," Calder answered. "Our readers . . . would have killed us for doing that. You're the little boy saluting his father. . . . No, no, no, they would have killed us for it."

You could not have asked for a more forthright explanation of John's place in the American psyche. *Even if the pictures were true,* Calder said, the *Enquirer* would not run them. (Since the tabloids linked John with various starlets every few weeks, the real blasphemy here was any suggestion that John might be gay.) To the millions of Americans who read the tabloids, John would always be that heartbreaking little boy, and they did not want to hear a word to the contrary. They would, in fact, lash out at anyone who suggested that the image and the reality were not the same—"kill" them, Calder had said, which was more than a little ironic.

· · ·

As he got to know us better, John seemed to feel more comfortable introducing his family to his employees. I met his sister, Caroline, when she visited one morning that winter and John showed her around the office. She was polite, but had a more reserved manner than John. He seemed almost nervous with Caroline, as if hoping that *George* would make a good impression on his big sister. I was anxious to do the same, so of course I got nervous and made a fool of myself.

A few nights before, we'd both attended the premiere of Mike

Nichols' new film *The Birdcage*. I was friends with Nichols' assistant; Caroline was friends with Nichols. During one raucous nightclub scene, Robin Williams' character had joked about Ted Kennedy's fondness for drink.

"I saw you at *The Birdcage*," I said to Caroline when John introduced us.

"Oh, really?" she said, her voice giving away nothing. "Did you enjoy it?"

"I did," I said. Then I remembered. "I mean, uh, except for that part about your uncle."

Caroline smiled, but the smile stopped at her eyes. "Which part?" she said sweetly.

"That part where . . . When Robin Williams . . . Um. Well. Never mind."

Caroline nodded cautiously and started backing out my office door. "Very nice to meet you," she said.

· · ·

One Friday morning in February 1996 John came into my office and shut the door. While I closed a computer file, he plunked down in a battered chair that I had scavenged from another floor. David Pecker ran a tight ship; we resorted to plundering unused offices and secret storerooms for furniture.

"There's something I need to talk to you about," he said.

"Okay," I said cautiously.

"I'm going to be spending more time on advertising calls, and I've decided that I need one person directly below me."

I nodded, trying to keep my face expressionless, but I was surprised. After Eric departed, John had said he did not want to replace him.

"It's going to be Biz," John said quietly.

I forced myself not to say anything for a second, but one turned into two, then a few. "Okay," I said finally. "Why?"

Because Eric and he had fought so much, John answered. "I don't need another male ego to compete with."

He sounded almost as if he were apologizing.

"Besides," John added, "I think it'd be good to have a woman as the executive editor of a political magazine."

Executive editor? Eric's title had been editor, which suggested more authority than "executive editor." John was promoting Biz, but he wanted the world to understand that *George* was still his show.

"We have a lot of female readers," John continued, "far more than any other political magazine. Biz is good for our image."

I nodded, unable to deny the logic. Even if many of our female readers were mostly interested in John, Biz was a great marketing tool, a fresh face in a journalistic milieu dominated by white men with bad haircuts and ill-fitting suits. But that rationale was a little insulting to Biz, whose many virtues had nothing to do with her sex. She was intelligent, cared deeply about good writing, and was a model of discretion. When Bob Guccione, Jr., her old boss at *Spin* magazine, was slapped with a sexual harassment suit, Biz would not speak a word against him. It seemed demeaning to say that she was being chosen because of her gender.

Maybe, I thought, she's just better than I am, and John doesn't want to say so. Maybe he's trying to be nice.

I must have looked concerned, because before he left John assured me, "Don't worry—I'm happy with your work."

I was stunned. I hadn't been campaigning to replace Eric—that would have felt like betrayal—but Biz's elevation hit me hard. I wondered why I hadn't seen it coming, and I was a bit shaken by how calculating John was about public relations.

Thinking it over in the days that followed, I came to the conclusion that emotional survival at *George* required keeping a safe distance from John. I could not forget who I was—an editor, a writer, a journalist who would be performing this work long after John Kennedy had moved on to other pursuits. Not a man who hung out with famous models and glitzy celebrities, but an ordinary man fortunate enough to love his work.

I would respect and protect John. I would do my utmost to stand by him. But I would not be seduced by him.

Six

On February 25, 1996, John and Carolyn took their dog, Friday, for a walk in Washington Square Park. It was a bright, sunny, unseasonably warm day. Her hair tucked underneath a red bandana, Carolyn was wearing sweats and sunglasses. John was similarly outfitted in sunglasses, cranberry-red shorts, and a light green sweater.

But what started as a pleasant Sunday morning stroll suddenly went very wrong. One moment the two lovers were walking along happily, the next they erupted into a knock-down, drag-out argument. John began shouting at Carolyn, Carolyn shouted back at John, and Friday looked on in distress.

Carolyn started shoving John, who pushed her back. His face contorted with rage, John screamed at Carolyn, "You've got my ring, you're not getting my dog!" Moments later he burst into tears and collapsed to the curb as if sucker-punched. Burying his head between his knees and tucking his arms around his legs, he curled into a ball.

Seeing John in such pain, Carolyn couldn't stay mad. She knelt down and, touching him gently, tried desperately to console him. It seemed to work. After a few moments, John slowly got to his feet. The two clasped hands and walked away, Friday trotting behind.

Unbeknown to the lovers, their quarrel was captured by a clandestine videographer and would be aired on a tabloid TV show a week later, after the program had a few days during which to promote its exclusive. Then the *National Enquirer* ran a cover story on "the brutal bust-up" that left America's "#1 hunk sobbing alone on the sidewalk."

In the office we circled the topic like airport guards around an abandoned suitcase. Even to those of us who'd seen John fight with Michael, the videotape of the clash was shocking. I knew that John had a temper and that Carolyn was no shrinking violet. But the violence of their rage presented a harsh contrast to the tenderness I'd seen between them.

John volunteered nothing about the fight, and we all shied away from the subject. Well, all of us except for Michael. He was furious that John hadn't told him about the brawl before its public screening. In the days before the videotape aired, no one knew exactly what it would show, not even John. This wasn't just a personal matter; everything he did could affect *George*. Michael and Elinore Carmody were both concerned: If the video showed John bullying Carolyn, how many fashion and cosmetics advertisers would we lose?

The fight, Michael told John after the show aired, would undermine John's credibility as an editor and *George*'s as a magazine. That it happened was bad enough; what made it worse was that he, Michael, could have used his PR skills to soften the blow.

Michael was right. Even though the video suggested that Carolyn was more the aggressor than John, the fight was bad for *George*. On *Saturday Night Live*, comedian David Spade joked of John, "Why don't you stop hitting your girlfriend and pretending to run a magazine?" To minimize the damage, Michael could have fed a pooh-poohing quote to a friendly columnist or stage-managed a public appearance by John and Carolyn. But John didn't want Michael that close, and Carolyn was even more adamant. If damage control was required, she insisted that she would do it. Michael wasn't the only one who had worked in public relations.

The fight in the park marked a turning point in Michael and John's relationship. Michael had attempted to stake his claim as John's closest adviser, and failed. Yet Carolyn lost, too, in a way I don't think she fully understood. The fight helped create an impression of her as high maintenance and melodramatic. Americans knew John as chivalrous, a gentleman; he had once met Daryl Hannah at the airport after she'd allegedly clashed with her ex-beau, the singer Jackson Browne. Now he was the one fighting with a woman. If he had changed, the public wouldn't blame him.

Though countless women would have traded places with her, Carolyn was in a situation where the odds of being disliked were much greater than those of winning America's heart. She was learning what Michael already knew: that everyone wanted to believe the best of John, even if it meant believing the worst of the people around him. Carolyn was flirting with becoming the next Yoko Ono or Courtney Love, the woman who steals a beloved man from his adoring public.

In principle, Americans should have taken to her; Carolyn wasn't American royalty, that oxymoron so often applied to John. She was, in fact, more typically American than he. She was not raised on ritzy Fifth Avenue, as John was, but in Greenwich, Connecticut, a suburb of New York. Greenwich is affluent, but Carolyn's parents were new there, not one of the town's snooty blue-blood clans. And like so many Americans whose parents came of age in the 1960s, Carolyn was a child of divorce; she was reportedly closer to her stepfather than to her father. She didn't go to a highbrow Ivy League college, but to middle-of-the-pack Boston University. Before becoming Calvin Klein's assistant, she had worked as a salesgirl in one of his stores.

If most people revered celebrity, John romanticized the ordinary, and Carolyn's everyday background was part of what attracted him to her. Her roots not only would give her the strength to be John's partner, they would help him stay grounded. Carolyn provided John a link to the lives of average Americans. At the same time, she was beautiful, passionate, and vivacious. She didn't seem to be at all intimidated by him.

People said John was like Jay Gatsby, and though that analogy had some merit—both men had seamless, seductive exteriors—there was an essential difference between the two. Gatsby knew who he wanted to be but denied who he was; John knew who he was, but not who he wanted to be. If anyone was Gatsbyesque, it was Carolyn. She was the social dreamer intent upon self-transformation. But as she herself would admit, behind her carefully constructed beauty there swirled a maelstrom of insecurity. Was she pretty enough for John? Strong enough? Did he really love her?

She wasn't book smart—Carolyn didn't read many books—but she compensated with ambition. At college she posed for "The Girls of B.U." calendar, which later embarrassed her. The calendar was testimony to how much work had gone into her current appearance. In her photo Carolyn looked girl-next-door sweet—big-eyed, big-haired, a bit Madonna circa 1985, nothing like the sleek fashion icon she would become. She seemed softer, more accessible than the woman who, in her need to protect herself, had adopted a hard shell. From the time she started being photographed with John, she felt pressure to look the part of his physical peer. But unlike John, Carolyn had to work for her looks. She subjected herself to injections of Botox, a bacteria that numbed the nerves in her forehead, so that she would not frown and develop wrinkles. She dieted herself rail thin, plucked her eyebrows until they were mere wisps, dyed her hair the color of white corn. She was sitting in my office once when John walked in and began stroking her hair. "Not so hard, okay, baby?" Carolyn said, squirming a little. "I've got so many chemicals in this hair, you're going to break it." She was half-joking, but only half.

I wished that the public could have seen John and Carolyn at their happiest, as they were just weeks later when they hosted a *George* party in Washington. Held on March 25, 1996, at the luxurious home of socialites Peggy and Conrad Cafritz, it was an intimate gathering of perhaps sixty people, including George Stephanopoulos, Secretary of Commerce Ron Brown, and Health and Human Services Secretary Donna Shalala. Chic, for Washington.

About an hour into the evening, after a cool spring night had descended, I saw John and Carolyn standing by a window near the bar. Someone was making a toast in the living room and the other guests had gravitated that way. With a mischievous smile, John slid the window open and dropped to the patio a few feet below. Carolyn slipped off her heels and followed, grasping the windowsill as John held out his arms and eased her to the ground, then reached for her hand. As they walked slowly through the moonlight, they stopped to kiss, Carolyn lifting her lips to John's. They didn't return until the party was winding down, and when they did, smiles danced around their faces like little waves lapping at the edges of a pool.

· · ·

After the brouhaha over the videotaped quarrel, things were quiet at the magazine for a few months. Biz worked ever more closely with John, Michael ever less so. I tried to avoid *George*'s politics and focus on the country's. After all, Bill Clinton was running for reelection against Kansas senator Bob Dole, and this was *George*'s time to shine, because nothing in politics is more entertaining than a presidential election.

In the second week of August, I flew to San Diego for the Republican National Convention with six or seven of my colleagues, including some new hires. One was Inigo Thomas, an eccentric Brit who smoked incessantly, drank as only British journalists can, and bore an uncanny resemblance to Austin Powers. The other new editor was Susannah Hunnewell, an incisive, sharp-tongued woman Biz hired away from the beauty magazine *Marie Claire*.

Our little band of travelers met John on the outskirts of town at the dilapidated Days Inn to which the Republicans had relegated us. The place looked like a cinderblock with air conditioners. On one side was a dive bar; on the other, a strip joint. A neon outline of a horizontal woman, her exaggerated curves like racetrack turns, blinked on and off in its front window.

Well, we weren't going to spend much time in our rooms anyway. The weather was balmy, the booze abundant, and the work minimal. Everyone knew that candidate Bob Dole didn't have a prayer of winning; there wasn't exactly a sense of urgency in San Diego. The only *George* representative who really had to work was Norman Mailer. Squeezing our budget to come up with a payment far larger than any we had previously made, Biz and John had commissioned Mailer to write two pieces on the '96 campaign for *George,* and the seventy-three-year-old legend was maneuvering around the convention, notebook in hand, digging for quotes like a cub reporter.

While the rest of us tossed back jumbo shrimps with cocktail sauce and sipped champagne at Steve Forbes' garden party luncheon, or devoured Wolfgang Puck's pizzas and listened to the Brian Setzer Orchestra on the San Diego esplanade, John avoided official events.

Not because he wanted to, but because his one attempt to participate had proven more trouble than it was worth.

On day two, John and Gary tried to get on the floor of the convention hall, where the delegates sat and members of the press wandered around in search of something, anything, to report. Maria Shriver was there, headset on and cameraman in tow, but she couldn't do much because people kept asking her for autographs. I was on the floor as well, hanging out with the South Carolina delegation. While the national anthem blared through the arena, Strom Thurmond, the nonagenarian senator from South Carolina, grabbed my shoulder with a withered hand, clutching me for support and liberating me only after "the home of the brave." He said not a word; he seemed to think I worked for him.

As Thurmond and I were getting acquainted, John edged on to one corner of the convention floor. Almost instantly the space around him started to crackle with energy like the horizon before a thunderstorm. At first John tried to be polite to everyone swarming around him, reaching for his hand, touching his shoulder, holding out programs and small flags for him to sign. But the mob kept growing; things were getting out of control. So he and Gary bolted, striking out for safety outside the building.

After that, John avoided the crowds. In the Days Inn's dingy but private conference room, he conducted an America Online chat to promote *George*. "How sick to death are you of people calling you John-John after all these years?" one e-mailer asked.

"No one I know calls me John-John," he sidestepped.

"Do you see politics in your future?" another wrote.

"Well, politics is in my present," John answered. "And for the time being, it is a fully engaging endeavor. Elective politics is one of those things that once you are in it, you do not leave voluntarily."

On Wednesday night we had thrown a party of our own at the San Diego Zoo. Greeted by the screeches of monkeys and the roars of lions cutting through the gentle night, guests entered the darkened zoo and walked down a narrow, twisting path bordered by thick foliage. At its terminus was a cafe with outdoor tables and warm yellow lights hidden in the trees, and that's where our party was held. We'd hired animal trainers to walk beautiful lion cubs on thick leashes. Roped off at the door, the press shouted questions and snapped photos of the arriving guests. The reporters went a little berserk when John strolled down the path, but he stopped and fed them sound bites about how good it felt to be in San Diego, and they simmered down.

The scene was mellow enough that people could actually converse. John mingled comfortably and departed before midnight. The rest of us lingered and drank in the moonlight. The *George* contingent tipsily closed down the party, arms around each other's shoulders, performing in an impromptu cancan line. A little unprofessional, but what the hell. This was our party, and we wanted it to last forever.

·   ·   ·

In Chicago two weeks later, the party wasn't in a zoo, it *was* a zoo.

I was in a taxi, stuck in traffic, perhaps four blocks from my destination, the Art Institute of Chicago. A cacophony of honking filled the night air. I stuck my head out the window and looked up the street. The traffic light switched from red to green and back again.

"Forget it," I told the driver. "I'll walk from here." I paid the man, hopped out of the cab, and started walking up the Michigan Avenue median.

It was August 27, 1996, and I'd flown into O'Hare Airport about three hours before. I had deadlines to meet at the office, but no way was I going to miss the *George* party at the Democratic National Convention. Everyone was going to be there—Democrats seemed to be more fired up about our bash than they were about Bill Clinton, and they were pretty fired up about Clinton. They could smell victory in November, and they wanted to party.

Originally we planned to host a soiree for two hundred or so at the Art Institute's nearby school—something exclusive and tasteful, which would have the added benefit of not costing a lot. But as convention time approached, desperate petitioners flooded our office with phone calls, faxes, and e-mails. How could they get on the list? They were a friend of a friend. . . . Even reporters who had trashed *George* in print didn't hesitate to call. We decided to move the party to the much larger Art Institute, but the guest list kept growing.

As I walked along Michigan Avenue, I saw what was blocking traffic. Flanking the long descending steps of the museum were steel crowd barriers, which resembled oversized bike racks. Behind them, hundreds of people armed with pads and pens and cameras stood waiting for the stars to make their appearances. Kevin Costner was expected, and so were Oprah Winfrey, Jerry Springer, Aretha Franklin, Chelsea Clinton, Billy Baldwin, Eleanor Mondale, and Chris Rock. And John, of course. He was the star people really wanted to see.

At the moment, though, since I was early—after all, I was working— no one had arrived except all those stargazers and a bunch of burly Chicago cops. And me.

I took a deep breath and strode up the long, rolling steps. I could feel people checking me out, wondering if I was someone they should know. A few snapped photos in case I was famous and they just didn't recognize me. I tried to walk as straight and tall as I could without tripping over any steps. At the top, I turned and looked upon the crowd. Maybe they were bored, maybe impatient, but in any case they were watching me. Is this what it feels like to be famous? I thought. The feeling of all these eyes upon you . . . It wasn't so bad.

And then I thought: It will be when John gets here.

He had landed in Chicago earlier in the week and passed the time appearing on *Oprah* and sailing on Lake Michigan. He also landed smack in the middle of a controversy. The September issue of *George*— marking our one-year anniversary—was on the stands. Its theme was women in politics. Its cover? The actress Drew Barrymore dressed as Marilyn Monroe on that infamous night in Madison Square Garden when she sang "Happy Birthday" to John's father. The ostensible reason? To mark Bill Clinton's fiftieth birthday.

That's what we claimed, anyway. But that explanation satisfied no one. The cover, wrote the anonymous scribes at Suck.com, a now defunct Generation-X web site, "is a blatant tribute to [John's] father (the Stallion)." Most commentators shared that opinion. How could John Kennedy pay tribute to the woman who had humiliated his mother in front of an arena full of people?

Around the office, we didn't know what to make of it. This had been John's call; none of us would have urged fooling around with Kennedy iconography. He had advocated the idea enthusiastically, but didn't provide much reason beyond saying that it was a sexy image. The cover would sell, we knew that. But John obviously had personal reasons for going with Barrymore as Monroe. Was he suggesting that he condoned his father's philandering? That he didn't take it seriously?

To the outside world, my colleagues and I adopted a party line. We're just re-creating a piece of Americana, we insisted. What's the big deal?

But privately, I felt the cover was a slap in the face, a setback to our attempts to get *George* judged on its merits. Sure, some people bought the magazine just for a JFK Jr. fix, but that wasn't satisfying. If we settled for such a small gratification, then we weren't journalists, just cogs in a machine peddling John F. Kennedy, Jr.

Naturally, the Drew Barrymore issue went on to sell twice the usual 100,000 copies we sold on the newsstand.

. . .

Our party filled up quickly after the doors opened at eight o'clock. Though we had stationed several bars inside the museum, most guests headed to the spacious rectangular courtyard, where waiters carried trays of hors d'oeuvres above their shoulders and the bars were less crowded. On one long side of the rectangular courtyard, our band—a young woman named Poe backed by a guitarist, a drummer, and a bass player with a shaved head—kicked in so loud you had to shout just to hear yourself.

It was a safe bet that no one like Poe had ever played a political convention before. (The GOP had featured Trent Lott leading a barbershop quartet.) Tall and slender with long, straight blond hair, she was wearing an oversize white T-shirt with her name on it, a black miniskirt, and knee-high black leather boots. Eyes closed, she wrapped herself around her microphone stand and sang, "You look like shit! What's your problem, bitch? Your legs feel like sandpaper!"

I sipped a vodka tonic and watched Poe stalk across the stage whipping her hair back and forth. I should have been working the party, but since you couldn't talk to anyone, what was the point? In San Diego, we'd known most of our guests. There were more than 2,000 people filling this courtyard, and probably 1,900 of them were strangers.

An anxious-looking Rosemarie Terenzio tapped me on the shoulder.

"John just got here," she said. She sounded a little frantic. "Can you just, uh, hang out by him?"

"Why?"

"It's getting weird," she snapped.

"Where is he?" I said.

She pointed to one corner of the courtyard, then bolted in that direction. I followed.

John looked like a fox cornered by hounds. There were people on every side of him, and more on their way. In the background, Poe was singing a new song. "I wanna kill you!" she yelled. "I wanna blow you . . . *away*!"

I caught John's eye, and he shot me a look of relief.

"Having fun?" I shouted.

"Stick around," he mouthed.

I nodded. At six-foot-three and 210 pounds, I was the biggest member of the *George* staff, and though I'd never played bodyguard before, I was willing to try. Something in the air made me more than usually wary about John's safety.

"I can do it in a church," Poe volunteered. "I can do it any time or place. But either way . . . I wanna kill you! I wanna blow you . . . *away*!"

"Maybe we should leave this corner?" I said.

John nodded and began to edge along the courtyard perimeter, shaking hands and saying hello to the people waiting—women, mostly, hovering in safe clusters of two and three, wearing their best party dresses, screwing up their courage to talk to John even as they pretended that they had just happened to find themselves standing next to him. I stood at his side and scanned the crowd. A few people asked if I could introduce them, which, if they didn't look like Charles Manson, I did. Most of them didn't; a large percentage were pretty women, but there were some men, political powerbroker types, and even a few wide-eyed teenagers. If John couldn't get rid of someone after thirty seconds or so, I'd tap him on the shoulder. And John would say, "I'm sorry—would you excuse me?" to the person monopolizing him, and we'd move along.

Our perpetual motion kept the crowds from getting too big, and as we moved we fell into a groove, like a waltz—*stop*-talk-go, *stop*-talk-go, *stop*-talk-go. John started to relax. That slightly desperate look vanished from his eyes. It began to seem as if he were actually enjoying himself.

I didn't realize it, but from inside the museum you could track our progress, because spotlights stationed in the courtyard's four corners illuminated John's every move, crisscrossing back and forth like at an old-fashioned movie premiere. Not to mention the flickering of strobe flashes around John. Looking down on us, someone told me later, was like looking at a huge conga line swaying through the courtyard, or a giant snake slithering along. You couldn't see John, but you could tell where he was by looking for the head of the snake. Everywhere he went, he pulled the party along with him.

I lost track of time, but at some point Elinore Carmody pulled John away to be photographed with executives from Neiman Marcus, the department store that was helping to sponsor the party. I was relieved of duty. Not long after that Poe, her hair damp with sweat and her makeup smudged, wrapped up her set. "Fly away," she sang. A slow song to kiss the party good night. "Fly, fly away . . . Nothing can stand in your way."

Though the bars were still busy, the Chicago fire department came and shut us down at about midnight. Too many people, they said. A fire hazard. Like they'd only just figured that out.

I returned to my room at the Hilton. I don't smoke, but I felt like having a cigarette. Too wired to fall asleep, I lay on my starched bed with its fire-retardant coverlet and pondered the scene that had just transpired—the adoring crowds reaching out to touch John, the energy bordering on anarchy, the love that felt like violence.

That, I thought, is what it will be like when John goes into politics.

Seven

New York quickens after Labor Day, especially in the media community, whose denizens return from their summer vacations with the reluctant knowledge that it's time to work again. Gone are the lazy summer Fridays where no one can be found at their desks past noon, the slow-moving Mondays when suntanned employees roll into offices just a little later than they would during any other season. *George* was no exception. We knew that we couldn't sustain the intensity of our party-throwing August. Congress was back in session, Bob Dole and Bill Clinton were teeing off against each other, and we had to find a way to make it all compelling.

But John seemed distracted in early September. He was skipping edit meetings, perfunctorily signing off on stories, and leaving the office early. His mood, however, was excellent; he was practically whistling through the corridors. Rose, meanwhile, was spending a lot of time on the phone with Ted Kennedy's office.

It could mean only one thing: After about a year and a half of dating, John and Carolyn were getting married. Everyone at *George*, I think, guessed John's secret. But no one said a word to him, and even among ourselves, we barely alluded to the possibility. That would have been bad karma, like a baseball announcer pointing out a no-hitter in progress.

John had hidden a clue in his October editor's letter (he wrote it in August), in which he talked of politics and love. "It's true that political life can be a strain on a marriage," John wrote. "The husband (usually) gets all the attention, while the wife is expected not only to give up her career but gaze adoringly during every photo opportunity. They have little privacy and even less time together. But in another respect, the crises and isolation of a public life create a sense of shared burden that can bring a couple closer."

Rereading that letter a few weeks after John wrote it, I speculated as to its intended audience. Was John writing this for our readers, or for Carolyn? Was it a warning or a promise?

I heard the news on a car radio on Saturday, September 21. "Sorry, ladies, the world's most eligible bachelor has finally called it a day," the broadcaster said. The wedding had taken place in a tiny white clapboard church—a former slave chapel with only a handful of benches and no electricity—on Cumberland Island, a little-known speck of land off the coast of Georgia. Not a single tabloid reporter or photographer was on hand to disrupt the ceremony. John had pulled it off.

Though I wasn't surprised, I couldn't stop smiling. It didn't matter that John hadn't told us or that we weren't invited. What mattered was that we'd kept his secret. That was our small part in the wedding.

First thing Monday morning, Rose left presents from John on our desks—cigars for the men, champagne for the women. A warm note accompanied the gifts:

To: All the Gentlewomen and Gentlemen of George
From: John
Re: Breaking News

I just wanted to let you know that while you were all toiling away, I went and got myself married. I had to be a bit sneaky for reasons that by now I imagine are obvious.

I wanted you all to enjoy these small tokens of gratitude and fellowship. You folks all do amazing work and it's an honor to have you as colleagues. This magazine has turned the corner, and it ain't because Fauntleroy does *Oprah*.

Thank you and good cheer to all.

P.S. Does this mean you'll all call me "Mr." from now on?

The note made me smile even more, because I knew how John must have enjoyed writing it.

At the same time, I couldn't help analyzing it a little—it's an editor's second nature—and I was struck by that offhand reference to Little Lord Fauntleroy. It was so casually dropped in that I wondered if John were well acquainted with the source, a sentimental novel published in 1886 called *Little Lord Fauntleroy*. Who read it nowadays? Why would John know it?

I later learned from a biography that John's mother had once listed "Little Lord Fauntleroy's grandfather" as a childhood hero. Doubtful that it could be a coincidence that mother and son both cited a nineteenth-century children's book, I dug up a copy. Written by Frances Hodgson Burnett, it's the story of an American boy named Cedric whose valiant father dies when the child is just a baby. Though the boy doesn't understand death, he knows that his mother gets sad sometimes, and he would "put his curly head upon her neck" to lift her spirits. "He did what he could, and was more of a comfort to her than he could have understood."

AMERICAN SON

Because his father had been an English lord, Cedric will also grow up to be royalty. But because Cedric doesn't know that, he remains innocent and unspoiled—*American* royalty, distinguished by humility and decency rather than the noxious affectations of the European aristocracy who take privilege for granted.

> He had big brown eyes and long eyelashes and a darling little face. . . . His manners were so good, for a baby, that it was delightful to make his acquaintance. He seemed to feel that everyone was his friend, and when anyone spoke to him, when he was in his carriage in the street, he would give the stranger one sweet serious look with the brown eyes, and then follow in with a lovely, friendly smile; and the consequence was, that there was not a person in the neighbourhood of the quiet street where he lived . . . who was not pleased to see him, and speak to him. And every month of his life he grew handsomer and more interesting.

It was a little unnerving, imagining the possibility of Jacqueline Bouvier Kennedy choosing this particular book to share with her children. Because John—as a boy, as a man—matched that description of Little Lord Fauntleroy in every way.

"I'm very glad I'm going to be an earl," Little Lord Fauntleroy says at the end of his story. "I didn't think at first I should like it, but now I do."

· · ·

While John and Carolyn honeymooned in Turkey, I embarked on a search for a wedding present. This was no simple task. The newlyweds hadn't exactly registered at Crate & Barrel, and what could one possibly buy for John Kennedy that he didn't already have? Adding to the pressure, John's office had filled with so many beautifully wrapped gifts that it looked like Whoville the night before Christmas. Every fashion designer in the world seemed to have sent the lovebirds something special.

After days of deliberation, I selected a small silver box with a lock in the middle and had it delivered to their apartment. I hoped it was both tasteful and symbolic.

About two weeks later, when John returned to work, we assembled in his office. Looking tanned and fit, he wore a vast smile on his face and a gold wedding band on his left ring finger. Rose had ordered muffins and coffee and fruit and champagne, and we toasted John and teased him about his secret preparations. He was flush with the glow of romance, so our jokes bounced off him like confetti.

"How's Carolyn holding up?" I asked John later that day, when things had quieted down a bit. As if to make up for missing the wedding, the tabloids had relentlessly tracked the newlyweds throughout their trip.

"She's doing just fine," John said proudly. "She knew what she was getting into."

Mostly what I remember from that day and the ones following is the way John kept repeating the words *my wife*—as in, "I was talking to *my wife* . . ." or "Well, *my wife* thinks . . ." He'd stop and unconsciously rub the ring on his finger and smile when he said those words, as if he were rolling around on his tongue a sip of the world's most succulent wine and never wanted to forget the taste.

Perhaps a week after John's return, I received a thank-you note in the mail. "Dear Rich and Nyssa," he had written on a thick white card with *JFK* embossed in black at the top. "Many thanks for the most elegant box with the Bauhaus legs. That was most thoughtful and I'll keep my pens and Milk Duds in it. Love, John."

That "Love, John" touched me. Not because I thought he did love me or Nyssa—our relationship was getting closer, but not that close. John was just so filled with happiness, he loved a lot of people right then. Especially those so pleased to see him filled with joy.

John had ample cause to hide his feelings, but he didn't, and that was both brave and inspiring.

· · ·

My own feelings about John were getting increasingly complex. He could be maddeningly contrarian, as when he chose Drew-as-Marilyn for *George*'s cover despite insisting that *George* wasn't the place to cover the Kennedys. But after the scary hurly-burly of the Chicago party, I felt more protective of him than ever—and I was discovering that John could return the favor.

In our November 1996 issue I wrote a "Where are they now?" story featuring players from past campaign scandals. Not the politicians but the civilians, people like Donna Rice, Gennifer Flowers, and Willie Horton, the furloughed killer the Bush campaign used to destroy Democrat Michael Dukakis in 1988. Rice had gotten married, changed her name to Donna Rice Hughes, and become a crusader against Internet porn. Flowers was starring in a road show of *Oh! Calcutta!* And Horton was locked up in a maximum security Maryland prison, where, somewhat nervously, I interviewed the aging murderer and rapist. "Despite overwhelming evidence, Horton insists that he didn't commit those crimes," I wrote. But we were tight for space, and I cut the first three words.

That edited line didn't please Massachusetts state representative Donna Fournier Cuomo, whose brother, a gas-station attendant, Horton had shot to death in 1974. In Cuomo's opinion, I had given a savage criminal a platform to proclaim his innocence. Well, not me, actually. By publishing my words, John had.

"I am taking this opportunity of the thirty-third anniversary of the assassination of your father to contact you," Cuomo wrote John on November 22. "I thought this day would provide you with a unique opportunity to identify with me and how it feels when someone you love is murdered." Instead, she insisted, John had whitewashed Willie Horton's brutality.

At the same time, Cuomo began pushing stories about John's callowness to the Massachusetts media. In Massachusetts, it doesn't take much to get stories about the Kennedys into the newspaper, and this was more than enough.

John showed me Cuomo's letter, and it made me feel awful. This woman's loss was tragic, but her outrage sounded opportunistic, and I'd gift-wrapped the opportunity for her to grab some ink by smearing John. November 22 was hard enough for him; he didn't come into the office on that day.

But John backed me up and refused to apologize to Cuomo. He knew he couldn't trust someone who was writing to him and talking to the press at the same time. "If I respond, she'll only publicize that, too," he said. "Anyway, you didn't do anything wrong."

"I appreciate that," I said, and I did. Plenty of editors would have written Cuomo a conciliatory note just to get her off their backs. Even if it meant undercutting their writer.

At about the same time, I became embroiled in an ugly spat with a journalist named Robert Sam Anson. A fearless, cantankerous reporter from the Vietnam era, Anson had written a devastating profile of *Washington Post* reporter Bob Woodward for *George* that I had edited, and when he expressed interest in tackling Senate majority leader Trent Lott, I quickly sent him a contract, which he signed with equal dispatch. He asked for an advance—his roof needed repair, he said—and I sent him that, too.

For the next six weeks or so, Anson assured me that he was making excellent progress—until one day late that fall when, without warning, he faxed me a note. He was very sorry, but he had just signed a contract with *Vanity Fair*. His new deal precluded him from writing for *George*. To be honest, he added, he hadn't made much progress on the Trent Lott story anyway. He'd been distracted because his dog had been hit by a car.

I was livid. Anson couldn't have signed a contract with *Vanity Fair* voiding his contract with *George*. Contracts don't work that way. And that line about the dog . . .

So I wrote a cranky retort. If I remember correctly, I said something about Anson updating the "dog ate my homework" excuse. I may also have mentioned that faxing a letter, rather than calling, suggested that Anson was not particularly proud of his behavior. But unlike my Maureen Dowd rant, I showed this one to John before mailing it.

"Fine," John said. "This guy's dissing us. Fire away."

Anson was not happy about my letter. He faxed me his veterinarian bill—"for your scrapbook"—and wrote John a truculent note. A couple days after receiving it, John summoned me to his office.

"I spoke with Robert Sam Anson," he said.

Uh-oh, I thought. "And?"

"I said, 'Robert Sam, I'm not sure why you wrote me—whether it's to say that you can't work for *George* or you're just mad at Rich,'" John continued.

Both, Anson had replied.

"So what'd you say?" I asked, letting a little hope into my voice. John seemed to be fighting back a smile.

"I said, 'Well, what do you expect Rich to do? I mean, you humiliated the guy. Every week I've been riding his ass about Trent Lott, and every week he tells me, Robert Sam's working on it, and then he gets this fax. You don't even *call* him.'"

Now John was starting to chuckle.

"So what'd *he* say?"

"Nothing, for a second," John replied. "And then he said, 'Well, the magazine's getting a lot better.' And I said, 'That's irrelevant. But it would be even better if you'd written that piece.'"

Vanity Fair wouldn't let him, Anson had insisted.

"So," John said, "I told him that I knew that wasn't true because I checked with Graydon Carter," the editor of *Vanity Fair*.

"You called Graydon Carter?"

John's eyes were twinkling. "Nope. But Robert Sam Anson sure thought I did."

. . .

It was clear that John couldn't have been happier with his marriage. But Carolyn's relationship with the media was proving to be a source of stress.

John had released only one photo of his nuptials to the press, a romantic image of the newlyweds walking down the church steps. Carolyn was wearing a long, flowing white dress that the designer Narciso Rodriguez created for her. (Our business side reported that Calvin Klein, Carolyn's old boss, was furious that Carolyn had not worn one of his dresses, and *George* never received another Calvin Klein fashion ad.) John was in a crisp tuxedo. He was kissing the white-gloved hand of his new bride. Carolyn's face was aglow with joy and love.

Ted Kennedy's office disseminated some key details about the ceremony: that John wore his father's watch. That his boutonniere was a cornflower, JFK's favorite. That Ted Kennedy and Caroline Kennedy Schlossberg had toasted John's mother. That a horse had nibbled on Carolyn's bouquet when she wasn't looking.

I had learned enough about the Kennedys to know that these weren't random nuggets, but precious gems painstakingly culled to add new luster to the Kennedy mythology. Ted Kennedy understood that, just as America needed John, so did the Kennedys; John was a powerful battery that could provide new energy to both. Inevitably, these personal touches were also political. Down the road, couldn't we all imagine that photo becoming a staple of campaign iconography? Wouldn't the gossamer images, the poetic touches, quickly become a heartwarming (if meticulously directed) scene in John's life movie? Of course they would. "Adieu, hunk, and best wishes," sighed one *Chicago Tribune* columnist. "With luck, an American tragedy may be redeemed in the wedding of JFK Jr."

Not everyone was so touched. Like the eternally single relative who parks herself near the buffet and hisses that the marriage will never last, Maureen Dowd couldn't resist sniping. Carolyn "is the new icon for our celebrity-addicted age," wrote the *Times* columnist. Blending "the worlds of Camelot and supermodels," Carolyn was "our new Obsession," a pun on the Calvin Klein perfume of the same name.

Though Dowd's was cleverer than most, such anti-Carolyn harping was common. What had she done to deserve such good fortune? Nothing, according to the conventional wisdom—she was a *publicist.* How had she landed John when so many before had failed? She *tricked* him. According to *New York,* Carolyn "appears to be almost a case study from the currently popular how-to *The Rules,*" the best-selling guidebook to snaring men. She was "cunning."

Maybe Carolyn should have expected such catcalls; no woman was good enough for America's son. But the truth was, she didn't always help her case. So admired in her former milieu, the haute couture she favored sometimes made Carolyn look severe and elitist. Moreover, whenever Carolyn appeared in public, she seemed to be scowling, which led numerous pundits to muse, Why *isn't* this woman smiling?

After all, she was married to JFK Jr. What could she possibly have to complain about?

Despite what John wanted to believe, Carolyn didn't seem prepared for her new status as style icon and First Lady-in-Waiting. Overwhelmed by the invasion of her privacy, she openly resented the photographers who pursued her wherever she went. It wasn't that Carolyn minded posing for photos. She'd posed for the B.U. calendar, after all. Since her college days, however, she had graduated to more elevated status as a behind-the-scenes producer in the fashion world. Not coincidentally, she liked to shape her image, to stage the shoot. Now she found herself in a situation she couldn't possibly control.

Her frustration weighed on John, who grew testy with his bride's harassers. In Hyannis Port in October, John threw a bucket of water on a photographer who called one of John's neighbors an "asshole." "You don't call women assholes!" John shouted. "Didn't your mother teach you that? I don't care if she got in your fucking way!" (John later bought the man a new camera.)

If the chivalry was typical of John, the short fuse with the press was not; he'd never previously done anything of the sort. And his temper kept erupting. In December John grabbed a photographer by his coat and threw the man on the hood of his Jeep Cherokee. In January 1997 John interrupted photographers who were playing with Friday while he and Carolyn brunched at Bubby's, a restaurant at the west end of John's block. "If you guys are going to be inhumane to my wife, you shouldn't pet my dog," John said.

· · ·

Despite the new pressures it added, John's marriage seemed to inspire him. His job, however, concerned him: As 1996 became 1997, he knew that the new year would be a challenging one for *George*.

The Clinton-Dole matchup had proved a snooze. We couldn't even get people to read the Norman Mailer articles, and they were good— no, great. The legendary writer had worked harder than reporters one-third his age. His unflinching examinations of Clinton and Dole were insightful, provocative, and beautifully written. But they generated little mail from readers and no buzz on the New York media scene. Maybe, in an era when the wisdom of age is casually overlooked for the beauty of youth, Mailer was insufficiently novel. Maybe the world wanted something fresher, trendier, more scandalous—or, simply, shorter. But the lack of reaction was demoralizing. Determined to put to rest the rap that *George* was all fluff, we'd spent a lot of money on one of America's finest writers, and he'd earned that money, yet no one seemed to care.

Now, with Clinton settling in for four more years, we had to convince readers that politics remained an urgent concern. The truth we could not concede—to them or to ourselves—was that, for most Americans, politics *wasn't* urgent. With the economy booming and the government divided, consumers were complacent and Washington gridlocked. Bill Clinton's competent stewardship of the Oval Office gave Americans little reason to worry. You don't need to hear from the pilot of a plane until you hit turbulence, and you don't really want to.

Instead, the public flocked to where the action was, the Internet and the stock market. Wealth and technology were the engines of 1990s America, not politics. As a result, magazines devoted to those subjects, such as *Fast Company* and *Wired,* started to look like doorstops. Even if no one actually read the things, they had buzz, and that was what advertisers demanded—and rewarded.

Magazines that helped consumers spend their new wealth also flourished. *InStyle,* which told its readers how to dress like celebrities, was starting to weigh more than the Manhattan Yellow Pages. *Martha*

Stewart Living helped consumers retreat from public activism by channeling their prosperity into domestic bliss. Also surging were the "lad books," sex-addled monthlies such as *Maxim* and *Stuff* that sported fleshy pictures of pop-culture Lolitas like peep-show signs.

George's circulation, meanwhile, had leveled off at around 430,000. That made us by far the biggest political magazine in the country, but it still fell short of the half-million mark we sought. That's what we needed to become the country's only *profitable* political magazine. After actually making a bit of money in 1995, thanks to our enormous first two issues, we had lost several million dollars in 1996. To win advertisers back, we needed higher circulation, but Hachette was reluctant to invest in direct mail to increase subscriptions. CEO David Pecker thought *George* could prosper without them and pressured us to pump up newsstand sales. Most new magazines take six or seven years before they turn a profit. Pecker didn't want to wait that long.

But driving up newsstand sales is a perilous road. Competition for rack space is fierce, and newsstand buyers are fickle. Magazines have to leap out and grab their attention. How? By slapping silly buzzwords like "Exclusive!" and "Hot!" and "Best!" on the cover. Or by touting a never-ending supply of lists: Top 10 Whatchamacallits, 50 Best Thingamajigs.

Problem was, all that cover glitz makes magazines look tacky, and that wouldn't suit *George*—or our biggest advertisers, upscale fashion houses like Armani and Versace. It wasn't their abiding interest in politics that prompted those companies to advertise. They were buying into John's elegance. We were confronted with a Catch-22: We needed more circulation to get more ads, but David Pecker's preferred strategy to increase that circulation might alienate our advertisers.

Headed into our third year, we needed new energy—and fresh bodies. In the fall Gary Ginsberg had departed for the high-paying pastures of a political consulting firm. Rachel Clark, one of our original associate editors, had taken a job at *Marie Claire* magazine. Rachel had clashed with Rose and thereafter felt denied access to John. Before making the decision to leave, she had lunch with John to talk things over. According to Rachel, John asked: "Why does everybody who gets close to me become rabid around other people who are close to me?"

So one morning in late January 1997 John gathered us in the forty-first-floor conference room, basically a shoe box with overhead lights. We'd just finished closing our February issue and, like many of our closes, this one had been exhausting and stressful—Biz was smoking more, Matt Berman was snapping at the young designers who worked for him, and I lost count of the nights I would call Nyssa at nine o'clock to promise her I'd be home soon. Now everyone was sleep-walking around the office, dreading the imminent onset of the next publication cycle.

While John waited for his staff to assemble, he leafed through a copy of *Flying*, another Hachette publication, gazing happily at the pictures of new planes. He was talking about taking flying lessons. He'd always wanted to learn to fly. Plus, the ability to fly his own plane would allow him—and Carolyn—to bypass the exposure of airports and commercial flights.

When everyone was seated, John began by asking us to consider why our last close had been such an ordeal. "It's important for us to be well rested, to have our strength up," John said, "because it's important to remember why we do this. Why we work late nights and week-ends to put out this magazine.

"You know I was in Washington for the inauguration of President Clinton," he continued.

While he was there, "dozens of people" had told John how much they enjoyed *George*. Not journalists or members of Washington's permanent political class, but real people. *George* was the first politi-cal magazine they ever *wanted* to read, they told him.

"We have created a paradigm shift in journalism," John said. By demonstrating the viability of a mass-market political magazine, we had changed how politics was covered. "Someday, we'll be able to look back on this and know that we created something truly new."

He had started slowly, but he was warming to his subject and the words began to come faster. He sounded almost as if he were talking only to himself.

"More and more," John said, "I realize how much of myself I've put into the concept of this magazine." Ever since he was a boy, he'd sensed a schism between the way he looked at politics and the way politics was reported to the public. To him politics was a noble endeavor, but the press never seemed to agree.

"There were only two ways I knew of to do something about this gap," John said. "One was to start a political career of my own. The other was to start a magazine."

But there were people who wanted *George* to fail, John said. The press did not want him to succeed, because the press did not want him to grow up. The success we'd had was only making resistance to the magazine more vigorous. "You can tell that we're accomplishing something in the way that our competitors are beginning to treat us." The criticism of our first year would be nothing compared to what we could expect this year.

"I've lost friends because they're feeling the sting of the ads that we're taking away from them, and they're pissed off about it," John said. "At first, they didn't take *George* seriously. Sure, *George* would have its two or three issues, its fifteen minutes, and then it would fade away and I would go back to being America's Prince Charming. But now they know that's not going to happen."

Editors at competing magazines were gearing up for battle, and that meant leaked, negative stories in the press, John said. So we had to replenish our strength. We would need it.

In the months ahead, John would prove to be right, but not for the reasons he thought. We would need our strength because John was entering a year of intense and painful self-examination and he would pull us along with him, like a whaleboat crew tethered to a harpooned animal, bouncing along the choppy ocean toward the unknown horizon.

Eight

In January 1997 the tension between Michael and John erupted again, and this time it was even worse. One day they were standing in front of Biz's closed door when the screaming began. "I want to see my editor!" Michael shouted. "She's not your editor!" John shouted back.

Suddenly Michael hurried down the hallway and past my doorway. One of his shirtsleeves was ripped near the elbow; John had apparently grabbed Michael with such force that he'd torn Michael's shirt. Moving into his office, John picked up the phone, called the facilities department, and asked for a locksmith to change the lock on his door.

A few minutes later, Biz and I were in John's office discussing stories for our next issue. As we sat around John's table trying to pretend that nothing had happened, a workman arrived and pulled out his tools. The next thing we knew, Michael reappeared and demanded that his lock also be changed. While John glowered, the locksmith said he'd need a work order, a bit of bureaucracy that stymied Michael, who retreated toward his corner of the hallway. After about five minutes Michael returned and said to the workman, "Why can't you just do it? Why can't you just change my lock?" The guy nervously responded that he had to have the paperwork. "Maybe I'll call David Pecker, then," Michael said.

His face flushed with rage, John was so angry it was a little scary. "Go ahead, Michael," he said. "Call David Pecker." He knew Michael would look ridiculous if he did.

Meanwhile, Rose kept scuttling in and out of John's office looking for his appointment book. Coming up empty-handed, she concluded that Michael had stolen it, which led to another confrontation with Michael, who denied any such charge. Minutes later, he was back outside John's office bearing the notebook in question. "Here," he said coldly. "You left this in my office." He tossed it on Rose's desk.

After that the fight fizzled, leaving the kind of uneasy quiet that comes from a lack of resolution. Two days later John had a beautiful new shirt hand-delivered to Michael, along with a note of apology. His gesture alleviated the immediate crisis, but not the enduring one: the two men were making each other crazy. How long could such an exhausting state of affairs continue?

At the same time, another potentially explosive situation had arisen. And though I stayed far away from anything have to do with Michael and John, I felt I had to weigh in on this new problem.

• • •

We all read other editors' stories on the *George* computer network, and that's how I stumbled across the Geula Amir piece that Biz wanted to run. She had never mentioned it in an editorial meeting; it simply appeared in the computer system.

Geula Amir was the mother of Yigal Amir, the young Israeli who had assassinated prime minister Yitzhak Rabin at a public rally in front of 100,000 people. "This is the story," Mrs. Amir wrote ominously, "of my search for the truth about the Rabin assassination."

I read on. Over the course of some 10,000 words—that's about ten solid magazine pages—Geula Amir claimed that her son had been set up. Yigal was a patsy, she insisted. He had been tricked by Israeli secret agents hoping to discredit Israel's right wing. The spooks would foil the "assassination" by filling Yigal's gun with blanks. By stopping the faux assassination, they would make themselves look heroic and the right wing horrific. "But something went terribly wrong," Geula wrote. The bullets were real. Rabin died.

I read in disbelief. The idea of staging a fake assassination was absurd; it would have been laughable if it weren't so offensive. It was as if, in 1964, Lee Harvey Oswald's mother had written an article proposing that her son was actually a pawn of the Democratic Party, which was hoping to smear the GOP. Only—oops!—he killed the president by mistake.

No, this story was classic conspiracy theory. It wove together isolated facts and wild suppositions about events that never happened into revisionist propaganda. Its purpose was clear: to rehabilitate Israel's right wing by blaming Rabin's assassination on his own government. Why this story had been brought to *George* was equally obvious. Published in John F. Kennedy, Jr.'s magazine, it would gain credibility and attract attention. The son of a slain president would be printing—and, by implication, endorsing—the deranged fantasy of an assassin's mother.

Why did Biz, who was smart enough to know better, want to run the piece? Partly, no doubt, because she was under pressure. After a year as executive editor, she hadn't hit any home runs. Her tastes were too alternative; she would have made an outstanding editor for the *Village Voice* or *The New York Review of Books*. To bolster her own position, she needed something, anything, to keep people talking about *George*. This story had been brought to her by Mrs. Amir's American "representatives," and Biz had seized upon it.

Yet there was another, less obvious reason why this article was winding its way like a parasite through *George*'s bloodstream. If *George* provided a template in which John could hash out his identity conflicts, it had also become a forum in which my colleagues and I debated everything we wanted to know about John but feared to ask. Conspiracy theories, sex in politics, assassinations—we redirected the questions we would not ask John into ideas for articles. The Amir story was the unhealthy conclusion of all this psychological transference, an unfortunate result of being so near someone about whom we had so much frustrated curiosity.

I knew I had to say something about the piece, but I wasn't sure when or how. As it happened, John asked my opinion of the article a couple of days after I read it. We were sitting in his office, which over time he'd decorated with personal touches. Outside the door was a huge painting of George Washington, which John had bought from a Brooklyn artist. Just inside a collection of presidential miniatures hung on the east wall. Above John's desk was a print of his father, a silk screen in grainy black and white against a red background. Farther along the wall hung a black-and-white portrait of Carolyn and Friday, who was sitting on his haunches, his ears perked, gazing up toward Carolyn. Her smiling face was shown reflected in a small round mirror hanging on a wall. Carolyn looked blissfully happy in a way she almost never did in public.

My mood, however, was anything but blissful. "I don't like this story one bit," I told John.

"Why not?" John said.

"You know what the linkage will be. You know what people are going to say about this piece."

"Yeah, I know," John said. He considered that for about a minute and said, "Is it too creepy?"

"It's definitely creepy," I answered. "But if you think the piece is credible, that shouldn't stop you from publishing it."

I didn't want John to kill the story because of Kennedy conflicts; I knew that argument could come back to haunt me. I wanted him to kill it because it was repulsive.

John asked if I thought the story was credible. If I thought that, say, *The New Yorker* would publish it.

"Never," I said. "It's pure conspiracy theory. You can't possibly prove it, but you can never disprove it."

John winced. That night, he took the article home to reread.

Meanwhile, another provocative story had come to my attention—and this one, I thought, *George* should publish.

.   .   .

I was checking in with one of my most trusted sources when he mentioned something that caught me off guard. "What would you say," he asked, "if I told you that a top Republican political consultant had an undisclosed history of spousal abuse?"

"I guess," I said slowly, "that I'd ask you to keep talking."

The story involved a man named Don Sipple, a political ad maker who had helped elect some of the GOP's biggest names, including Bob Dole, Missouri senator John Ashcroft, and Texas governor George W. Bush. Sipple had a rocky personal life. He'd been married three times and divorced twice. In 1992, he had sued his first ex-wife, Regina Sipple, for custody of their son, Evan. At the custody trial, Regina testified that Don had beaten her. Sipple's second wife, a respected Washington lobbyist named Deborah Steelman, told a similar story. Yet the judge still granted Don Sipple custody.

A wife-beater gets custody of his son? I asked my source why.

Well, he said, the case was tried in a small town in Missouri, where Don Sipple had helped elect a governor and two senators. Plus, one of Sipple's character witnesses was the chief justice of the Missouri supreme court.

I whistled softly. "That is interesting."

For the next several days I thought long and hard about whether to pursue this story. It certainly wasn't the kind of piece John had created *George* to publish; it wouldn't brighten our readers' opinion of politics. The only really negative articles we'd published had been about journalists.

Yet wasn't this a legitimate story? Sipple was a behind-the-scenes player who may have used his political power to influence the outcome of a legal proceeding. For several 1994 campaigns, Sipple had created anticrime advertisements playing on women's fear of violence. Didn't people have the right to know if high elected officials were taking advice from a violent man?

At our next edit meeting, we gathered in John's office, and John went around the circle asking people their ideas. When he came to me, I said cautiously, "I've got something kind of unusual."

I laid the story out in quick strokes. An uncomfortable silence ensued.

"What do people think?" John asked.

My colleagues didn't exactly jump to volunteer their opinions. There was some hemming, a bit of hawing, but no one would take a stand yea or nay. This was sensitive stuff, and they wanted to see which way John was leaning.

"And this guy was Bob Dole's media adviser?" John asked eventually.

"Yup," I said. "He urged Dole to attack Clinton's character."

"And there are court records?"

"There are," I said.

"And you would write this?"

"I don't think this source will talk to anyone else."

John sighed. "All right," he said. "Go ahead."

. . .

In our March 1997 issue we published the Geula Amir story; John had decided to defer to Biz. Once he made his decision known, I said nothing further about my concerns. No point in prolonging a fight I'd already lost.

But John didn't sound comfortable with the story. In his editor's letter, he conceded that Geula Amir's representatives surely brought the article to *George* "hoping that my own family history would bring added attention to their story. . . ."

He added, "In no way is it intended to be an objective examination of the events surrounding the assassination. It is, however, a compelling look at one facet of an insular, conservative religious community within Israel. It may raise interesting questions. It may not."

I shook my head in frustration. Such wishy-washy rationalization made John look weak, and it hardly explained his decision to publish a wildly irresponsible piece of journalism.

What did explain it? I still can't say for sure. Did John want to give Biz a show of confidence? In part, I suppose. Did he run the piece because everyone would expect him not to? Yes, to some degree. "Counterintuitive" wasn't just one of John's favorite adjectives, it was a way of life for him.

Yet I think there was something more. Maybe John was acting on a deeper motivation. As his encounter with Oliver Stone had suggested, John wasn't ready to talk about his father's death. But the Amir story may have been his way of edging closer. Try as he might to avoid the subject, John couldn't help but be drawn to it—even if only through surrogates.

The article might have helped John, but it hurt *George*: Those news organizations that didn't ignore the story mocked it. The Amir piece, said the *New York Post,* was "about as convincing as a similar plea would be from O.J.'s mother, if O.J. had killed Nicole Simpson and Ron Goldman in front of dozens of witnesses and been videotaped in the act."

This time, unfortunately, the *Post* got it exactly right.

.   .   .

I knew that John was protective of Carolyn, and that she needed him to be. But I didn't realize how urgent that was until April 1997, when John and Carolyn hosted a *George* table at the White House Correspondents Dinner, an annual event featuring politicians and reporters at the Washington Hilton.

The gala took place in the hotel ballroom, a subterranean cavern that holds some seven thousand people, most of whom seemed to converge around our table. The bolder ones snapped photos of John and Carolyn; others took pictures of friends who just happened to be standing in front of the couple. The after-dinner speaker made a joke about the size of Ted Kennedy's head and a bowling ball bag; I caught a glimpse of John, who wasn't laughing.

When the ceremonies wrapped up, it felt as if the guests unanimously decided that the nearest exit lay just past our table. We couldn't stay seated; it was like being buried to our necks in sand as the tide rolled in. So my colleagues and I stood and formed a human V in front of John and Carolyn and plowed through the hordes. As photographers backpedaled, we forged ahead fast enough to keep a crowd from coalescing but not so fast that John and Carolyn couldn't keep up. John took Carolyn's hand and guided her behind our moving wall. We passed through the lobby quickly, so that John and Carolyn never felt the crush. Not until we were out of the hotel did we break formation. Since the photographers assumed that John would have a limousine, none bothered to follow us.

Pleased with our escape, we walked a few blocks south on Connecticut Avenue to the Jockey Club bar at the Ritz-Carlton, where we were staying. The bar was small and very dark, a safe haven. While John eased off his tuxedo jacket and sipped a scotch, Carolyn sat next to associate editor Susannah Hunnewell and began to rant. That was insane! she fumed. What a bunch of amateurs! No rope lines, no guards! Don't these people know anything about security?

A woman who never lacked for an opinion, Susannah tried to get a word in edgewise. But Carolyn was just warming up. That kind of thing would never have happened in New York! If Washington is going to have this kind of dinner, they'd better figure out how to do it right. They have to keep people in line! Otherwise, someone's going to get hurt. My God!

Carolyn's tirade made me uncomfortable, for I had always believed that one of Washington's best qualities is its everyday interaction between ordinary citizens and famous, powerful politicians. She seemed to be advocating a clear-cut distinction between the two as something not only necessary, but desirable. I wondered if she really believed what she was saying or if she just needed more time to get used to the crush of attention, and hoped it was the latter.

She was struggling, that much was clear. In the months after the wedding, Carolyn couldn't seem to figure out what she wanted. She had quit Calvin Klein in late 1995, and showed no burning desire to get a new job. At one point in John's life, he hadn't felt like working, either.

He filled his time with adventure and athletics, but Carolyn did not share those enthusiasms. To her husband's frustration—voiced to at least one of my colleagues—Carolyn didn't like to work out or rollerblade or kayak.

To pass the time, she did like to shop, and at Christmas in 1996, John had gathered us in his office to give every member of the staff a gift picked out by the two of them. Considerably more personal than the *George* watches of 1995, the gifts reflected John's growing understanding of us as individuals rather than simply employees. My present was a Montblanc fountain pen—a well-chosen gift, since I collected pens, though I couldn't remember ever having mentioned that to John.

Because Carolyn rarely ventured out in public except to shop and dine, corresponding images kept landing on the gossip pages. Carolyn tried on Hush Puppies at Tip Top Shoes on West 72nd Street; Carolyn comforted a salesgirl who was yelled at by an obnoxious customer at Ralph Lauren on Madison Avenue; Carolyn extravagantly tipped a Hyannis Port waitress, whispering that she remembered what it was like to wait on tables. There was something oddly poignant about such episodes. It was as if Carolyn was trying to reconnect with people whose lives were simpler than her new existence—as simple as her life once had been.

• • •

Since the shirt-tearing fight in early January, Michael Berman had become a virtual nonentity within the office. Often as not, he didn't even bother coming to work, and his absence was hurting our ad sales. His relationship with John may have been deteriorating, but Michael could articulate the vision of *George* and he was a hell of a salesman.

Then, in April, we learned why Michael had been only going through the motions: After months of negotiations, John and Hachette had bought Michael out. *George* had started with a trio of leaders—John, Michael, and Eric Etheridge. Now there was only John.

Hachette named Michael head of the company's television and film production department. Hachette had only a minimal presence in those businesses, but that wasn't the point. John wanted Michael gone, and Michael had negotiated a strategic departure.

Some weeks later, on Michael's first day at his new job, I bumped into him in the elevator and we had a brief, awkward chat. A few minutes later, his secretary called—Michael wanted to have lunch with me. Caught by surprise, I agreed. But the second I hung up the phone I began to question the wisdom of that decision. So I walked down the hall and told John of Michael's request. "Tell me if this is a problem," I said.

He frowned. "It's okay, I guess."

About half an hour later, John came into my office. Actually, he said, he'd prefer if I didn't have that lunch. Michael, he continued, never wanted John to grow up. He'd paid a lot of money to get free and clear of his old partner, and he didn't want to start that "whole head-game routine" again.

"I'm happy to cancel the lunch," I said. "I don't want to get caught in the middle."

So I called Michael back and canceled. "I'm sorry," I told him, "it's just not a good time. It's nothing personal."

But it was personal, and the whole thing made me feel dirty. Michael might have descended into moody and erratic behavior, appearing more concerned about his standing with John than the success of the magazine he had cofounded. But John himself had explained why. *Everybody* who got too close to John was sucked into the maelstrom of his celebrity. And everyone caught in that maelstrom lost the independence that John had liked about them in the first place.

My recognition of this truth unnerved me. How could we work with John every day, forming a kind of family in the office—which was what John wanted, what he *needed,* to feel comfortable working with all these journalists—without getting so close that we lost our own identities? The very intimacy that John needed in order to work with us could also destroy us.

In the short term, John clearly felt relief over Michael's departure. He hated fighting with Michael and didn't like the man he became when he lost his temper. With Michael gone, John always kept his office door open, walked the hallways more, and seemed to laugh more, too.

But Michael's exit also rattled John. He had lost both his business partner and a friend of almost fifteen years. In his business and his personal life, John was now more alone, more isolated, than before.

·   ·   ·

During the winter and spring of 1997, trouble was breaking out in the Kennedy family. First it was reported that John's cousin Michael, a son of Bobby Kennedy who lived in Cohasset, Massachusetts, had carried on an affair with his children's teenage baby-sitter. The girl's family was furious, and the Massachusetts press was swatting Michael like a piñata.

Also in Massachusetts, congressman Joe Kennedy was fielding some bad press of his own. In 1991 Joe was divorced from his wife, Sheila Rauch Kennedy, and soon after married one of his congressional aides. But to remarry within the Catholic Church, Joe had to have his first marriage annulled. Annulments are hard to obtain, so Joe had used family connections within the Catholic hierarchy to secure one. For Sheila Kennedy, the experience was devastating. How do you tell your kids that, in the eyes of God, they are the products of an unsanctified union?

I had met Joe and Sheila Kennedy some ten years before, in the winter of 1986. A cub reporter in Washington, I was covering something called the Grate American Sleep-Out for *Washington City Paper,* the local alternative weekly. To protest homelessness, members of Congress were sleeping on grates behind the Supreme Court.

It was a frigid night, and everyone was struggling to stay warm. Joe Kennedy showed up late, around ten—the last congressman to arrive. The TV crews on hand swarmed around Joe as he dished out sound bites, fast and confident, like a short-order cook slinging hamburger patties.

After the TV crews packed up and pulled out, Joe and Sheila unrolled their sleeping bags on the frozen ground with the rest of us. I picked up my pen and paper to interview them. With markedly less enthusiasm than he had displayed for the cameras, Joe said a few words, then nodded off.

While Joe snored away next to us, Sheila talked to me for another twenty minutes. An expert in public housing issues, she spoke eloquently about their relevance to the homeless. It was a shame, I thought, that she wasn't the one elected.

Now, six years after her divorce, Sheila was publishing a book, *Shattered Faith: A Woman's Struggle to Stop the Catholic Church from Annulling Her Marriage.* The timing was terrible for Joe; he was planning to run for governor in 1998, and the story of his aggrieved wife certainly wouldn't help with the women's vote.

John made no bones about the fact that the press coverage of his cousins' personal problems troubled him. These were private matters, he said. He was irritated that Joe's wife was writing a book, and angry that Massachusetts prosecutors were weighing a statutory rape case against Michael. He fumed that it would be the first time that such charges had been filed in Massachusetts since the Pilgrims. If Michael weren't a Kennedy . . .

At the same time, my investigation into the story of Don Sipple was progressing. Reporting the article was slow, difficult work. Neither of Sipple's ex-wives wanted to speak with me, and from the brief contact I had with them, I got the distinct impression that, despite the fact that they had been separated from Sipple for years, both women were physically afraid of him. Many of the participants in the custody case were also reluctant to talk. One who did received an anonymous, threatening phone call: "You shouldn't have talked to that reporter," said a male voice. "That was a dumb thing to do." Another person I'd had a conversation with dissolved into tears. No one seemed to feel right about this unnoticed custody trial in a backwater southern town.

After months of reporting, I finally felt prepared to talk with Don Sipple, and we met in his office at the Watergate. It was as awkward an interview as I've ever conducted. A handsome man with thinning blond hair and a sharp, intelligent face, Sipple refused to say why his ex-wives might have accused him of abuse. "I cannot speak for them," he said. "All I can say is, it never happened. It's fiction."

But as I would write in the story I finished and gave to John in late May, it didn't sound like fiction.

·   ·   ·

"I have to tell you," John said to me one afternoon in early June, "I'm not comfortable with this story."

He certainly looked uncomfortable. As usual, he was impeccably dressed, in a tan summer suit, white shirt, and pecan-colored tie. But his body was taut, his hands clenched in front of him. We were sitting in his office with the door closed. On the table between us lay a printout of my article on Don Sipple.

"What do you mean?" I said. "Uncomfortable how?"

"I'm not so sure that Don Sipple is a public figure," John said. "He's no James Carville."

Sipple's obscurity might expose *George* to a lawsuit, John continued, because libel law makes it easier for private people to sue than public figures.

"Sipple's been profiled in magazines and newspapers," I countered. "Besides, a trial is a public proceeding. It's next to impossible to sue someone for reporting on a trial."

I was starting to feel uncomfortable myself. When I'd given John my story, I'd attached a memo apologizing for its formidable length of some seven thousand words. But the article deserved the space, I said, because it would be widely read and discussed. It had never occurred to me that John might not like it.

John drummed his fingers on the table. "Still, Sipple's not an elected official," he said.

"No," I admitted, "but he helps elect them."

Journalists needed to write about such men, I argued. They were the secret powerbrokers of politics. I mentioned Dick Morris, who had allowed a prostitute to eavesdrop on his phone calls with Bill Clinton. That was trivial compared to what Don Sipple had been accused of.

John didn't look convinced—or like he wanted to be convinced. "Whatever happened was a long time ago," he said.

It doesn't feel that way to the women he hit, I almost responded. But that wouldn't have helped my case. I was beginning to suspect that nothing I said would help. Something about this article just didn't sit right with John.

"This is the story that I told you I was going to write in the editorial meeting," I said. "You signed off on it then."

It was a weak argument and I knew it.

He twisted in his seat. "I know," he answered. "But maybe we should wait. Publish it next year, during the election. *If* Sipple's still advising George W. Bush."

"That would look as if we were targeting Sipple," I said. "Then we'd really be in legal trouble."

"There's one other thing that bothers me," John went on. "The way it's written. . . . It's as if you're judging Sipple. You have a prosecutorial tone."

And then I knew what the problem was: At the very moment two women were accusing John's cousins of bad behavior, I had written a story about two women accusing a man of bad behavior. I had handed it to an editor who sat in the courtroom during the rape trial of his cousin, William Kennedy Smith, to show his support for the accused. Whose father's reputation had been tarnished by accusations that he'd exploited women. Whose uncle had accidentally driven a woman off a bridge, then fled the scene.

That I had spent months reporting the story; that I had the facts down cold, backed by court testimony and on-the-record quotes; that people had risked their jobs to speak with me—none of that mattered. What mattered was that I had written a story exploring one of the most sensitive subjects in John's life—men mistreating women. And I'd come down on the wrong side.

My heart sank. How could I possibly have thought that John would publish this story?

Yet there was more journalist in John than there had been two years before, and he struggled with the decision. On the one hand, he was confronted with exactly the type of article he never wanted *George* to publish. It had been only a matter of time before he would have to face such an editorial moment of truth. But he probably hadn't expected that the provocation would come from a member of his own staff.

On the other hand, John knew that this article would attract attention for his magazine. He also knew how hard I'd worked on the story, how much emotion I'd invested in it. So as our conversation wound up that day, he said he wanted more time to think.

He asked Rose and Carolyn for their opinion. They urged him not to publish the article. You don't want to condone investigating people's private lives, they said. Think of the precedent. How could you criticize others for doing to you what you will have done in your own magazine? "This story has no place in *George*," Rose told one of my colleagues.

John also sought the advice of my fellow editors—Susannah, Inigo, and our newest hire, Jeffrey Podolsky, a Diet Coke–swilling refugee from *People*. Torn between their old roles as journalists and their new ones as JFK Jr. preservationists, they equivocated. They knew what John wanted to hear them say. And when I asked what they had told him, they wouldn't look me in the eye.

As for Biz, she would not share her recommendation with me. I didn't push her. If she wouldn't volunteer her vote, I knew what it was.

A few days later John called me back into his office to tell me his decision: He would not run the piece. I was free to shop it elsewhere, he said. But I would have to sign a release saying that I had reported the story outside the scope of my *George* duties. The document was a legal fig leaf in case Sipple sued, but I signed it. What choice did I have?

The rejection left me listless and despondent. I couldn't concentrate or even see the point of working. The Sipple piece was the biggest story of my career. I was certain it would have given *George*'s credibility a shot in the arm. Most important, it would have brought a wrong to light. And now it was dead in the water.

I considered quitting. Hell, I'd already lasted longer than most of the original staff. Working at *George* was like riding a bucking bronco.

There'd be no shame in being thrown now. Wasn't quitting the only way to salvage some self-respect?

I started putting out feelers to editors at other magazines.

Although I don't think John expected me to, I did sell the story elsewhere—to *Mother Jones*, a small, liberal magazine based in San Francisco. *Mother Jones* didn't have the visibility *George* did. But it had no sacred cows, no psycho-editorial conflicts. They couldn't wait to print the piece.

Little did I know that publishing that story in another magazine would put me on yet another collision course with John.

Nine

A few weeks later, on July 16, I saw the photo. Sudie Redmond, our managing editor, showed it to me just before it was sent to the printer.

The picture was to accompany John's September 1997 editor's letter. It showed John sitting in a dark room, gazing at an apple dangling above his head. His arms were wrapped around his knees. Though his groin was shrouded in shadow, John appeared naked.

I quickly learned the details. John had posed in his office one night just a few days before. He and Matt Berman, our creative director, and the fashion photographer Mario Sorrenti had come in after everyone else had left for the day. Sorrenti, who was known for persuading his subjects to disrobe, had snapped the picture. (Matt added the apple later, via computer.) But John only looked naked—he had left his boxers on. And according to Matt, John had Sorrenti shoot the photo with a Polaroid camera. There would be no incriminating negatives to turn up on the Internet or in the *National Enquirer*.

The photo would play off the cover, a disturbing image of the waif-model Kate Moss, shot in profile, naked against an Eden-like backdrop as a deer licked hungrily at her hand. (The background was fake, the deer real.) She was supposed to look like Eve. Which would make John Adam.

It occurred to me that John had lost his mind.

One thing was for sure—this wouldn't have been happening if Michael still worked at *George*. Certainly Michael wanted John to exploit himself, but only in ways that were consistent with the rest of the magazine's editorial content.

Then I read the editor's letter that accompanied the picture. John had written it at the last possible moment, and as was the case with the photo, he hadn't asked for his editors' opinions. Whatever he was trying to do, he obviously didn't want to be talked out of it.

His editorial began with a quote from Jack Nicholson on how women are different from men: "They're stronger and smarter and they don't play fair."

The words that followed became the most hotly debated prose ever published in *George* and probably the most misunderstood words John ever wrote or spoke. They are worth quoting at length:

> I've learned a lot about temptation recently. But that doesn't make me desire it any less. If anything, to be reminded of the possible perils of succumbing to what's forbidden only makes it more alluring. But while I'm playing Hamlet with my willpower (should I or shouldn't I?), there's always the distraction of gawking at the travails of those who just couldn't hold back. We can all gather, like urchins at a hanging, to watch those poor souls who took a chance on fantasy and came up empty-handed. . . .
>
> I read an article recently that gave a name to the kind of temptation I'm talking about. It's not a striking body or a pile of money or a new toy. Rather, it's the inevitable byproduct of living a respectable life. The author surmised that the more we live a life governed by conventional norms of proper behavior, the nicer and more responsible we force ourselves to be, the further we drift away from the essence of our true selves—one that's impulsive and rude and ruled by passion

and instinct. Give in to yourselves, like Mike Tyson and chomp off your tormentor's ear, and become an outcast; conform utterly and endure a dispiriting and suffocating life.

I've seen it up close in the past year. Two members of my family chased an idealized alternative to their actual life. One left behind an embittered former wife and another, in what seemed to be a hedge against his own mortality, fell in love with youth and surrendered his judgment in the process. Both became literally poster boys for bad behavior. Perhaps they deserved it. To whom much is given, much is expected, right? The interesting thing was the ferocious condemnation that met their excursions beyond the bounds of acceptable behavior. Since when does someone need to apologize on television for getting divorced?

But nonetheless, there was something comforting in watching the necessary order assert itself, even for me. The discontents of civilized life looked positively benign when compared to the holy terror visited upon the brave and stupid. . . .

Back when *George* began, John's editor's letters had sounded stilted and impersonal. This one managed to strike a tone that was at once confessional and evasive. Was this progress?

In some ways, yes. The new intimacy of his voice marked a vast improvement over the self-conscious formality of his early efforts. But if John's letter revealed that his literary sensibility had evolved, it spelled disaster for *George*. His soul-searching had nothing to do with the contents of the issue; it would both overwhelm and undermine them. You might as well just tear out all the other pages in the magazine.

And though many people would say, so what, John is more interesting than *George* anyway, that reality wasn't easy to accept if you worked there. We devoted ourselves to the articles we assigned, researched, edited, fact-checked, copyedited, proofread, laid out, and libel-checked. We did our best to balance the challenge of publishing a magazine with the duties of working for a celebrity. Yet John's letter—and especially his disinclination to discuss it with the rest of us—suggested that he didn't much respect us for our labors, that he could (and would) trump our work any time he wanted to.

John had every right to print whatever he wanted, of course. It was his magazine. When people like Maureen Dowd or Donna Fournier Cuomo criticized *George,* it wasn't Biz or me who took the heat, but John. Even so, this editor's letter felt like betrayal. We had vowed to protect John's privacy. Now, it seemed, John was repudiating our efforts by baring his breast before the world.

And how would Carolyn feel, reading about her husband's flirtation with temptation? One year after their wedding, John was publicly lamenting the tedium of a conventional life. Even if this wasn't meant to be a commentary on his marriage, the world would interpret it that way.

Clearly John was aware of how marriage had changed his life. He and I had recently eaten lunch at Gallagher's, a steakhouse on 52nd Street. He knew that I was upset by his decision on the Sipple piece and asking me to lunch was an olive branch. Gallagher's was a dark, unfashionable, old-time place; John could eat there and be relatively sure he wouldn't be hounded. And its portions were huge, to match his appetite.

In person, I simply couldn't stay angry at John. His charm was too great, his company too enjoyable, and we had a pleasant meal. John wolfed down a salad and steak hash with a side of thick asparagus and an immense portion of strawberries with whipped cream for dessert. Walking back along Broadway, we talked about the October cover, which was to feature Elizabeth Hurley. He fell silent for a few steps, then abruptly turned to me and said, apropos of nothing, "I wonder if that's why Elizabeth Hurley won't marry Hugh Grant—because she's afraid that if she's not single anymore, she'll lose her juice."

Just as he was that day on the street, John seemed, in his letter, to be thinking out loud.

. . .

In the explosion of publicity that the letter instigated, John would be accused of criticizing Joe and Michael. But he wasn't—he was defending them. He didn't say they deserved to be "poster boys for bad behavior," but that they were *turned into* poster boys. In fact, John insisted, his cousins' only mistake was "to make excursions beyond the bounds of acceptable behavior," as though statutory rape was some kind of social gaffe. The alternative to such excursions was "a dispiriting and suffocating life." John—the kayaker, the aspiring pilot, the reluctant politician—could relate.

So could I. We're all human. We all feel temptation. Yet shouldn't John have shown at least some sympathy for those damaged by his cousins' behavior? Michael Kennedy had seduced a teenage girl entrusted to the care of his children. She would surely live with the psychological aftershocks for the rest of her life. And Joe Kennedy wasn't being chastised for getting a divorce, as John wrote. He was faulted for having his marriage annulled. John was smart enough to grasp the distinction. Why didn't he? And why didn't he write one single generous word about these women? He had referred to Sheila Kennedy as an "embittered former wife," without conceding that she had a legitimate reason to be bitter.

Why was John so unequivocal? Only one answer made sense: Because his loyalty—to his family, his gender, the way the world was when his father was president—trumped his logic. To John, these women were not victims; they hadn't played by the rules.

The pattern was impossible to ignore. From Don Sipple to Mike

Tyson to William Kennedy Smith to Michael and Joe Kennedy, John instinctively sided with men accused of malfeasance. Especially when they were Kennedys.

Maybe he was right in doing so. Or mostly right. If I had learned anything working with John, it was that you couldn't believe what the press wrote about his family. I had seen how people acted strangely around the Kennedys, did things they weren't proud of. Maybe later they couldn't admit it and instead blamed the Kennedys. Surely much of what was said about John's family—perhaps most—wasn't true.

But some of it was. And John, staring up at that dangling apple, did not want to admit that sometimes bad behavior wasn't the woman's fault.

.   .   .

In July 1997, *Vanity Fair* published a profile of Rudy Giuliani alleging that the New York mayor was sleeping with his press secretary. (Both denied it.) The story had sparked a tabloid frenzy and *Vanity Fair* was reaping a publicity bonanza.

In the last week of July, John convened a not-so-routine editorial meeting. He had only one thing on his mind: What did we think of *Vanity Fair*'s revelation? Should *George* publish that kind of story?

The room was silent. We were already on edge, waiting for the controversy we knew John's letter would provoke. Now John was asking whether we should print exactly the kind of invasion of personal life that his letter appeared to criticize.

We've always said we wouldn't do stories like that, someone finally said.

I know, John answered. But should we?

Vanity Fair didn't exactly nail the story, someone else offered.

Their proof was tenuous, and if you're going to run that kind of piece, you'd better get it right.

John scrunched up his face. The answer pussyfooted around the question, and he hated that.

Rudy's fair game, a third person responded. He's Mr. Morality, closing down strip clubs all over the city. You can't crack down on other people's sex lives while indulging your own.

John thought about that, tapping his fingers on the table. I'm not sure that's reason enough to write that he's having an affair, he said.

I was reluctant to weigh in; John's decision not to publish the Sipple article felt to me like the elephant in the room. But I spoke up anyway.

"If Rudy's got a mistress on the public payroll, of course it's a legitimate story," I said. "He's abusing the power of his office. That's not even a hard call."

Looking unhappy, John said nothing, and the conversation petered out. Finally John seemed to realize that no one else was talking. He looked around the room and shook his head. "I don't know," he said. "It just doesn't feel right."

A few days later, John went on vacation. First he traveled to an air show in Oshkosh, Wisconsin, where he confessed to the show's surprised attendants that he had loved flying ever since he was a kid in the White House. "Must have been all the helicopters landing on the front lawn," he said.

John then departed for a kayaking trip in Iceland, where the media wouldn't be able to find him when the issue came out. He'd done the same thing—fled the country, to court fashion advertisers in Italy—back in April 1996, just before the much-criticized Sotheby's auction of his parents' belongings.

Also that first week of August, *Mother Jones* published the Sipple story. The media response was, to put it mildly, underwhelming. Behind the scenes, Sipple was prevailing upon political allies to put the squeeze on reporters at newspapers and TV stations. If he could keep the story off CNN and the networks, and out of the *New York Times* and *Washington Post*, it might just disappear without a trace. That article is garbage, his surrogates whispered. It was supposed to run in *George*, but John Kennedy killed it. If John Kennedy doesn't believe what his own editor wrote, why should you?

"I've never heard anything like this," one *Washington Post* reporter confessed to me. "You can't believe what these guys are saying about you."

But Sipple did have one problem. In an off-year congressional race taking place in New York, a Republican named Vito Fossella was running to replace congresswoman Susan Molinari, who had resigned to care for her new baby. Fossella's media adviser? Don Sipple. Fossella's employment of an alleged wife-beater was something his Democratic opponent was starting to talk about.

On August 8, Sipple quit Fossella's campaign. "It is amazing to me," he wrote in a letter of resignation, "that false allegations, made by a marginal magazine that will be the subject of libel action, can send otherwise reasonable people into a frenzy."

On August 11, I was invited on CNN-fn, the network's business offshoot, to discuss the story. At the same time, word of John's letter was about to leak. The New York *Daily News* had somehow acquired a copy before our issue hit the stands. The *News* ran a relatively small item on the eleventh. The next day came the first real spark of a media firestorm. The *New York Post* ran a story headlined, JFK JR. SCOLDS HIS SCANDALOUS COUSINS.

That did it. Suddenly John's photo and letter were everywhere—newspapers, TV, radio, the Web—and everywhere the story was the same. JFK JR. BREAKS KENNEDY RANKS, BASHES COUSINS, read a headline in the *San Jose Mercury News*. Our office was flooded with similar press clippings from all over the world. "A crack," Dan Rather intoned, "has developed in the legendary solidarity of the Kennedy family." *Boston Globe* columnist Mike Barnicle wrote that John had "the body of Joe Piscopo and the brain of Sonny Bono" and sounded like "some thin-lipped, dim-witted, bad-backed polo player whose empty head can barely retain enough limited cocktail chatter to get him through a dinner with that international moron, Princess Di."

Even the *New York Times*, usually above weighing in on pop culture controversies, piled on. "It may be unfair to analyze Mr. Kennedy's essay as if he actually meant to say something in writing it," said an unsigned editorial. "The fact that he has attached a picture of himself in a discreetly lighted state of nudity suggests that the editor of *George* does not regard his prose as much of a draw."

At least *he* signed his name to what he wrote, I thought. I was a little shaken; I'd read the *Times* since I was an eight-year-old book-worm, and I couldn't remember such ad hominem commentary appearing in its venerable pages.

The irony was that John had *defended* his cousins, and it didn't require a microscopic deconstruction of his letter to show that. So why did the tabloids report that John was guilty of "dissin' cousins"? And why did so many other newspapers, magazines, and television shows follow suit?

There were several explanations. First, news outlets routinely repeat each other's mistakes. Second, in a slow summer news cycle, the lure of a Kennedy family feud was too delicious to resist.

But I think that there was a third reason the media insisted on mis-understanding the piece. Consciously or not, the press simply did not want to believe that John was defending his cousins. That would make the editor's letter harder to write about, hence less profitable. How else could so many journalists read a line like "Since when does someone have to go on television to apologize for getting divorced?" and interpret it as criticism of Joe Kennedy?

The public also accepted this take on John's letter, but perhaps for a different reason. After all, if Americans conceded that John was sticking up for his cousins, they would have to admit that he was a more complicated and in some ways darker figure than the golden boy they had always envisioned.

The *National Enquirer*'s Iain Calder had said that if his publication printed something contrary to its audience's image of John, "Our readers would kill us." Well, John himself had presented a contradictory image. And because they could not kill him—they *needed* him— they denied the meaning of his words.

. . .

On August 12, the morning after John's letter hit the news, I stepped onto the set of CNN-fn's *Washington Unwrapped* wearing a black suit and royal blue tie, my face caked with orange makeup. I was prepared to discuss Don Sipple, and host John Defterios did ask some questions about my article. But to my dismay, he then pulled a bait-and-switch. The conversation went like this.

Defterios: "The other thing I want to talk to you about is the column put forth by John-John, or JFK Jr., about his cousins becoming poster boys. . . . What was the motivation behind that, would you say, on his part?"

Me: "First, I guess I'd want to say that that quote has been taken out of context a little bit on the part of the New York tabloids. They have him saying that his cousins are poster boys [for bad behavior]. He actually says, as you put it, that they have become poster boys.

"John was writing a column about the temptation to stray from a conventional life and he raised it in that context. He, I think, was aware that it would cause some controversy, but John knows what he's doing."

Translation: *You don't really think I'm going to answer that question, do you? Truth is, I don't think that John knew what he was doing. He never dreamed his words could be twisted as they were.*

Defterios: "Okay. To make the link between the two, then—Don Sipple—is that fair territory? And are the Kennedy clan fair territory in a case like this with their infidelities or domestic violence?"

Me: "I'm not really in the position where I could talk about the Kennedys. I would say that domestic violence is a serious issue. It is a legal issue and I think it's of a seriousness that is perhaps greater than some of the other things that we have said of people in politics lately."

Translation: *If you think I'm going to touch that one in public, you've lost your mind.*

I was sweating as I yanked the earpiece out of my ear and walked off the set. I had tried to assume a bland and uncontroversial tone, but just talking about John's letter made me queasy. No matter what I privately thought of that letter, I still felt protective of my boss. John had enough people criticizing him without me joining the pack.

A day or so later I flew to Washington to appear on the CNBC talk show *Equal Time* and discuss my story. This time it was a fellow guest, *Newsweek*'s Eleanor Clift, who put me on the spot.

Clift: "I want to know, though, why you didn't do [this story] for *George* magazine, why you went to a more alternative publication?"

Me: "It would have been a precedent-setting story for *George,* and we've never really done that kind of story before."

Co-host Harry Shearer: "And you would have had to take your shirt off."

Me: "Which would have kept anybody from reading the article."

Feeling pleased with myself for squeezing out of a jam, I took the shuttle back to Manhattan. Strolling into my office, I found a manila envelope on my desk. The green stub of a registered mail receipt was glued to the outside. Inside was a court filing: Don Sipple was suing *Mother Jones* and me for $12.5 million.

. . .

John returned from Scandinavia in the third week of August and promptly headed to Hyannis Port for a family weekend. He knew he had some fences to mend.

After that, he returned to work. I didn't talk to him about the "poster boys letter," as it had quickly become known—no one wanted to bring it up—but I did have to tell him about the Sipple lawsuit.

"I've got some bad news," I said. "Don Sipple's suing me."

He nodded as if he wasn't surprised and said, "I'm sorry to hear that."

"I mention it because there's a very good chance that, if it goes to court, he's going to call you as a witness. To ask why you didn't want to run the piece."

John nodded. "Of course. He'll try to say that. . . . Well, just let me know what I can do."

"It could get ugly," I said.

"Don't worry about it," he responded, the tone in his voice reassuring.

That helped—a lot. In the preceding weeks, I had pushed myself to try to understand John's point of view, and my anger had subsided. With my story actually published, it had become easier to appreciate the awkward position in which I had placed my boss. That the article had made national news restored my confidence; I'd proved that I could publish my work without my colleagues' help. Besides, my exploratory job interviews had convinced me that no other workplace could possibly be as fascinating as *George*. I wasn't quite ready to jump off the bronco after all.

The awkwardness was not quite over, though. Like ex-spouses at cocktail parties, my controversy and John's continued to bump into each other. On Thursday, August 28, CNN was planning to air a story on Don Sipple. A CNN producer told me that Sipple's first wife, Regina, had agreed to go on camera. I waited for the broadcast feeling as jittery as if I'd just downed a triple espresso. How could Don Sipple possibly sue me when his wife was going on television to accuse him of abuse?

But at the exact time the story was slotted to air, Joe Kennedy held a press conference. He would not run for governor of Massachusetts, he announced. He needed to devote more attention to his personal life.

CNN covered Joe's press conference live and bumped the Sipple segment. The producer told me she didn't know when it might run now. *If* it would run.

In the middle of that afternoon, John walked into my office and sat down. I tried to straighten the clutter of magazines and government reports that I never quite found time to read; John always urged us to keep our offices neat. He said nothing, and so I waited. He would talk when he was ready. He looked tired. Just around the sides of John's temple were a few strands of gray. I'd never noticed those before.

Perhaps a minute passed as John stared out my window toward the swamps of New Jersey.

"Did you hear?" he said finally.

"I did," I said. "I'm sorry."

"I didn't see the announcement," John said. "What are people saying?"

People were saying that John had helped drive Joe Kennedy from the governor's race, but I didn't want to tell him that. He looked low enough as it was.

Instead I told John about a rumor making the rounds. *Boston* magazine was apparently preparing an article on his cousin Michael. Rumor had it that Joe had called Michael's baby-sitter "the little slut." Furious, the girl's family planned to exact revenge by leaking negative stories throughout Joe's campaign.

John shook his head. "That doesn't sound like Joe."

"No," I said, "it doesn't." Joe wasn't exactly a women's libber, but neither was he a misogynist.

"Anyway," I said, "Joe apparently figured there was just too much craziness going on. He wouldn't be able to run a decent race."

I winced. John's letter had contributed to the insanity and we both knew it. Joe could have survived his wife's book; he could not beat that and the perception of John's disapproval. After all, John was the good Kennedy.

John gave a deep sigh. He was still staring out the window. I finally turned around and looked myself. Occasionally you could see the president's helicopter flying over the Hudson, when Bill Clinton was visiting New York. If you peered between the buildings, you could spot the aircraft carrier *Intrepid,* now a floating museum, moored at 48th Street. Surprisingly often in the summer and fall, fires burned in the toxic swamps across the river.

"You know, I wouldn't be surprised if Joe got out of politics entirely," John said quietly. "I bet he quits the House."

"I could understand why," I said. "Sometimes you'd have to wonder if it's worth the grief."

"In fact," John went on, "he *should* get out of politics." There was a little life in his voice now. "He'd be a *great* businessman. He's incredibly good with people. And he's a great father to his kids."

He turned his head and looked right at me and said, "No matter what you do in politics, if you're a great father, then you've done something meaningful."

I just nodded. This felt like dangerous ground.

"I don't know, there's something crazy about being in politics," John said, shaking his head in frustration. "You get hit with all this criticism. You don't have any real power. And you don't make any money. I mean, Joe has to *rent* an apartment in Massachusetts. Because of alimony, because he has to have a place in Washington. . . . He's a forty-five-year-old man and he doesn't even own a house."

"He doesn't?" I asked, slightly stunned. A Kennedy couldn't afford a house?

John shook his head no.

"Well," I said, "if it's not for the money or the power, maybe people go into politics for the attention. Because they're not cut out to be movie stars, and politics is the next best thing."

"Yeah, I guess," John said. But the look on his face suggested he didn't think very highly of that idea.

. . .

Two days later Nyssa and I were riding in a taxi down Sutter Street in San Francisco. I had flown out to meet with the editors and lawyers at *Mother Jones*. The magazine was putting us up at a quaint little hotel called the Rex, and we were trying to forget the $12 million lawsuit hanging like a scythe over my neck and pretend that we were on a romantic getaway. It wasn't easy, but I was glad to be there with her. We both loved San Francisco—the clean, salty air, the hilly streets, the feeling of healthiness that New York lacks. Besides, I hadn't been a very good boyfriend the past few weeks.

We were headed to dinner when the cabdriver turned up his radio. There were news reports from France—something about Lady Diana and a car crash. Fortunately the princess was not thought to be seriously injured.

When we returned after a few hours of hearty seafood and warming red wine, Diana was dead.

Oh, Jesus, I thought. That poor woman, killed trying to flee photographers.

I couldn't help but wonder if all the paparazzi who had devoted themselves to Diana would now shift their attention to John and Carolyn.

· · ·

On Monday morning I was grilled by *Mother Jones* lawyers. They probed like sadistic surgeons for any slip-up, no matter how small, I might have made reporting my story. They told me to expect that Don Sipple would hire a private investigator, dig up any dirt on me he could. If the case went ahead, we would do the same to him. Maybe we'd see if he had any ex-girlfriends with dark stories to tell. I must have looked surprised—I *was* surprised—because they explained that such espionage was standard operating procedure in these matters.

That afternoon, the *Mother Jones* editors and I gathered around a television in a local bar: CNN was finally running its story. Too nervous to eat, I stood and stared at the television. The screen was filled with reports from England and France about Diana's death. After too many long, frustrating minutes of CNN's hourly news, the serious face of investigative reporter Brook Jackson came on-screen. "The kind of story Regina Sipple tells is all too familiar," Jackson said. Seconds later, the television showed a photograph of Regina, looking calm and composed. "I was injured a number of times," she said.

It was the Monday of Labor Day weekend—not a lot of people were watching CNN. But I couldn't have cared less. Because seeing

CNN flash the cover of *Mother Jones,* hearing those words from Regina Sipple's mouth, was the affirmation I'd been waiting for.

Months later, a California court would throw out Don Sipple's lawsuit and award some $50,000 in legal fees to *Mother Jones.* Sipple appealed the ruling, but an appellate court denied his motion. We had won, and won big. More than ever I regretted that the story hadn't appeared in *George.* Such a slam-dunk ruling would have been great publicity for the magazine. Nothing earns a magazine respect among its peers like fighting and winning a libel suit.

I told John that he wouldn't have to testify after all. "Congratulations," he said, sounding genuinely pleased. "I'm glad it worked out."

.   .   .

In our November 1997 issue we ran a photo essay about Lady Diana called "The Mourning After." It didn't have much to do with politics, but John felt strongly that Diana's death was too central—and, frankly, too commercial—to ignore. People were so interested in her, *George* had to do *something.*

In truth, running the piece was a mistake; some cultural moments were simply beyond *George*'s scope, and pictures of a princess's funeral didn't fit in a magazine about American politics. John's decision to publish the photo essay reflected his deep sadness about Diana's death. But it was also a sign that sometimes he himself wondered just how relevant politics was to the age, or if celebrity was all.

As if to compensate for the photo essay, in his editor's letter John wrote of another death that had attracted far less attention than Diana's but was, he implied, a greater loss: that of Mother Teresa. Although this letter didn't generate a ripple of press, it was heartfelt and moving. It was a shame that the media didn't publicize this one as it had John's letter of two months before, because—unlike that earlier letter—it displayed the clarity John possessed, the maturity and perspective he was capable of:

"As I write this, it has seemed like a month of funerals, and the outpouring of raw feelings has the cynics squirming like saltbugs after a spring rain.

"A few contrarians are finding fault with Mother Teresa now that she's in a pine box," John wrote, referring to a previously published attack on the nun by *Vanity Fair* writer Christopher Hitchens. "How better to display independent-mindedness than to slag a future saint?"

More than a decade before, John wrote, he had visited Mother Teresa's orphanage, and she had asked him to drive her to the airport to pick up a shipment of donated clothing. "Mother's hands, with thick, arthritic knuckles, looked as if they were made of clumps of wood, and were disproportionately large for her tiny body. . . . I remember wondering how much suffering must have seeped into those fingers.

"I've never seen one person provoke as many small acts of kindness from strangers. The three days I spent in her presence was the strongest evidence this struggling Catholic has ever had that God exists."

But people weren't paying attention to her passing, John pointed out. Not compared to the media frenzy surrounding the death of a beautiful, beloved celebrity. "How many people remember every detail of Diana's death but virtually nothing of Mother Teresa's?"

In time, I would look back at this letter in sadness, for it was both a remembrance and a prophecy. Mother Teresa and Lady Diana represented the two extremes of John's existence, the call to service and the lure of celebrity. Stuck somewhere between the two paradigms, unable to discard either one, John hoped to merge them—in his magazine and in himself. He had to acknowledge the power of celebrity, but he never had any doubt that service was more important.

Ten

Thank you, God!" associate editor Susannah Hunnewell proclaimed as John walked up the wooden steps of the Beaverkill Valley Inn. "What a sight to see first thing in the morning!"

Biz Mitchell and Matt Berman, who were also sitting on the porch, almost choked on their coffee. Even John looked embarrassed by the comment, so typical of Susannah's propensity to blurt out whatever came into her head. But I couldn't blame her. In fact, I admired her candor. She was simply expressing what all the women on staff felt about John but would never say to his face.

It was early November 1997. We were encamped at the Beaverkill because John had decided we needed a retreat. He knew his staff was still shell-shocked from the backlash against his "poster boys" editor's letter. None of us had enjoyed the public flogging that John and *George* had received. So John wanted us to rediscover the fun of working at the magazine.

But the truth was, *George* wasn't always fun for John, and he needed this getaway as much as we did. Mentally, he'd been bruised by the outcry over his editor's letter. Physically, he felt cooped up in the office, with its stale air and claustrophobic cubicles and sickly fluorescent lights. Too much time there and he drooped like an unwatered plant. So, more and more, he traveled. There was a trip to Cuba to meet Fidel Castro for an interview that was never published (Castro refused to be taped); an excursion to Tibet to interview the Dalai Lama; a journey to Vietnam to interview a former Viet Cong general.

While on those trips, John would usually tack on a few days for hiking or kayaking. On his return, he brought us presents: T-shirts from Martha's Inn in a town called George, in Washington State; Somerset's shaving oil from England; white silk scarves blessed by the Dalai Lama; fire-truck red notebooks with a Communist logo from Vietnam. I'll never forget the time a conservative Republican senator visited *George* and sat surrounded by nattily dressed journalists scribbling in notebooks emblazoned with the seal of the Vietnamese Communist Party. That pretty much confirmed all his suspicions of the liberal media.

When John was away, we missed his energy, and Biz was hard-pressed to pick up the slack. Leadership held no joy for her. She preferred to hole up in her office, smoking and kibitzing with Rose behind a closed door. When she wanted to communicate with the rest of us, she'd send interoffice e-mails or have her assistant distribute her multiple-page, single-spaced memos. Perhaps Biz remembered the price that Eric had paid for not recognizing the limits of his authority, and simply erred on the side of underasserting her own. But without John, we drifted.

The magazine itself had been wildly inconsistent over the course of 1997. A strong issue would be followed by one that strayed far from our chosen terrain. The pressure to boost newsstand sales still had us splashing celebrities on the cover, even when they had no political connection—sex symbols like Jenny McCarthy, a *Playboy* Playmate, and Pamela Anderson Lee, also a *Playboy* Playmate. Such choices, which were made by John, Biz, Matt, Rose, and Carolyn, gave our critics ample ammunition. Even more demoralizing, they hinted that we ourselves had lost confidence in *George*'s mission, perhaps even grown bored with politics. In truth, the failure was not of vision, but execution.

The only publicity *George* had generated in recent months came from the Geula Amir piece and the poster boys editor's letter. Neither helped our image, and their sensational nature all but eclipsed the solid, smart political reporting that consistently ran in the magazine. Nor were we cheered when John distributed a memo informing us that the poster boys issue had sold 170,000 copies on the newsstand, about 70 percent above our average. "Nudity works!" John scribbled in the margin. The joke fell flat.

Meanwhile, as if to set the record straight about his feelings toward the Kennedy family, John began trying to shoehorn its members into *George* in flattering ways. He asked me to talk with his cousin William Kennedy Smith, who was organizing a group of doctors against land mines. Perhaps somewhere down the line *George* could write something. (Matt Berman would design a logo for the group.) Cousin Bobby Kennedy penned a screed decrying the environmental policies of GOP governors; I hosted a cocktail party for *George* subscribers at which Bobby gave a short speech.

For our December 1997 issue, which we put to bed before heading to Beaverkill, John featured Ted Kennedy in a photo essay called "Legends of the Hill." Kennedy's black-and-white portrait, shot by celebrity photographer Herb Ritts, required extensive retouching to mask the ravages of age and alcohol—the loose cheeks and bulldog jowls. But John revered Teddy, as he called his uncle. Why not use his magazine to burnish Teddy's image? In the end result, Kennedy looked handsome, healthy, and iconic.

The picture of *George,* however, could not be so easily touched up. So on the first Sunday in November, bundled up in jeans and wool sweaters and heavy coats, we convened at a Hertz rental garage in Midtown. Piled into three white vans, we were soon making our way up the West Side Highway and over the George Washington Bridge, then turning north, winding along the Hudson River toward the Catskill Mountains.

It was cold and pitch-black when we pulled in at the Beaverkill Valley Inn, a rambling, unpretentious house near a trout-fishing river in Lew Beach, New York. John had rented out the entire place. On the first floor was a parlor with board games such as Monopoly and Life that I hadn't seen since I was a kid. The cozy dining room was stocked with fruit and cookies. In the basement were ping-pong and pool tables, which some of us quickly staked out. The bedrooms upstairs were spartan chambers with twin beds, hardwood floors, throw rugs, and bedside tables—but no telephones. Cell phones were scarce back then, so when I wanted to call Nyssa to wish her good night, I had to wait in line for the pay phone in the basement.

We city dwellers looked self-conscious in our little-worn outdoor gear, and some of us didn't even try to dress for the country. Matt Berman's downtown uniform of black pants and untucked shirts didn't include sensible shoes. Inigo Thomas, the Englishman, wore the same beige corduroys, dress shirt, red cable-knit sweater, and tweed blazer every day. Jeffrey Podolsky, who smoked imported cigarettes and had his shirts custom made, strolled into the inn with the head of his teddy bear poking out of his duffel bag.

Out of the office, in the middle of nowhere, we resembled bright-eyed schoolkids on a field trip. For the next four days we would be sleeping, eating, and playing in intimate quarters. I felt a little as if I'd joined the cast of *The Waltons.*

. . .

"Here's where we stand," John said.

It was Monday morning after breakfast. Wearing lace-up boots, blue jeans, and a long-sleeved T-shirt, John was holding forth in the inn's conference center, a converted barn about a hundred feet away from the inn. Sipping coffee in a cheery upstairs room flooded with sunlight, we sat around three long tables connected in a U-shape. John ambled back and forth in front of us like a college professor leading a seminar.

"Our business staff tells me that *George* competes for ads with four other magazines," John said. "*Vanity Fair, GQ, Esquire,* and *Men's Journal.* Here's how the ad count for those five magazines breaks down."

He picked up a marker from the tray of a white bulletin board and began writing.

GQ	—	31.6%
VF	—	30.3%
MJ	—	14.3%
G	—	13.1%
E	—	10.1%

Our goal for 1998, John said, was to knock *Men's Journal* out of the number three spot. We also intended to increase circulation. At the moment, we sold some 430,000 issues a month. The plan was to launch a direct-mail campaign to double that number in four years.

I whistled under my breath. If we had almost a million readers, no one would be laughing at *George* anymore.

This was all good news, John emphasized. Especially if we considered that *George,* unlike those other magazines, didn't have the natural advertising constituency of publications showcasing fashion or technology; that it dealt with weightier subjects than our competitors; and that it was read almost equally by men and women (something that advertisers actually disliked, believing it decreased the efficacy of targeted advertising). *George* was pretty darn successful for a political magazine. And though some of this was clearly attributable to John, not all of it was. *George* had struck a chord among people who didn't normally read political magazines.

The bad news was that advertisers thought the magazine erratic. They couldn't always tell what typified a *George* story, and sometimes we couldn't either, judging from some of the articles we'd printed. "*George* focuses on the people in politics," John said. "So let's talk about the people we write about."

As John wrote our suggestions on the board, we compiled a list of words to describe people who epitomized the optimistic spirit of *George*. Our heroes were "future-oriented" and "dreamers" with a "sense of purpose." They were also "authentic, innovative, attractive, and complex." And they were "survivors."

It occurred to me that all we were really doing was describing John, who wore those descriptions as comfortably as an old sweater.

Next we outlined our villains. They were "hypocritical, self-serving, self-righteous, pompous, corrupt, self-interested, smarmy, self-promoting, phony, elitist, racist, and sexist." And, John said, adding the coup de grâce, "disloyal."

John looked at the board and nodded. All right, he said. We've talked about character traits, now let's talk themes. Which ones make for compelling magazine narratives?

We were warmed up now, so answers bounced back like rubber balls. Scribbling as fast as he could, John scrawled, "Strange Bedfellows. The Outsider. Triumph over Adversity."

And one other: "Rising Star–Falling Star/Icarus."

· · ·

I carry with me so many pictures from those four days. . . .

I remember how bright the stars were at night. In New York City, you can always see celebrities, but you can never see stars.

I remember the cool, smooth feel of the hardwood floor when I swung my feet out of bed in the morning.

I remember John waking up early to do yoga in the basement.

I remember the tension thick in the air at mealtimes, like smoke off a frying pan, because everyone wanted to sit with John, but no one wanted to seem obvious.

I remember that, because New York had a mayoral race and we were going to miss Election Day, John brought a stack of absentee ballots.

I remember drinking beers and arguing with John about the New York Giants. He was rooting for Dave Brown, the team's woeful quarterback, because the New York sportswriters thought Brown was a bum. I agreed with the sportswriters. Brown *was* a bum, at least when it came to completing passes. But John couldn't resist an underdog. He loved Patrick Ewing, the New York Knicks' beleaguered center, for the same reason.

I remember that John had his handyman, Effi Pinheiro, bring Friday from Manhattan in a car-service sedan. When Friday spotted John from a hundred yards away on the lawn, he shot toward his master as if he'd been fired from a cannon.

But most of all, I remember the long and strange hike we took that Monday afternoon.

Manmade trails carved through the rambling woods and hillsides that surrounded the inn, and after lunch John asked if anyone wanted to go for a walk. About a dozen of us did, and at around three o'clock the group set out on a leaf-covered path leading uphill into the woods behind the inn. The clouds hung so low that afternoon, there appeared no space between earth and sky. Fragile sunbeams struck the hillside at strange, off-kilter angles. A steady breeze slowly rocked the tree branches, as if the hills themselves were swaying back and forth. The leaves had fallen from the trees, leaving the countryside cloaked in Puritan gray, but the rough grass in the clearings was still green.

Wearing boots, sweatpants, a blue sweatshirt, and a slightly goofy ski hat, John led the way. Friday trotted alongside him, and the rest of us trailed slightly behind; John kept a brisk pace. After about half a mile, we began to separate into clusters. Thanks to my own long legs, I found myself walking with John twenty or thirty yards ahead of the others. As we walked, we chatted. He was relaxed and expansive; I'd never seen him more at ease than he was then, hiking along this autumn hillside, basking in nature and in the family he had created for himself.

We spoke of the beauty around us and whether one could live amid such wilderness yet still enjoy a satisfying career. I mentioned playwright David Mamet, who lived in Vermont. John cited novelist William Kennedy, a resident of upstate New York. (Both men had written for *George*.)

So one could live in the country and stay productive, we agreed, and John admitted that he dreamed sometimes of fleeing the manic urgency of New York City to settle somewhere quiet. Not too far from the city, but enough to escape it.

John in the suburbs? I found that hard to imagine. I'd grown up in the Connecticut suburbs. They were boring. Suburbs existed for ordinary people with ordinary lives, people like me.

"I don't know, John," I said. "I have a hard time picturing you living anywhere but Manhattan."

"Maybe," John said. "But sometimes I think it'd be great to have a big country place and fill it with children. And dogs."

I had to smile at that. I remembered the story Gary Ginsberg had once told about John's old German shepherd Sam, who was so surly that John's mother finally gave Sam to a Secret Service agent who lived in the country. Sam, Gary said, "had bitten everyone but John."

"Where would you live?" I asked. "If you left the city."

Maybe Greenwich, John said, because that's where Carolyn's family is and she'd like that, being near her family. Or maybe somewhere in the Hudson River Valley. He had a fantasy of commuting to work by boat.

"Maybe it's time to think about helicopter lessons," I suggested.

John laughed. "I have to learn to fly a plane first."

"How does Carolyn feel about leaving the city?" I asked.

"She's all for it," he said quickly. "She's freaked about raising kids in the city. She thinks they'd be endlessly harassed."

"Like she is?"

"Mmm-hmm."

"Well . . . would they be?"

He'd reassured Carolyn that things hadn't been so bad for him as a kid, John said. He'd never felt in danger; he'd had a reasonably normal childhood.

"So what did Carolyn say to that?" I asked.

"She said that that was easy for me to say, I had Secret Service agents guarding me."

"She's got a point."

John responded that he'd never really felt "protected," and he'd never really felt in danger.

"Well, the Secret Service agents were always around somewhere, right?"

"Yeah."

"So you *were* always protected?"

John nodded. "Yeah."

"Well then, would you ever really know what it's like not to feel protected? Because it never happened. You couldn't know, could you?"

John thought about that as we walked along, the dry leaves crunching under our feet. We had left the inn well behind.

"Maybe not," he said. "Maybe not."

Anyway, he continued, the move out of the city couldn't happen anytime soon. He already owned too much real estate. Besides his loft, he was part owner of two houses that he could never sell, the Kennedy compound at Hyannis Port and his mother's home in Martha's Vineyard.

"I understand about Hyannis Port," I said. "But couldn't you sell your mother's house, if you had to?"

I don't think so, John said, and laughed a little. I don't think people would understand.

"Well, do the two houses serve different purposes for you? I mean, do you go to different houses for different reasons?"

John thought that over. "The one in Hyannis, that's much more like my father's family. Lots of people around. Very social. Whereas my mother's house is very much like she was. Beautiful and isolated." His next words particularly struck me. "It has," he said, "a terrible beauty."

It was approaching four o'clock. A couple of people had turned back, and we stopped in a meadow to let the rest catch up. The temperature had dropped a few degrees, the wind had picked up, and the sun was starting to fall behind the hills. It wasn't quite day and it wasn't quite night, but that hour at the beginning of winter before blackness descends and you can't believe how quickly the daylight retreated.

I snapped a photo then. It looks like something you might find on an album cover from the 1960s—nine of my colleagues, five women and four men, bundled up like hippie children, standing and sitting in the wild green grass, the tree line in the background, a glint of sun wrapping around the clouds. Their faces are smiling and carefree, like utopians who've discovered the perfect site for a commune. John is kneeling in the grass on the far side of the picture, pulling Friday tight against his chest, kissing the top of his head.

John wanted to keep going, and so we climbed onward, upward. As the crow flies, we were maybe two miles from the inn, but on the twisting paths, it was longer. We walked in a northern direction for another fifteen minutes or so before agreeing that it was time to head back. Even if we simply retraced our steps, we were an hour away from the inn, and there wasn't an hour of daylight left.

John dropped to one knee like a quarterback and drew a circle in the dirt with his finger. "We're here," he said, making an X at six o'clock on the circle. "And this is where we need to be." Another X, at three o'clock.

"This way," John said, pointing upward toward a ridgeline. The other side of the ridge, he explained, had a beautiful view of a clearing, and beyond that lay the inn. If we climbed up there, we'd have a straight shot home.

That's not right, I thought. The ridge in question lay to the west, in the direction of the setting sun. But the inn was toward the east. John wanted to take us 180 degrees the wrong way.

I thought about saying something, but hesitated. What if I was wrong? What if it was my sense of direction that had gone awry? After all, John was the outdoorsman. Then again, what if I was right? No one likes to be shown up.

What the hell, I thought, as John led us toward the setting sun. Where's the harm in getting a little lost?

A few hundred yards later, we were standing on the edge of a long-running ridge and looking down upon . . . a forest. There was no clearing. No inn. Just oak and maple and birch trees on a rocky, leaf-covered hill.

John started making his way down the slope. We followed, grabbing on to tree limbs and leaning backwards to keep our traction on the slippery leaves. Someone banged a knee painfully on a rock, and the rest of us waited while she gingerly flexed her leg. When the ground leveled, we bushwhacked single-file through the woods, stepping around trees and over fallen limbs, pushing branches out of our way, releasing them gently so they didn't slap back into the eyes of the person following.

It was almost dark now, the shadows growing longer until they started to connect. The conversation that had bubbled along during our walk dried up. We were tired, our weariness compounded by anxiety. I shivered and zipped up my jacket. Walking behind John, I couldn't see his face, but I could tell from the way he was looking around, seeking out avenues through the trees, that he had no idea where he was going.

We could be seriously lost here, I thought, and wondered how long it would take a search party to find us once darkness fell completely and we really started to feel the cold.

. . .

No more than five minutes later, we walked straight onto a path. Sheer luck. One second we were navigating through dense woods, the next the trees seemed to part before us and we emerged onto a downward-sloping, manicured trail that must have been fifty feet wide.

No one said a word, not even a joke to cut the tension. No one wanted to remind John that he had gotten us lost. And, maybe, no one wanted to admit it. But I took a close look at John's face as we re-assembled, and I saw a look of deep relief.

We started walking again. Probably because we needed a break from the intensity, John and I fell into a conversation about movies. I told him about a screening I'd attended not long before, a film the studio wanted *George* to cover but that wasn't right for us. The movie was called *The Game*.

John's head jerked around. "Really?" he said. "I know that movie."

While he was with Daryl Hannah, John explained, she had urged him to read a script that had come her way. It was the screenplay for *The Game*, and Daryl told John he "needed" to read it. So he had.

In the movie, Michael Douglas plays the scion of a wealthy banker. He's a handsome, wealthy financier who dresses beautifully and exudes confidence. But inside, he is haunted by the tragedy that he witnessed when he was a little boy. In Douglas' mind he incessantly replays his father's suicidal plunge from the roof of their family mansion. He sees his father's body, broken and bleeding, on the driveway pavement. Those flashbacks are shot in grainy sepia footage, like an old home movie. Douglas asks the family maid, "What was my father like?" She asks why he wants to know. Douglas replies, "I wonder how much of him there is in me."

On Douglas' fortieth birthday, his younger brother, played by Sean Penn, gives him what can only be called a life game. The player doesn't know when the game starts, how to win it, what its rules are, or even who is playing. The game is produced by a mysterious corporation, which begins by putting Douglas through a rigorous series of physical and psychological stress tests.

Once the game has begun, Douglas quickly finds his life descending into madness. The family home he still inhabits is vandalized. His bank accounts are plundered. He falls for a beautiful but mysterious blonde he's not quite sure he can trust. One night a taxi driver jumps out of his cab while Douglas is in the backseat. When the taxi plunges into San Francisco Bay, Douglas nearly drowns in the icy black water.

In this world without rules, isolated by experiences that no one else can even believe, much less relate to, Douglas must question every previously accepted fact of his identity—the impact of his father's death, the value of his work, his choices for the future. Soon he stops denying the bizarre reality of the game and works merely to survive it. Desperate for money, he is forced to sell his father's gold watch, his most treasured heirloom.

At the film's climax, a despondent Douglas leaps off the top of a skyscraper. Plummeting earthward, he is certain that he will die in seconds. But it's all part of the head game; the company has constructed a giant bubble that breaks his fall. Douglas lands smack in the middle of a birthday party attended by all the participants of the game, including his brother, Sean Penn. It's like a reunion in heaven, except it gives Douglas new life. Because in re-creating his father's death, he has finally exorcised that tragedy from his psyche. At last he is free to enjoy the beauty of life on his own terms.

"What'd you think of the movie?" John asked me.

I didn't enjoy it, I answered. I found it surreal in a way that defied credibility. No one would play a game like that, even if such a thing existed. "As if you could survive a fall from a skyscraper."

John stopped walking and turned to me. "Are you kidding?" he replied. "That movie is my *life*."

He stopped then, as if maybe he'd said too much. A few minutes later, we spotted the warm yellow lights of the inn shining through the trees.

· · ·

We returned to Manhattan on Thursday, November 6, to attend our second anniversary party, which we threw at a hot new restaurant called Asia de Cuba. It was a great party but an odd crowd. Larry

Flynt, the publisher of *Hustler* magazine, was there—we'd run a story on the recent film *The People vs. Larry Flynt*. Donald Trump was there, too, with two tall, dressed-to-kill models in tow, so thin they looked as if they'd been stretched. Donna Rice Hughes, the antiporn crusader, was on hand, along with Conan O'Brien, Sheryl Crow, Dick Morris, George Stephanopoulos, and the Reverend Al Sharpton. The mau-mauing minister was surrounded by a trio of massive body-guards. John posed for a picture with Sharpton, whose enormous bulk was cloaked in a checkered blue suit and bright yellow tie.

A week or so after the party, John decided that he wanted to run the picture with Al Sharpton on his editor's letter page.

Don't do it, I said.

Usually I wouldn't have questioned John about anything on his editor's letter page, but after the poster boys fiasco, I was determined to speak out when I thought that John might not be considering the possible repercussions of his actions.

Sharpton is a bigot and a charlatan, I added. He's an anti-white racist, and our readers won't like seeing you with him. That's the kind of picture that could come back to haunt you. I didn't say, *If you ever run for office,* but I thought it.

John would have none of it. Sharpton was a legitimate politician who had run for mayor against Rudy Giuliani, he argued. He wasn't about to dump on him just because everyone else in the press did.

The conversation ended there, and John ran the photo along with his January 1998 editor's letter.

· · ·

In the third week of December, John gathered us in his office for the now-annual distribution of Christmas presents. Once again he and Carolyn had chosen elegant gifts for everyone—cuff links from Paul

Smith, silk scarves from Henri Bendel, a set of Hermès ashtrays. I received a monogrammed silver letter opener from an exclusive New York jeweler. John had spent thousands of dollars of his own money on these gifts.

He also passed out small cards bearing a quote from retired Giants quarterback Phil Simms, who had led the team to two Super Bowl victories but never gotten much respect for it. "You may not win them over," the card read, "but if you hang around long enough, you'll wear them out."

Feeling inspired, I took the train to Connecticut to spend Christmas with my family. John traveled to Vero Beach, Florida, to commence flying lessons.

Eleven

I awoke on January 1 convinced that after a rocky twelve months, the worst was over. My distaste for the Sharpton photo aside, our good karma was back. For *George* and John, 1998 was going to be an excellent year.

That sense of optimism lasted until I picked up the morning paper and read that Michael Kennedy was dead. Vacationing in Colorado, he had collided with a tree while playing football on skis.

John cut short his flying lessons to attend Michael's funeral. When he returned to the office, he looked like a pummeled boxer in a late round, weary and struggling to stand. However unintentionally, John had caused Michael pain, and now Michael was dead, and John would never get to see the wound he had inflicted heal. Joe out of politics, Michael dead—was John's touch a curse?

I asked him if he was holding up okay.

"That," he said, " was the hardest funeral I've ever been to."

Michael's death seemed to spark an impatience in John, and at our next editorial meeting, he lit into us. The magazine was uninspired, the writing tepid, the stories lackluster. We had to do better. He wanted to commission muckraking pieces detailing the Justice Department anti-trust case against Microsoft and investigating the most corrupt cities in America. Those stories were about things that mattered: government fighting for the underdog and the betrayal of the public trust. He wanted *George* to get serious.

But much as John wanted to spotlight the perils of corruption and the virtues of Justice, the cabinet agency where he had once worked, he couldn't escape the Scylla and Charybdis of presidents and sex. *George* was about to be handed its biggest story, one that would pervert his magazine's mission in a way John had never imagined. The nation was about to meet Monica Lewinsky.

On Saturday, January 17, Internet columnist Matt Drudge posted his now notorious scoop about the president and the intern on his web site. On Monday, John convened an editorial meeting in his office. Biz and Inigo and Susannah and Jeffrey Podolsky and I could hardly contain our excitement. Bill Clinton had just hit the media hive with a stick, and even though we couldn't cover this story with the immediacy of television or the daily press, we were buzzing along with the rest of the swarm.

Well, all of us but one. As my colleagues and I leaned forward in our chairs, arguing over what facets of the story *George* could tackle, John said little. Instead he fidgeted in his seat and stared out the window. The irony was inescapable: The press was hunting down an unfaithful president, and the magazine owned by the son of a famously libidinous president was racing to join the pack.

We got several stories rolling that afternoon. Biz would ask up-and-coming novelist Darcey Steinke to profile Monica Lewinsky. Feminist Naomi Wolf, who had started a column on cultural politics for *George,* would write about sexual harassment in the workplace. John chose to interview former senator Gary Hart, whose career had been cut short by alleged adultery a decade earlier. My task was to assign a profile of

Vernon Jordan, the Clinton confidant who had aided Monica Lewinsky in her job search. The reporter I chose was a rising star in Washington. A staff writer at *The New Republic*, he'd written two other stories for me. They were good pieces; this writer had a flair for unearthing the perfect colorful anecdote. His name was Stephen Glass, and he would further contribute to John's education—and my own.

· · ·

Adrenaline was not the only reason to cover the Clinton scandal, nor even the main one. That was profit. The media industry was growing like a vine in the mid-1990s, shooting upward on old platforms such as television and making inroads into new ones like the Internet. The press barons needed content to fill those costly web sites and countless cable TV shows. But because they were pouring money into building the means of distribution, and because the industry was increasingly run by huge corporations like General Electric and America Online, the bean counters didn't want to pay much for what they called "content."

All of which is to say that Bill Clinton chose exactly the wrong moment in history to fool around with an intern. Compared to other forms of entertainment, politics is cheap to produce, and Clinton filled the content gap. The more disturbing scandal of 1998 was not so much the president's hapless relationship with a young celebrity-worshiper, but the self-justifying manner in which the press staged a media circus that would enrich its producers and make stars of its ring leaders. Dwight D. Eisenhower had warned the republic of the military-industrial complex, but Bill Clinton was under assault from the country's burgeoning political-entertainment complex.

Though controversial when introduced, the idea of covering politics as entertainment, without apologies, had spread like a virus since *George's* debut. Comedian Bill Maher had hit the big time hosting

AMERICAN SON

Politically Incorrect, a show that assembled actors, rock stars, sex symbols, and, occasionally, politicians to discuss issues of the day. Mike Nichols was making a movie from the bestselling *Primary Colors, New Yorker* writer Joe Klein's political roman à clef. And of course there was the feeding frenzy of cable television shows—*Hardball, Rivera Live, Crossfire, Equal Time, Washington Unwrapped, The Beltway Boys.* How many journalists depended on Bill Clinton to make a good living?

And *George* was part of that overheated climate. Our magazine was the first media venture explicitly dedicated to the proposition that politics and entertainment had become inseparable. Much as it pained John to admit it, it was no coincidence that Monica Lewinsky had actually wanted to intern at *George.*

John had always wanted his magazine to emphasize the human drama of politics. Like ABC's *Wide World of Sports,* we would cover the thrill of victory, the agony of defeat, and so on. Now, simply to stay relevant, *George* had to dig into politics' seedy side. If we were to succeed, we had to cover the president's sex life. John had never anticipated this turn of events, and if he had, it is hard to imagine he would ever have started *George.*

· · ·

The scandal issue that we mapped out in January hit the stands in mid-March. "Sex in High Places," the cover blared, and we delivered the goods. Darcey Steinke skillfully portrayed Monica Lewinsky as a confused and vulnerable girl. Infused with a deep sympathy for its subject, John's interview with Gary Hart provided perspective from a man who'd undergone a hazing comparable to the one Clinton was getting. The juiciest story was Stephen Glass' profile of Vernon Jordan. "Vernon Jordan is a Washington wise man who talks sex with Bill Clinton when no one else is listening," Glass wrote. "What do the

· 180 ·

president and Vernon Jordan have in common?" asked one anonymous source. "They both like younger women." There were quite a
few anonymous sources sprinkled throughout Glass' article.

John had been uncomfortable with this story from the get-go. That
was in part, I think, because while in law school, John had written Jordan a letter asking for career advice. On top of that, the article sounded
like something that might have been written about John's father. In fact,
it sounded like something that *had* just been written about his father.
Even as we were preparing the Jordan piece, John was fuming over *The
Dark Side of Camelot,* a new book by investigative journalist Seymour
Hersh that rehashed all the old innuendo about JFK's sex life and added
some tawdry (and much questioned) new tidbits. When John picked up
the issue of *Time* featuring Hersh's book on the cover, he briefly flipped
through it, then angrily hurled it down.

John knew that Vernon Jordan had a reputation as a rake. But he
had deep misgivings about depicting Jordan as, he said sarcastically, "a
poonhound." Sex appeal, John argued, was just part of Jordan's charisma, a by-product of the man's confident, forceful personality.

So I wrote a sentence to address John's concerns and inserted it
into the story. It read, "Jordan is, by all accounts, a man of immense
charisma and intelligence whom both men and women find compelling." It was an awkward sentence. You could sense the conflict
behind it, the "but" that was about to follow. Ironically, it also helped
establish the credibility of the article and its ensuing sexual gossip. "I
always wear a bra around Jordan," Glass reported one unnamed Washington woman lamenting. "Otherwise he stares at my tits."

"Are you sure about all this?" John had asked me before we went
to press. "It's tough stuff."

"I'm afraid so," I said. "Steve's a good reporter."

The situation became still more awkward when the art department discovered what seemed a telling photo—Jordan at a party with

his arms draped over two beautiful movie stars. One was the actress Famke Janssen. The other woman, smiling and holding a drink, was Daryl Hannah.

I quickly showed the photo to John. "Do you have a problem with this? It works for the story, but . . ."

He looked at it for a second and said, with an in-for-a-penny tone in his voice, "If it works, use it."

The prurient details of the article got picked up in newspapers all across the country. Whether it appeared in the *National Enquirer* or *George,* sex always sold.

Jordan himself didn't comment publicly on the story. At least, not until the revelations about Stephen Glass burst into the headlines.

• • •

On April 25 we shuttled to the capital for another White House Correspondents Dinner. Since my first one in 1996, the event had become even glitzier, with celebrities such as Anne Heche and Ellen DeGeneres showing up to flirt with politics for the horde of reporters and photographers in attendance. A rope line in the Hilton lobby, about a hundred feet from where John Hinckley had shot Ronald Reagan seventeen years before, restrained fans who yelped and squealed as one star after another walked into the hotel. Sharon Stone! Tim Russert! Salma Hayek! Paula Jones! I was glad for Carolyn's sake that she had decided to skip this one.

Arriving late to avoid the free-for-all, John slipped into his seat just as the dinner was starting. He sat in amazement as Bill Clinton addressed the crowd, an annual rite for the president. How Clinton could stand and crack jokes before the people who, come the next morning, would return to prying into his sex life was beyond John's understanding.

Dinner over, the *George* crowd hustled our boss past gawkers and photographers and through the hotel doors. But as we started down the block, one young man pursued us. He had long, unkempt brown hair, his shirt was untucked on one side, and he was waving something in his right hand.

It was a tense moment. People rarely chased John. Photographers did, sometimes—but whatever this guy had in his hand, it wasn't a camera.

As the man caught up to our group, I saw what he was carrying—a dog-eared copy of *Esquire* with John on the cover—and I breathed a sigh of relief. "Hey, John Kennedy!" he shouted. "Hey, John! Will you sign this?"

John looked like he wished he were invisible. "Sorry, no," he said.

Thrusting the magazine toward John, the man followed us as we headed down a dark side street. "C'mon, man," he whined, his voice hungry. "Just one autograph. That's all I want. One little autograph. What's the big deal?"

While John kept walking, staring fixedly straight ahead, several of us simply stopped in front of the man. For a few seconds he looked as if he were considering trying to get past us, but instead he slumped and shook the magazine angrily in John's direction.

"Asshole," he said. "What's the big fuckin' deal?"

. . .

On a Monday morning several weeks later, I walked into my office and saw the red light on my phone lit up. "I've left *The New Republic*," I heard Stephen Glass say on my voice mail. "I'll be leaving Washington for a while." He sounded scared.

I yanked the phone out of its cradle and called Glass. What was going on?

He'd made mistakes in a story he'd written for *The New Republic*, he told me. *TNR*'s editor had fired him.

"Just mistakes?" I asked. Everyone made mistakes. It was unfortunate, but didn't usually merit the ax.

"Yeah," he said. "I can't really talk about it now."

"Well, keep your head up," I said. "You'll get through this. Call when you can."

But Glass had lied to me, and not just then. Over the next few days, I learned along with the rest of the world that Stephen Glass was a serial fabricator. Relying upon a fervid imagination that many novelists would envy, he had invented facts, sources, and anecdotes in dozens of stories for *The New Republic* and other magazines. He had been caught only after concocting an article about a computer hacker infiltrating a company called Jukt Micronics. A technology reporter named Adam Penenberg thought Glass' tale improbable and tried to confirm it. He could find neither the company nor the hacker—because they didn't exist.

Glass' deceit hit me hard. I had spent hours brainstorming with him, discussing ideas, suggesting lines of inquiry, certain that I was helping this good-natured young man become a better journalist. All the while, he was teasing out my vulnerabilities, playing on my vanities, assessing how better to dupe me. Like Herman Melville's confidence man, he appeared before his victims in a form they trusted, winning their confidence, then betraying them, leaving them awash in disillusion. Glass knew that I was desperate to land a scandal scoop, and he'd given me just what I wanted.

But my soul-searching would have to wait. The immediate question was the Jordan profile. How many of the naughty bits it contained were figments of Glass' perverse imagination? I scanned the backup materials he'd sent our fact-checkers. One anonymous source he claimed was George Stephanopoulos, whom I promptly telephoned.

"I have no right to ask you this," I said, "so if you don't want to tell me I'll understand. But Stephen Glass says you were a source for his story on Vernon Jordan. Did he ever interview you?"

"Nope," Stephanopoulos replied. "Never even called me."

And so it went. Once we had shed our patina of trust, it was a simple matter to see with sharper eyes: The Jordan story was a tapestry of previously reported facts, distorted half-truths, and outright lies. We would have no choice but to run a major correction.

Deeply disturbed, John called me at home at eleven o'clock on the night of June third. That afternoon, Jordan had called to complain about the story. "We don't hear a thing from him for weeks, and now he calls," John said, sighing. "What exactly is wrong in that story?"

"It's hard to know for sure," I answered, speaking softly. Nyssa was asleep in bed next to me, a pillow pulled over her head.

I told John that I'd been able to reach Glass only once more, at his parents' house in Illinois. "I'm in a bad way," he had said. "My parents are worried that I might do something . . . extreme. Someone's with me all the time. I can't talk right now."

When he felt up to talking, I had replied, I would appreciate his help determining what was true and what wasn't. I hung up irritated. Glass was implying that he might attempt suicide. True? Or just another manipulation? I hated that I even had to consider the possibility.

John absorbed all that information without comment; that a journalist would make things up was hardly a shock to him. "I think I need to apologize to Jordan personally," he said. "But not professionally."

"It's the other way around, John," I said. "We didn't publish that story because we dislike Vernon Jordan. It was just business."

Besides, if anyone should apologize, it wasn't John; I had not only been Glass' editor, I had been his advocate. This mess was my fault.

Carolyn agreed that he shouldn't apologize, John said. She thought it was going too far to use the words *apology* or *regret* in whatever he wrote.

"Actually, that's not quite what I meant." I had to be careful—this was not the time to contradict Carolyn. "You don't have to say 'I apologize.' *That's* making it personal. But to say something like 'We regret the error'—journalists do that all the time."

The next day John ignored both my advice and Carolyn's and wrote Jordan a letter of apology. It was something his mother would have done—a proper, mannered communication between two peers, privately conveyed, so that the outside world could not listen in.

He would also address the fiasco in his July 1998 editor's letter. "As editor-in-chief," John wrote, "I am ultimately responsible for the contents of this magazine. It is a responsibility I welcome, both when our work succeeds and, in this case, when it falls short of our standards."

That was something his father's example had taught: Take responsibility for your mistakes, and people will respect you all the more. JFK had done so on a matter of immensely greater gravity, the Bay of Pigs, but the principle was the same. Glass had written for other magazines, such as *Harper's* and *Rolling Stone,* whose editors never addressed his fabrications with anywhere near John's candor. The man once mocked as a journalistic dilettante had acted more professionally than some of the industry's most esteemed veterans.

When Jordan received John's letter, he promptly leaked it—or had someone else leak it—to Howie Kurtz, the influential media reporter for the *Washington Post*. GEORGE'S SORRY STATEMENT OF AFFAIRS, read the June 8 headline. Wrote Kurtz, "It's not every day that John F. Kennedy, Jr., sends a contrite letter to the subject of a *George* magazine article. . . ."

John was floored that Jordan had shared the contents of a private correspondence with a reporter. Jordan's hardball did, however, teach him a useful lesson. His mother's manners meant little to the snipers in the D.C. jungle. If anything, they made him vulnerable.

When dealing with Washington, John needed to be a Kennedy. Because that was how Washington would treat him.

. . .

After Michael Kennedy's funeral in January, John had resumed his flying lessons, and in the succeeding months he pored over tables and charts and textbooks, immersing himself in the task of getting his pilot's license. I had never seen John work as diligently as he did to prepare for that pilot's exam. In the past, he had never used his top-of-the-line Apple computer. He wrote in longhand on a legal pad and had Rose type his hard-to-decipher, left-handed cursive. (John's spelling was like wandering through a tag sale—you never knew what you might stumble across—and his handwriting was a labored series of dips and swoops.) Now he got an America Online e-mail address, JKGeo@aol.com, and surfed the Web for maps and weather reports. In early May, he earned his license to fly small planes.

John happily answered questions about flying when *USA Today* interviewed him about the newly released *George Book of Political Lists,* a move to extend our brand into book publishing. "The only person I've been able to get to go up with me, who looks forward to it as much as I do, is my wife," John said. "The second it was legal she came up with me." Now, "whenever we want to get away, we can just get in a plane and fly off."

He flaunted his enthusiasm like a kid at show-and-tell. He loved to chat about planes with the editor of *Flying* whenever he bumped into the man in the hallway. After he bought his first plane, a four-seater Cessna, John asked if I wanted to see a photo the way a new father asks if you want to see baby pictures. Before I'd had a chance to respond, he was logging on to AOL and going to a Cessna Web site. He was still proudly eyeing his plane when I left his office a few minutes later.

Some of the staff wondered whether John's enthusiasm wasn't leap-frogging his abilities. Later that summer, John offered to fly another staff member back from the Cape. Leery about flying in a small plane, she debated whether to accept John's offer and asked Gary Ginsberg for his opinion. "What's the downside?" Gary joked. "You either get a free ride home with the boss, or you get to die with John Kennedy."

My colleague decided to fly with John. The two took off late in the afternoon, and flew smoothly and uneventfully down the New England coastline. But by the time they neared the New Jersey airport where John kept his plane, the sky had grown dark, and the ground below had become a confusing kaleidoscope of multicolored lights. His passenger pointed out a string of blue that looked to her like a runway, but John disagreed, maintaining that it was a highway. As they continued on, an air traffic controller came on the radio to warn John that he was overshooting the runway. John promptly banked the plane in a circle, and landed without further incident.

After taxiing to a stop, John turned to his passenger and apologized. It was, he explained, the first time he'd ever done that.

· · ·

Given the choice between the public and the press, John instinctively sided with the public. He knew that Americans found the saga of sex in the Oval Office entertaining. But he also believed that they could separate that melodrama from Bill Clinton's job performance. Unlike, say, the people reporting on it.

In his interview with *USA Today,* John was asked to comment on the Clinton scandal. "It's making people really reflect on what matters in their leaders," he answered. "People are really concerned with the capacity to govern and not just someone's personal life."

One day that summer John walked into my office pointing to an article on the front page of the *Times*. Clinton had made a statement about Lewinsky while traveling overseas. "But many in the White House press corps were dissatisfied with the president's explanation," the article said. John jabbed the newspaper with his finger. "Why the hell should the president have to justify himself to the press?"

On that point, he never wavered. During an edit meeting a few weeks later, John grew incensed when his own staff criticized the president. We were preparing a year-end issue ranking the "best and worst" in politics in 1998, and Bill Clinton was to be our "least valuable politician."

John had been so quiet I wondered if he was even paying attention, but suddenly he erupted. The public is right not to care about this scandal, he proclaimed. So what if Bill Clinton had fooled around with Monica Lewinsky? The man worked hard. Who were we to judge him? The president, John declared, was just "loving life."

Silence around the table.

Biz tried to change the subject, saying that the liberal media was angry at the president for signing a punitive welfare reform bill.

"Biz, that's infantile," John snapped, and she recoiled as if slapped. The rest of us were equally shocked—such harshness was unlike him, especially with Biz.

Anyway, John continued, he had a different perspective, because "the media is doing to Clinton what it has been doing to my family for the past thirty years." It was wrong to judge a president by his personal life. By that standard, John said, FDR would also have been *George*'s least valuable politician. "So would my father," he pronounced.

I don't remember anyone having an answer for that.

The scandal may have demoralized John, but it also forced him to hone a political philosophy to counter its depressing reality. Acknowledging that *George* needed the buzz, he would allow his staff to chase scandal stories. But he was determined to offer Americans an alternative. He proposed an affirmation of government based upon three tenets: realism about politicians' personal failings, appreciation for their sacrifices, and greater public participation in civic life.

"The scandal," John said in an AOL chat, "has revealed an important facet of the American people, which is that they are not swayed by endless nay-saying regarding politics. They recognize real achievement. They want their leaders to produce and do well. They respect our government institutions, if not always the people who run them. And they have realistic expectations about what people in public life can and should accomplish."

Over the course of 1998, John detailed this philosophy of patriotic realism through his writings in *George* and in increasingly frequent public statements. Few paid attention to John's theorizing, because it did not involve his personal life and there were no semi-naked pictures next to his writings. But John's words provided a sense of the leader he was becoming. He was, you might say, composing a platform.

The introduction of John's argument came in his March 1998 editor's letter. The issue coincided with the release of two movies about politics and sex, *Primary Colors* and *Wag the Dog;* the latter featured a president who fakes a war to cover up a sex scandal involving himself and a Girl Scout. Those films eerily paralleled events in Washington, John wrote. "Turn on the news and go to the movies and one thing becomes clear: Hellish torment awaits those who mix an undisciplined libido with a political career." The language was strong, to match John's empathy for any politician living through such misery.

One month later, of course, our "Sex in High Places" issue highlighted the scandal. But at the same time, it also featured Tom Hanks, star of an HBO series on the space program, on the cover. In his editor's letter, John admitted that he abhorred the Lewinsky coverage in his own magazine. "The last few months have made vivid that enduring paradox of American politics: It brings out the very best and worst in all of us," he wrote. "Accordingly, in this issue we endeavor to offer you a bit of both, from a behind-the-scenes look at a scandal-soaked Washington, D.C., to a reminder of the glittering success of the Apollo space program . . ."

This month *George* brings you the "worst in all of us"? John might as well have been holding the magazine with one hand and his nose with the other. Was it mere coincidence that the countervailing example he provided, the space program, was largely begun during his father's administration? John was reluctant to say explicitly that his father should be a model for a new generation, but he was edging in that direction.

Just after that issue came out, John cited another source of inspiration from his father's administration. At *Time* magazine's seventy-fifth-anniversary gala on March 19, he rose to toast JFK's secretary of defense, Robert McNamara, long vilified as the architect of the Vietnam War.

McNamara "served his country with exceptional loyalty, integrity, and dedication," John said. "And after leaving public life, he kept his own counsel, though it was by far the harder choice.

"Years later, Robert McNamara did what few have done. He took full responsibility for his decisions and admitted that he was wrong, and judging from the reception he got, I doubt many public servants will be brave enough to follow his example.

"So tonight I would like to toast someone I've known my whole life, not as a symbol of the pain we can't forget but as a man, and I would like to thank him for teaching me something about bearing great adversity with great dignity, an adversity endured only by those who dare to accept great responsibility."

I was less convinced than John was of McNamara's courage; he'd waited a long time to make that apology. But I admired the guts it took to deliver that toast in front of a roomful of American artists and intellectuals, who by and large scorned and shunned McNamara.

To help compose an August photo essay on American heroes, John proffered his nominations. "For the sake of variety," he wrote in an interoffice e-mail, "I'm choosing great underdogs who have triumphed over—yes, you guessed it—great odds."

They were:

> Hon. John L. Lewis
> Yogi Berra
> Hon. Bernie Sanders
> Norman Mailer—for his underdog literary sensibility
> Arthur Imperatore
> Dennis Rivera
> Mugsy Bogues
> Anthony Lewis—ditto Norman
> Betty Friedan
> Rodney King
> Richard Jewell
> Gen. Shalikashvili
> Madeleine Albright
> Susan McDougal*

---

*John's list included, respectively, the Georgia congressman who'd been savagely beaten during civil rights protests; the former New York Yankee; the self-proclaimed Socialist congressman from Vermont; the writer and pugilist; the developer who founded a ferry service between Manhattan and New Jersey; the head of the New York hospital workers' union, and a friend of John's; the diminutive pro basketball player; the *New York Times* columnist and First Amendment crusader; the feminist author; the victim of a beating by Los Angeles police officers; the security guard wrongly accused by the press of planting a bomb during the 1996 Olympics; the chairman of the Joint Chiefs of Staff; the Secretary of State; and the Clinton friend who was jailed for refusing to testify before independent counsel Kenneth Starr.

John was probably the only American not paid to do so who referred to our elected representatives by their official designation, "Honorable." But in an old-fashioned way, he believed they *were* honorable.

In contrast, John had serious questions about those he suspected did not serve with honor and loyalty. Around this time, Claire Shipman, the NBC White House correspondent whom I'd hired as a columnist, was writing a profile of George Stephanopoulos for the magazine. The piece focused on Stephanopoulos' break from President Clinton and his decision to write a book about his former boss. Why was Stephanopoulos writing this book, and to what extent did the very act of doing so constitute a betrayal of the president?

When Shipman finished a draft in the first days of March, I showed it to John. He didn't normally want to see stories that early in the editing process, but I knew he was deeply interested in this piece. John returned it with these comments.

> To what extent was Bill Clinton responsible for George Stephanopoulos' current misfortune? A little heavier thinking on the issue of loyalty. A little tougher. He looks a little indiscreet about this. Could George really not have known [how controversial his book would be]? And if that's true, what does it say about George? Should it have a quote from a psychologist on what GS needed to do? Examples from other worlds of people who've had to make the same break?

After Shipman's story came out in May, the subject came up again at an editorial meeting. "This guy owes everything he is to Clinton," John said. "And now he's writing a tell-all?"

"What a scumbag," Inigo Thomas said.

"That's a little harsh," I said. "Doesn't it depend on what he writes?"

And we were off to the races debating the nature of loyalty, one of those minefield conversations during which what we were really hashing out—the terms of our relationship with John—went deliberately unspoken. Somehow, I thought, I doubt that editors at other magazines have discussions like this.

John mentioned Dee Dee Myers, Clinton's press secretary–turned–talking head, whom he also dubbed disloyal.

"The person who's truly disloyal," I said, "is Dick Morris. Clinton treated him just fine, all things considered, and now Morris makes a living taking shots at him." But weren't Myers and Stephanopoulos of a different order? Clinton had treated them shabbily, yet they appeared to have struggled with their decision to talk about him.

"They're all scumbags," Inigo reiterated. "You just don't do that."

Perhaps, John mused, there was something about Clinton that was partly responsible for this disloyalty, either in his choice of the people he surrounded himself with or because he created misgivings among his aides. On the other hand, John added, Clinton adviser Harold Ickes had never said a word about anything and probably never would. That was admirable, but increasingly rare. How could one go into politics without the expectation of such discretion?

Maybe, I suggested, loyalty is owed in proportion to the character of the person to whom it is owed.

"Yeah, maybe," John said. "But Stephanopoulos couldn't even wait until Clinton left office. A president has a right to expect better."

· · ·

While John struggled with his philosphical ambivalence toward the Lewinsky affair, the rest of us had a different problem. After our strong start covering the scandal in *George,* we had lost momentum, and our coverage had lost focus. The story had created a schism between John and his staff that was paralyzing the magazine. We knew that the human elements of this drama were perfect for *George,* but sensing our boss' disapproval, we hesitated to cover the story full-bore. Inevitably our coverage of the year's consuming event felt tepid. The nadir came in August, when we put then little-known actress Charlize Theron on the cover. She had absolutely nothing to do with politics, and John knew it. I think that's why he chose her. He was fed up.

Every Monday the *New York Post* runs a feature called "On the Newsstand" in which it rates new issues of magazines. Our August issue prompted the writers of "On the Newsstand" to declare, "*George* isn't worth the pulp required to print it." Regarding that issue, the *Post* wasn't entirely wrong. Yet, with John's permission, Biz responded by writing a two-page letter criticizing the *Post*'s methodology. That prompted "On the Newsstand" to stop mentioning us entirely, which was worse than a negative review. Magazines can live with people saying bad things about them. But if people aren't saying *anything* about them . . . that's trouble.

Early in 1998, the economic news had been promising; John distributed a memo stating that *George* had again topped *Esquire* in January ad pages. That win was especially gratifying for him. In its year-end issue for 1997, *Esquire* had published a nasty satire of John's editor's letter photo, a series of computer-generated nudes purporting to be outtakes from the original photo session. Most of the time John accepted teasing with grace, but the *Esquire* parody stung. So on his memo, John had drawn an arrow to the word *Esquire* and wrote "Oops! Nudity *doesn't* work."

That January bump had turned out to be a fluke, however, and our internal turmoil only intensified. Later that month, publisher Elinore Carmody left the magazine. Her relationship with John had been prickly. Elinore worked hard to convince advertisers that they belonged in *George*, but within the office she made clear her opinion that the magazine's editorial quality was inconsistent. Some months earlier, they had disagreed over a back-cover Mercedes ad, a photo of Marilyn Monroe with a Mercedes emblem on her cheek. Tearing out the ad, John wrote a note and left both on Elinore's desk: "I wish someone had informed me of this beforehand." Elinore didn't appreciate the gesture. Landing Mercedes was hard enough.

Publisher number three had arrived in March. He was a genial fellow named Stephen McEvoy who previously sold ads for Hachette's "car books," *Road & Track* and *Car & Driver*. None of us could quite understand how working at *Car & Driver* qualified you to be publisher of a political magazine. Whether or not McEvoy could have made a difference even if he were the world's most experienced publisher, I don't know. But over the next few months, *George*'s ad count continued to dwindle, and the magazine began to shrink visibly.

For wage slaves in the backbiting world of glossy magazines, few phenomena are as demoralizing as shrinkage. Readers might think that editors scan their competitors for explosive stories or hot writers. We do, eventually. But our first act upon receiving our rival magazines is to lift them like a butcher assessing a quantity of sliced cold cuts. Heft means ads, and ads mean your magazine is hot, and a hot magazine means job security and more money at Christmas.

When shrinkage hits, everything sours. Suddenly budget woes trip you like a rope tied between trees. Don't assign this story—too expensive. Don't shoot an original portrait. Cut this story in half, we don't have the pages. It's like being on a lifeboat where the portion of your rations is slashed and slashed again.

Worst of all, shrinkage usually means compromising your principles—like when we started accepting ads from the National Rifle

Association in which gun buffs like Tom Selleck touted the joys of packing heat. At *George's* inception, John and Michael had announced that we would not accept ads from political organizations, but now that policy was abandoned. Our readers were confused. One woman wrote, "John F. Kennedy, Jr., of all people . . ."

When I cautiously informed John that many readers found it distasteful that he would publish ads from the NRA, he winced and said, "I know, I know. But we need the pages."

That fall John entered into discussions on the future of *George* with Hachette CEO David Pecker. The company's contract to publish the magazine was expiring at the end of 1999, and Pecker apparently thought that he had John over a barrel. In its fourth year of publication, *George* was further from turning a profit than in its first. A well-sourced rumor had it that Pecker had one very specific demand for John: Biz Mitchell had to go.

As I would learn later, John would not agree: Biz was loyal to him, and he to her. But he knew Biz was struggling. He had asked Inigo and me to prepare a report on how the magazine could function more smoothly—conspicuously omitting Biz from the exercise. He was also conducting one-on-one lunches with the senior editors to discuss *George's* problems, and his line of questioning always led back to Biz. Three years as executive editor had sapped her energy and may well have contributed to the decline of her marriage: Biz was getting a divorce. Thinner than ever, with dark bags underneath her eyes, she looked utterly exhausted.

Meanwhile, the office dramas had prompted me to evaluate the state of my own personal life. Things with Nyssa were wonderful, but we'd been living together for three years now. Was I taking her for granted?

Maybe it was because Susannah Hunnewell had left *George* to have a baby, or Biz's marital problems, or that romantic image of

Carolyn on John's wall. Perhaps I had finally recognized that life with John was such a roller coaster, I needed someone to help me stay grounded. Whatever the impetus, I finally realized that it was time to make my bond with Nyssa permanent.

One October weekend we traveled to Fisher's Island, a tiny swatch of green off the coast of Connecticut. On Saturday afternoon, we walked through a wildlife refuge on the island's southern shore. The air was still warm. Sunbeams sliced through the canopy of leaves, and a salty breeze blew in from the ocean. I could hear the faint crashing of waves from the beach a few hundred yards away.

On a narrow, rock-strewn path overlooking the cresting surf of Block Island Sound, I got down on one knee and proposed to Nyssa, and I could not speak when her eyes filled with tears and she said yes.

Twelve

On Thursday evening, January 7, 1999, John walked into my office and pushed the door shut. His eyes were red and puffy. Slumping down in a chair opposite my desk, he put his head between his knees.

For a minute, maybe two, he sat without moving. Staring at the industrial gray carpet, he didn't say a word, and my office was heavy with the awkward silence that comes when no one wants to speak first. It was about six o'clock, and most of the staff had left for the day. Through my window, I could see cars crawling like steel insects up Eighth Avenue forty-one floors below, the square white lights of New Jersey apartment towers lining the Hudson, the red blinking beacons of planes descending toward Newark and La Guardia and JFK.

Still John said nothing.

He's going to fire me, I thought. But what for?

I took a deep breath and sat up straighter in my chair. Every roller-coaster ride has to come to an end. Might as well get this one over with. In some ways, it would be a relief.

"Spit it out, John," I said.

• • •

The morning before, the *Post* had published a story that rocked our office. JOHN JR. SEARCHING FOR NEW NO. 2, blared its headline. Media reporter Keith Kelly reported that "John F. Kennedy, Jr., is searching for a hands-on editor for his *George* magazine to try and bring it to the next level. . . . Calls to Kennedy and other magazine officials were not returned."

Our doors slammed shut like mousetraps. Manuscripts lay unread while we turned our editors' eyes to the *Post*, sniffing out clues to the aricle's sources and credibility. Ominously, the story contained hints of an inside job. That line about taking *George* "to the next level" was a leaker's way of spinning the idea that the trouble did not involve a fight between John and Hachette. Nor was it about hanging a failing editor out to dry. It was about making *George* even *better*.

Was the story true? We had no idea. But because of the article's careful wording, we all suspected that it had been planted by someone at Hachette. It appeared that someone wanted to get rid of Biz without hurting *George* any more than necessary.

Would his own publishing company really double-cross John? Even by the slippery standards of the magazine business, that would be vicious work. But it was possible, and David Pecker (or someone following his directions) became an instant suspect. Pecker was a hard-nosed businessman with a sizable ego, and Hachette scuttlebutt had it that he had tired of being eclipsed by John. Besides, Pecker revered the bottom line, and *George* wasn't paying off.

Whoever it was who'd leaked the story, he had forced John to make a Solomonic choice. If the report was true, John could have confirmed it to Keith Kelly. But even if he were looking to replace Biz, John wouldn't have wanted to release the news on someone else's terms. And he certainly wouldn't have wanted Biz to learn of her obsolescence through the *New York Post*.

Of course, if the story wasn't true, John could simply have said so. Yet even if he had issued a vehement denial, the smear would stick to Biz, buzzing around her reputation like a cloud of mosquitoes. Her power, her credibility, and her ability to do her job would be undercut.

So behind our firmly closed doors, we debated the story's final line, "Calls to Kennedy and other magazine officials were not returned." For John not to say anything—that looked bad for Biz. He would have denied the story if he could. Unless . . .

Unless John hadn't heard about the call. That was what Rose claimed, and it was possible. John and an instructor were flying his plane on a cross-country trip. If John was in the air when the call came in, he could have been unreachable until after Keith Kelly's deadline.

We wanted to believe that scenario. Because if Rose had spoken with John and he hadn't responded to the *Post,* then it was all true, and John had been outmaneuvered. That was an unnerving prospect. And much as I had disagreed with Biz on editorial matters, I took no satisfaction in seeing her humiliated. No one deserved that kind of treatment.

As soon as Biz arrived at work that Wednesday, she retreated into her office and shut the door. In the rare moments when she did venture into the hallway, she fluttered like a hummingbird, a flurry of motion with very little movement. At once fascinated and horrified, we knew that we could do nothing to help her. Rose spread the word that John was returning to the office. But while he was en route for the next day and a half, John did not call—at least, not that Rose mentioned—and Biz's discomfort grew increasingly hard to witness.

Watching her twist in the wind might have been the most upsetting aspect of this power game. John had always assumed that his enemies would target only him; I don't think he had ever considered the possibility that someone would move against him by picking off one of his colleagues. We all felt vulnerable, for if John couldn't protect Biz, then none of us was safe.

Maybe that was a truth we needed to learn—that no matter how close we might feel to John, we were all expendable. He was the franchise. We worked for John only while we were of use to him, after which loyalty was irrelevant. As Eric Etheridge had learned, the second we became a liability, we could be removed. There could be no damaging the franchise.

Denying that logic was useless, but accepting it was hard. Wasn't it part of the deal that if we did all we could to protect John, he would return the favor? Or were we really just pawns, to be sacrificed in intrigues the details of which we weren't even privy to?

When he returned late that Thursday afternoon, John disappeared into Biz's office, where he stayed until moments before walking into mine and shutting the door.

.   .   .

"Spit it out, John," I said, and he shook his head as a dog shakes off water. Slowly, he pulled himself together, sitting up in his chair and lifting his head, imposing discipline upon his body.

He spoke in a flat, weary voice. "Biz is leaving *George* and you are the new executive editor."

I wish I could remember my immediate response, but I cannot. I remember only that I didn't feel a hint of pleasure. Who wants to receive a promotion from a man who looks like he's just had his heart torn out?

"What's going on, John?" I said.

Picking his words carefully, he said that Biz had been dragged into a fight. He had been negotiating with Hachette over a television spin-off of *George*. Hachette had given away some rights that John had insisted upon keeping. When John found out, he fought to reclaim them. That had complicated—and probably terminated—the television deal.

The *Post* story, John said, was David Pecker's revenge. He wanted to show his displeasure with John; he also wanted Biz gone. One shot, two kills.

"I don't want this job if you were pressured into giving it to me, if I'm some kind of transition figure," I said.

He shook his head no. "Your name had come up a long time ago. I just had . . . a different timetable." He gave a bitter laugh. "Obviously."

"Don't worry about the way this is happening," he went on. "That article in the *Post* . . . that was just business. Just business."

He sounded as if he were trying to remind himself of that fact. Or convince himself.

John asked me to say nothing about the promotion until we announced it the next day, when he would tell the press that Biz had left because of "creative differences." He said he trusted me and that I had shown discretion at *George*, but that he could not overemphasize its importance now. Being who he was, he said, the fact that he knew and trusted me was extremely important to him.

"We'll talk more tomorrow," John said. "I have to go home."

And that was how, after three years and seven months working for John Kennedy, I became the executive editor of his magazine. The manner in which I was promoted wasn't exactly what I had hoped for. But I took comfort in the words of Phil Simms: "If you stick around long enough . . ."

I had, somehow, stuck around, even though I had not particularly expected to. The roster of spin-offs was long. Of the original eight editors, only John and I remained.

·   ·   ·

On Friday morning, Biz didn't come in to the office. John held a meeting with the staff at which he announced the change, and the stunned expressions on people's faces reminded me of the meeting at which John had announced Eric's departure. That Biz was leaving was not entirely a shock, but no one could understand why her exit had been handled so awkwardly.

The next days were a whirlwind of interviews, lunches, and advertising calls, a frantic blur of early mornings and late nights and early mornings. Exhausted, I would sometimes come into work having selected my outfits haphazardly. When John arrived, he'd tease, in his best Irish brogue, "Get dressed in the dark again, did you, Rich?"

When I got home at night, Nyssa and I would sit on our bed and plan our wedding, tapes of prospective bands playing in the background. The nuptials would take place in early September in Stowe, Vermont, a quaint little town that had become our escape from Manhattan. The ceremony would be held in a simple white New England chapel smack in the middle of Main Street; the reception would follow at a picturesque hilltop manor with a stunning view of nearby Mount Mansfield.

Wedding-planning consumed what little free time I had, but I didn't mind a bit. I was a lucky man. Somehow I had landed a dream job and the woman I'd always dreamed of. And Nyssa, who had taken a new position in public relations at CNN, understood about the demands on my time. She knew how hard I had worked for this opportunity. I wanted to give her a wedding as beautiful as—well, as beautiful as John and Carolyn's. That wasn't within our reach, but she deserved it.

Biz's ouster and my promotion had sparked a minor outpouring of press about *George*'s ostensibly shaky finances and how many editors John had gone through and whether I could provide the needed shot in the arm. Most writers thought not. "Would this magazine exist without John?" one commentator sniffed. But critics had been saying that for years. Besides, John *was* there, so the point was moot.

Anyway, there was work to be done. Determined to boost morale, I never shut my office door, walked the hallways frequently, and held weekly editorial meetings. I purged *George* of everything unconnected to the nexus of culture and politics, such as the horoscope column Biz had favored. I even took Keith Kelly, the journalistic bane of *George*'s existence, to lunch at Gallagher's, where he did his best to dig up news about John and I did my best to obfuscate. How could I stay mad at this old-school tab reporter? True, he covered *George* as if it were a soap opera. So? It *was* a soap opera.

John recovered quickly from his malaise. In the end, Biz's exit was a relief to him. After months of vacillation, he'd been forced to cast aside someone he cared about. But having done so, no matter how awkwardly, John moved on. Once he made a decision, he never looked back.

Perhaps my best qualification to be John's number two was the history I now had with him. After four years testing the limits of what he would publish, I knew when to push him and when to leave well enough alone. When I assigned a profile of Eleanor Mondale, it was clear that her past as the wild daughter of vice president Walter Mondale was to be the article's focus. Back in 1995, John would never have published such an intimate story about a politician's child. In 1999, the piece made for great reading. John knew it and ran with it—happily.

John also told me the story of a mother-in-law of a prominent politician who was being treated at the National Institutes of Health. He thought the politician, who had let the press know of his visits to the hospital, was exploiting the woman's illness for political gain. But in reality, John said, the politician rarely visited his mother-in-law.

As you might expect, the treatment of a sick mother was a sensitive point for John, who didn't much like the man in question anyway, and when I asked him if he was thinking about a story, he answered, "Well, I've been wondering about that." Drumming his fingers on my desk, he thought for a bit, then said, "You know, let's leave that one alone."

He knew this information, he explained, because his cousin Anthony Radziwill was a cancer patient in the same hospital ward. The story was probably too personal to publish—but if we did, it would be obvious how we'd found it. Teddy Kennedy had used his pull to get Anthony into that treatment program, and John feared drawing attention to Anthony's presence. Anthony Radziwill was like a brother to John. He'd been the best man at John's wedding, and John had been the best man at his. The last thing John wanted to do was jeopardize the care Anthony was receiving.

In other ways, though, the lines between John's family and his work at *George* continued to blur. That spring, he would write an editor's letter praising the work of senators John McCain and Russ Feingold for their promotion of campaign finance reform. He also gave them the annual Profiles in Courage Award through the Kennedy School at Harvard. That was the kind of Kennedy-*George* synergy that worked for everyone involved.

At the same time, the awards prompted John to remember his father. I walked into my office one day with Matthew Saal, an associate editor, to find John sitting in front of the television I had inherited from Biz, who had inherited it from Eric. He was watching a black-and-white videotape of his father delivering a speech; the *Today* show was running a piece on the Profiles in Courage Award and a producer had put this tape together. John watched with a rapt expression, as if he were trying to absorb every word his father was saying. Once, I think, John would have quickly shut off the television if someone had come into the room while he watched his father. Now, he let us join him, and for several minutes the three of us sat without speaking and listened to JFK.

. . .

During my early months as *George's* executive editor, I got one lucky break: With the Lewinsky scandal finally ending, political reporters could actually write about politics again. Even more than the coming presidential campaign, the biggest story of spring 1999 was the New York Senate race looming in 2000. Longtime senator Daniel Patrick Moynihan was retiring. Hillary Clinton had been visiting New York a lot lately. Would she run for the Senate? Speculation abounded.

John and I argued over the possibility. He insisted that she would, that she was making all the moves one would make before announcing a candidacy. I couldn't believe a woman who had endured such political heat would choose to stick her head in that particular oven again. John, however, was so convinced he was right, he bet me $100 that Hillary would throw her hat in the ring. I was far from certain that I would win—John's political intuition was rarely wrong—but if betting John would help keep him engaged with the story, I would gladly lose the money.

I needn't have worried. John was more than interested in Hillary's political maneuvers; he was irritated. He thought Hillary was demeaning the role of First Lady by covertly running for Senate while insisting that her New York forays were necessitated by White House duties. She was tainting a nonpartisan job with partisan activities.

I had relocated to Biz's office, which shared a wall with John's, and one morning he stormed in carrying a *Times* article about a trip Hillary had taken to Binghamton, New York. "Can you believe this?" he said. "Since when does the First Lady have to travel to Binghamton?"

I let that pass. "What's on your mind, John?"

"I want to say something about it," John said.

Specifically, he wanted to write a *New York Times* op-ed slamming Hillary's "abuse" of her position.

Whatever he wanted to get off his chest, I suggested, he should do so in his own magazine. *George* needed buzz, and if John criticized Hillary Clinton, his words would generate a firestorm of publicity. Who could speak with more impact on the role of the First Lady than the son of Jacqueline Bouvier Kennedy?

The inevitable controversy could help *George*. Instead of tabloid headlines, the magazine would make serious news. John's words would have a genuine *political* impact.

But in another way, an attack on Hillary could hamstring the magazine. If the First Lady did run, her likely matchup with New York mayor Rudy Giuliani would be 2000's most exciting campaign. If John blasted her, Hillary 2000 wouldn't be returning our phone calls, you could bet on that.

After sleeping on it, John chose to keep his peace. He didn't want to jeopardize *George*'s ability to cover Hillary's campaign. That decision represented a quiet watershed for him. Four years earlier, John would never have placed *George*'s interests ahead of his private passions. Back then John had seen his concerns and *George*'s as two separate paths. Sometimes they were entwined, but just as often they conflicted.

Now he believed that his future was inextricably linked with *George*. If the magazine proved to be a long-term success, John could progress to the next phase of his life with a win under his belt. If *George* went bust, he would be an unemployed former editor and lawyer. That would be more than a perception problem. It might make John himself wonder if he was really capable of greater things.

So *George*'s uncertain future weighed on him. As he had before the magazine launched, John once again began to wake at five in the morning, worrying about his magazine and his future. One day that spring he said to Gary Ginsberg, "If *George* fails, am I a failure?"

. . .

On the morning of Tuesday, March 2, John and I were standing in a stairwell outside a banquet room at Le Cirque, the fashionable Madison Avenue restaurant. Dressed in a conservative navy suit, a white square neatly tucked into his breast pocket, John was sitting on a step going over his remarks with a Montblanc fountain pen, crossing out words and scribbling revisions in the margin. Next door, a herd of reporters impatiently awaited John's entrance. The George Washington impersonator we'd hired to mingle with the crowd couldn't entertain them much longer.

In the back of John's head was another kind of buzz, the chatter of political commentators speculating that John too might make a bid for the New York Senate seat. There was a lot of it that spring. He had been doing this *George* thing for four years now. Wasn't it time to cast aside this amusing but time-wasting digression? He could simply fold *George,* say he gave it the old college try. After all, no one really expected a political magazine to turn a profit.

John wanted to puncture this trial balloon while announcing something that was, in fact, pretty small potatoes: We had hired former New York senator Al D'Amato to write a column. That news would usually merit a few lines in a newspaper. But John knew that if he scheduled a press conference now, reporters would flock to it. His misdirection was "a little bait-and-switch," he admitted, but nothing wrong with having some fun at the press's expense. More important, he would be exploiting the political interest in him to help *George*. Like jump-starting a car with the battery from another engine.

At the appointed hour, I walked out before several rows of cameras

and reporters to introduce John. I remembered that first press conference in Federal Hall; I'd watched that one from the balcony. Now here
I was, unknown and jittery, on the stage introducing John. I kept my
remarks short and got out of the way as soon as possible.

John walked out carrying his speech in one hand. "This morning,"
he said, "we have a very special announcement to make."

He looked and sounded confident. An outsider would never have
known that he was nervous.

"But first," he continued, "a brief political note. As a magazine editor, I am supposed to remain neutral in all political races. But sometimes one feels so strongly about a candidate, an exception must
be made."

John paused for effect. "As you know, there has been much speculation about the race for the New York Senate in 2000. Everyone has
been wondering whether a certain woman who has remained behind
the scenes for many years, a woman who many feel has been the real
brains behind a certain powerful man, would be a senator New Yorkers could be proud of. Well, I know that she would, and today, I would
like to throw my support to that woman."

As one, the crowd leaned forward, tape recorders held high, pens
perched over open notebooks. Was John actually going to endorse
Hillary Clinton? She hadn't even entered the race!

"I'm talking, of course, about Al D'Amato's mother, Antoinette."

When the disappointed groans died down, John introduced
D'Amato, who beamed as he took the microphone. "Do you have any
idea the mischief I can do?" he joked to the reporters about his new
writing gig. "You've been torturing me for years."

D'Amato promptly turned to John and suggested that he run for
mayor of New York in 2001. When John merely smiled, his Republican
admirer swiveled to face the surprised media again. "I'm just telling

you, in two or three years . . . I mean, a Kennedy leading this city? Pretty good!"

Suddenly the temperature in the room seemed to have shot up. Reporters' hands were waving, their voices clanging against each other like swords in a medieval joust. Did D'Amato know something he wasn't telling? Would John consider it?

John looked both bashful and bemused. "Not today," he said, shaking his head at D'Amato in mock frustration.

What about the Senate race? Would Hillary run?

"I'm sort of betting she will," John said, looking in my direction. "I have a large bet with Rich."

Well, could he see himself *ever* running for office?

"I can see myself lying on a beach in a hammock, so I can see myself in elective office."

That's an interesting way to put it, I thought. All or nothing.

The press conference broke up soon afterward, and the next morning we got decent play on the D'Amato hire. But the suggestion that John might run for mayor? Every local paper and TV station had something to say about that prospect. My favorite commentary was this exchange from Fox's *O'Reilly Factor*. A guest pointed out that John "could have a career as one of those celebrities who you know for just being famous."

To which host Bill O'Reilly responded, "Yeah, but he doesn't want to do that. He wants to live up to his father's legacy, and the only real way he can do that is to get into politics."

O'Reilly didn't get that revelation from John, who had never publicly said anything of the sort. But from all I'd seen, he was exactly right.

At the same time, John received regular warnings of just how much the rules had changed since his father's era. The very next night, March 3, ABC aired Barbara Walters' interview with Monica Lewinsky. John invited us to watch the interview at the Downtown Athletic Club, one of the myriad gyms to which he belonged. An old stone building just north of the Holland Tunnel in lower Manhattan, the club bore no resemblance to the clinical steel and glass cages most modern health clubs resemble. It looked like a dungeon, its machines something repossessed from a torture chamber.

We gathered in the dining hall, a shadowy, cavelike space with televisions hanging from the ceiling and a bar running along one wall, at about eight o'clock. John had bought dinner, and we served ourselves from a buffet while getting drinks from the bar. There was, I believe, just one other club member in the room, a wrinkled man in a wrinkled suit, his tie yanked down from his unbuttoned collar. He was sitting alone, drinking at the bar, staring at nothing in particular.

As Walters filled the screen, then Lewinsky with her glossy pink lipstick, we fell silent. Within minutes John looked like he was sitting through a root canal. When Walters asked Monica about her infamously stained blue dress, John audibly groaned.

The man at the bar picked that moment to walk over and tap John on the shoulder.

"You're John Kennedy, right?" he said. The words came out *Zhaaaan Kinnnn-uhhh-dy*. Sitting next to John, I could smell the oily vapor of gin and sweat and tobacco oozing from the intruder's pores.

"That's right," John said coolly.

"Nice to meet you," the man said. *Nize ta meetcha*.

"Nice to meet you, too."

The man leaned over toward John. "Hey, didja know that your father and my father were both in the Harvard Alumni magazine once?"

"No, I didn't," John said.

"Yeah. Uh-huh. The same page, even."

"Really?" John said.

The man swayed for a second, waiting for something more. When John said nothing, he frowned and said again, "Well, nize ta meetcha," and walked back to the bar, where two of our interns, attractive young women who'd just graduated from college, were sitting.

The man sat next to them and leaned over to ask if he could buy them a drink. "Can you believe that guy?" he said, flipping a thumb in John's direction. "I tell him his father and my father knew each other, he doesn't even give a damn."

When Monica's interview was over, we gathered our coats and exited into the frigid night. The downtown streets were dark and deserted and a little creepy, and most of us had arranged to be picked up by a car service. But John demurred. He was in no hurry, he said. He wanted to walk back to North Moore.

While waiting for my own ride, I watched as he climbed the steps of a concrete pedestrian bridge that arced over the traffic descending into the Brooklyn-Battery Tunnel. The bridge was flanked by wire fencing on both sides, and streetlights cast small circles of unforgiving white light on the beige concrete. John looked like he was walking behind the barbed wire of a prison camp.

I saw a heavyset man coming John's way from the other direction and tensed for an encounter, but John had a sailor's cap pulled low over his forehead and the man walked right by him. Then, about three steps later, the guy did a double take and turned full around. As I watched him, he looked at John, and I could tell exactly what he was thinking: *Hey, that was JFK Jr.!* And then: *What the hell is JFK Jr. doing walking by himself in this neighborhood?*

John gave no sign of noticing. His head down against the wind, he continued his solitary walk through the shadows and spotlights.

.   .   .

What I didn't know until later was that, at the time, John was indeed considering running for office. After all those years, all those maddening questions like a never-ending ringing in his ear, he had finally been tempted. Maybe it was because *George's* financial woes were wearing on him. Or maybe it was that, in a little over a year, John would be forty, and even John couldn't stay Little Lord Fauntleroy forever. Those few strands of gray in his hair had been joined by a few more. John knew that potential in life is like capital in politics. If you don't use it, sooner or later you lose it.

That spring, John was approached by several friends active in New York Democratic politics who urged him to run for Moynihan's Senate seat. They could provide him with the money and the political infrastructure. And imagine the volunteers! John would be the pied piper of politics. As for the press, well, John was guaranteed more free media than any Senate candidate in history. In fact, anything candidate Kennedy might need would be provided for him. All he had to do was say yes.

But there were drawbacks, too. Running meant John might have to take on fellow Democrat Hillary Clinton and probable Republican foe Rudy Giuliani. Both would have been formidable opponents. Both had been laboring in the trenches of elective politics for decades. Both knew the ins and outs of the legislative process, the arcana and minutiae of public policy. And both were used to the rough-and-tumble of political life. Rudy and Hillary not only could take brutal personal and political criticism, as John could. They could also dish it out. And that, John had never had to do.

Could he have won that Senate race?

In my opinion, easily.

After all, some 40 percent of New Yorkers would have beaten themselves about the head and face rather than vote for Hillary Clinton, and at that point in his administration, about the same number found Giuliani equally distasteful. No one felt such animosity toward John.

On the contrary. John's decency would have won votes from people who disapproved of the Kennedys, and those who revered the family would have recognized that John embodied its most attractive qualities. He would have won votes from straight women and gay men who found him physically attractive. From senior citizens who thought of him like a son. From baby boomers who considered him both a peer and a leader. From young people who saw him as a role model. From minorities who saw an heir to a civil rights legacy. From Manhattanites who appreciated John's love for the city and upstaters who shared his ardor for the outdoors. From working people who thought that John F. Kennedy, Jr., was, all things considered, a regular guy, and celebrity buffs who thought that he wasn't. From anyone tired of partisanship, tired of being disillusioned, tired of having no one to believe in.

Maybe some of those were the wrong reasons to vote for a political candidate. Maybe they weren't substantive or serious enough. But that is the way most people vote. Do they like a man? Do they trust him? Do they think he is a good person? On those counts, John was unbeatable. And was there ever a candidate more suited for television?

Why might people have voted against him? His lack of conventional political experience, perhaps—although John possessed far more inside knowledge of politics than many candidates for higher office. Perhaps the suggestion that he was not smart enough. But John in action would have dispelled that myth pretty quickly. The reasons to vote against him were not compelling.

I would have voted for John because although he inherited power, he did not lust for it. And because if John fulfilled the potential he carried within him, he could one day restore a luster to the presidency that the United States had not seen since John's father was president. If he were finally able to put his misgivings about politics behind him—and I think John would have—he could restore our faith in the power of politics to improve people's lives.

Finally, I had another, more personal reason to support John. Four years before, I had not known him, and what I did know had made me skeptical. I was a career journalist, which, at the time, had made me distrust John and John distrust me.

But much had changed since then. After four years of being startled, disappointed, moved, infuriated, puzzled, shocked, impressed, and educated by John Kennedy, I had come to respect this man. With *George,* John had made himself vulnerable, taken chances, made some mistakes, gotten lambasted in the press, and tried to accomplish something for his country—even as he labored to resolve his own existential conflicts. Just as John wanted our readers to do with the politicians we profiled in *George,* I had come to see him in the fullness of his identity, and, rather than harping on his flaws, I had learned to appreciate his commitment to public service.

So, yes, I believe that John would have won that campaign for the Senate in the year 2000. And then, maybe eight years down the road, maybe twelve, he would have run for president. Having seen not just John's talents but also the reverence in which Americans held him, it is hard for me to believe he would not have won that race as well.

But he wasn't quite ready. So much was happening—his cousin Anthony Radziwill's health continued to decline; *George's* future was cloudy, and John had invested too much to let it founder without him. As he had said in a February interview in *Brill's Content* magazine, "This enterprise has consumed almost six years of my life. It came at considerable personal risk. There were a lot of people who would have loved to see this be a farce, and it hasn't been. And you know, I don't really care what people think as far as my involvement. I care what the people who work here think."

And there was one other issue: Carolyn. John knew that his wife had not fully adjusted to her new role. She was neither entirely comfortable nor entirely happy, and she certainly wasn't sure what she wanted to do with herself beyond being John's wife. So when interviewer Steven Brill popped John the inevitable question—Would he run for office?—John's answer was telling.

"Obviously [George] brings you right up against politics, and I like that," John admitted. "Do I feel a frustration about being an observer, not a participant? Sometimes, yes. That's my background. That's what I have in my blood.

"But yet, would I want to go in [to politics]? Not at this juncture of my life. I just got married. My wife likes her privacy."

Which wasn't to say that Carolyn wasn't growing more at ease with the public and the press. At a May charity benefit sponsored by George and the actor Paul Newman, Carolyn told gossip columnist Mitchell Fink of the Daily News that she no longer read about herself because "I don't want to know." The gossip "has nothing to do with how I live my life. I have problems and issues just like anybody. But I'm a happy person, and maybe a better person for not knowing."

When not talking to reporters, Carolyn felt even more comfortable expressing herself. Near the end of the same dinner, she wandered over to my table, and with a big smile on her face whispered sweetly into my ear, "I can't believe I've had to sit next to that thug Puffy Combs all night."

According to the tabloids, Carolyn had been delighted by Biz's departure. JEALOUS CAROLYN PLEASED AS JFK'S TOP EDITOR QUITS, the Globe declared. "It's either her or me!" the paper's "sources" had Carolyn declaring.

That was absurd. John and Biz never had even a flirtatious relationship, much less a sexual one, and Carolyn knew that—she liked
Biz. But for whatever reason, Carolyn did come by our offices more
frequently that spring than she had in the past year or so. If John was
on the phone, Carolyn would often wait in my office. Sitting with her
legs draped over the side of a chair, her long blond hair spilling toward
the floor, Carolyn made me a little afraid to move. In any event, keeping her entertained was always my priority. We never talked about the
disagreements John and I had had in the past, though. My apparent
apostasy during the Don Sipple brouhaha was now forgotten.

When John was finished with whatever he was working on, he
would come in and stand behind his wife, gently stroking her hair or
more firmly massaging her back. Teasing him, she would pretend not
to notice and carry on talking to me, until he would throw up his
hands in mock frustration and stalk out. Then Carolyn would smile
and ease out of her chair and amble into her husband's office, sometimes shutting the door behind her.

The two were delighted to hear of my impending wedding. John
reacted with the enthusiasm that happily married people often get
when they hear of others taking the plunge. They so love the club,
they want everyone to join. "Congratulations on your engagement!"
he wrote teasingly on the cover of a Pirelli tire calendar, each page
emblazoned with a Herb Ritts photo of a tempting model—a joke gift.

Carolyn's reaction was different; she asked about my marital
plans with a single-minded intensity. When she discovered that I
hadn't yet bought Nyssa's engagement ring, she peppered me with
questions about the size and cut of the diamond Nyssa wanted. When
I asked about her ring, she said that John had given her diamonds
from a piece of his mother's jewelry. There was a brief pause as we
both recognized how unhelpful that was. "You know who you should

call?" she said hastily. "Who could get you a wonderful diamond? Maurice."

"You think so?" I said. Maurice Tempelsman, an immensely wealthy diamond importer, was Jackie Onassis' companion during the last years of her life.

"Definitely," she insisted. "I'll give you his number." And she did.

I never did call Tempelsman. I hadn't met him, and I would have felt silly, pestering him about buying a diamond on an editor's budget—like calling Bill Gates for help buying a computer. But Carolyn had made the gesture sincerely, and I appreciated that.

. . .

As part of his campaign to revive interest in *George*, John gave a speech before the American Society of Magazine Editors on April 28. ASME is the guild of the magazine industry, a trade association whose most prominent function is an annual awards banquet. The ASME National Magazine Awards are steeped in intramural politics, and it sometimes seems like their purpose is to reward a popular editor who's about to get fired or die—or who's served as a judge for several years. Nevertheless, magazines that win trumpet the news to advertisers and readers as if they'd just received the Nobel Prize.

George had never won an ASME award. So John was going to give the editors what they had been requesting for years—himself, in the flesh. If that was the game, John, who wouldn't even give interviews when launching *George*, was finally willing to play.

About two hundred people gathered for lunch at the Harvard Club that Tuesday. It was a stuffy place, filled with dark mahogany panels and faded red carpet and stoically uncomfortable furniture. Oil portraits lined the walls like the ghosts of Establishments past.

We sat down to a lunch of baked salmon and salad slick with the inevitable raspberry vinaigrette dressing. As the equally inevitable white cake with raspberry stripes was being dispensed, an ASME official stood to introduce John. "He's like a member of the family," the woman said, "and when he became an editor, we were delighted to have him join us in the family business."

John began by recapping. Why had he started *George*? Well, "for the first time there were people in government that didn't look like our grandfathers. They looked like me and people I was friends with."

A standard stump speech—I started daydreaming. But then John started saying some unusual things, some personal things, and I snapped to attention.

"That was the commercial reason behind it," John said. "The second was a more private one, which, four years later, I can talk about openly. Based on my life experience, I had a unique perspective on public life. I grew up feeling that people in public life were heroes, that their lives were difficult, they were often misunderstood by people on the outside and that this illusion of power and high living was really misinformed. I didn't understand why movie actors were the only ones who could sell magazines and why people in entertainment were the only heroes of popular culture. I thought if I could parachute behind enemy lines, in a way, and join the journalistic profession, that I could begin to let my perspective about politics seep in and maybe influence the presentation of politics."

During the question and answer period, John again veered back and forth between the professional and the confessional. "How much time do you spend on covers and what is your favorite part of the job?" asked one questioner.

He took the second half of the question first. "I like the challenge of this enterprise. I feel that this is a new enterprise in which the odds are stacked against me and we have to persuade people. This sense of mission animates the people who work at the magazine."

Exactly right. As far as we were concerned, it was *George* against the world. Or at least the upper crust of it.

"I probably spend less time on the covers now than when we started," John continued. "In the beginning, we were trying to bundle up so many ideas into one image within the magazine. . . . And sometimes we were more successful than others. You get ground down, and you realize that the exigencies of the marketplace demand that you play by the same rules as everyone else. In the beginning, we could take more chances. And now, as an ongoing business, we have to be more responsible.

"Plus," John went on, "I also like to tweak this whole aspect of family history that has been—it was like water with a tennis ball and a hose, and it was building, building, building. I wanted to comment on this personal aspect. Some of this pressure needed to be let out. You had this generation before me which just kind of stopped. Everything was frozen, and this icicle was bigger and bigger and bigger and was just about to drop. I used the covers to address some of these inchoate feelings I had about politics and celebrities and about those ideas, in a way that I understood."

I sat open-mouthed. Three years after the Drew Barrymore cover, John had finally explained himself. Did this audience have any idea how long it had taken John to be able to say these things? How hard he had worked to reach this point?

The next question was, "Having covered politics from so many perspectives, have you ever considered running for office?"

"No one's ever asked me that question," John joked, to laughter from the crowd.

"Yeah, sure," he continued more seriously. "But that happened way before *George*. In fact, I think that I've always had the perspective of running for office. I remember going to clambakes at my uncle's house when I was four years old, and there were strangers walking through the living room, and they were paying ten thousand dollars to do it. I knew that side, but I was intrigued by the other side.

"The frustration I have these days is that sense that I think everybody has when you read about the Internet and the reach that the Internet has, which is, Am I relevant? Am I making an impact or a difference?

"I think that if you're in politics you feel the same thing. You've got to wonder if you're just the beach ball for everyone to play with and bat around, or are you really doing something? I think that politicians' greatest achievements come after they die because everyone says what great stuff they did and how full of achievement their life was. But when they're living, they never get that kind of accolade.

"It's a long twisted answer, but . . . it's something that I struggle with a lot, and I'm glad Hillary Clinton's running for senator so I won't have to have anyone ask me to think about it."

The audience thought he was kidding.

"How do you feel, in hindsight, about the picture with the editorial in which you posed nude?" the next questioner asked.

"I wasn't nude," John replied. "But that got a lot of attention, and really that was born out of—I think my cousins got a raw deal. Anyone who read that letter would know that I wasn't condemning my cousins. . . .

"Joe was on the cover of a magazine for 'men behaving badly' at the same time when Michael was having his problems. Prosecutors in Massachusetts were talking about the first statutory rape trial probably since the Pilgrims. I thought there was something wrong here.

"Part of what I wanted to do with that photograph was say that the human frailties that my cousins were suffering in the public forum were those which we all have, including myself. The picture worked in the sense that I got as much grief from the picture as my cousins got. And then it was done with. I wasn't going to start a career talking about my family."

As far as I know, not one sentence of John's speech made its way into print. Given that he'd bared himself before a roomful of journalists, such reticence was astounding. But I wasn't entirely surprised. "He's like a member of the family," John's introducer had said, and John had promptly made his audience feel like they were members of his family. And once you were a part of that inner circle, you wanted to protect him. You couldn't, of course. But you wanted to.

Thirteen

John had watched with disbelief as congressional Republicans attempted to impeach President Clinton. Had Washington gone crazy? Impeaching a president because he had lied about an affair? All Clinton had done was try to keep private what wasn't anyone else's business in the first place. So after the Senate finally put an end to the saga in February 1999 by voting against impeachment, John was determined to make a statement reflecting his frustrations. He chose the occasion of the spring White House Correspondents Dinner to do it.

Since 1987, when reporter Michael Kelly of the *Baltimore Sun* had invited Fawn Hall, Oliver North's document-shredding secretary, to the banquet, it had become customary for every news organization to host a celebrity. Not, mind you, that they had conceded any link between politics and celebrity . . .

In the past, John had been our requisite star, but this year he wanted to up the ante, and raise *George*'s profile. We arranged to have four tables at the May gala and John invited Sean Penn, the actress Claire Danes, Gucci's master designer Tom Ford, Clinton loyalist Harold Ickes, and *Hustler* publisher Larry Flynt.

This last invitation was deliberately confrontational. In 1998 Flynt had offered a $1,000,000 reward to anyone with evidence of a politician's infidelities, an attempt to shame hypocritical politicians attacking Bill Clinton. That offer had made Flynt less than popular in Washington. Even the press corps briefly paused from lighting a bonfire under the president to scorch Flynt. The pornographer never had to pay out, but at the end of the year he published *The Flynt Report,* a rundown of scandals connected to pro-impeachment politicians. John's invitation to Flynt was an aggressive declaration of where his sympathies lay.

Writing in the *Washington Post,* the very same Michael Kelly would call Flynt's presence at John's table a "revolting spectacle," pointing out that the *Hustler* publisher had once printed pictures of John's mother surreptitiously taken while she was sunbathing topless on a Mediterranean beach. In truth, John was conflicted about the invitation, but he liked Flynt. (Having spoken with him at our second anniversary party, I had to agree that Flynt was an unexpectedly thoughtful and likable character whose mind was considerably more subtle than his magazine.) John admired Flynt's resilience and instinctively stuck up for anyone sneered at by the mainstream media. Moreover, like John's first interview subject, George Wallace, Flynt was in a wheelchair as the result of an attempted assassination, and John was sympathetic. Finally, John thought, at least Flynt was honest about being a pornographer. Could the White House press corps say the same?

On the Saturday of the banquet, we hosted a pre-dinner cocktail party at the Four Seasons for our less notorious guests, a group of *George* advertisers. But for half an hour after the party started, there was no sign of either John or Carolyn. The guests were getting restless when John suddenly showed up alone, wearing a button-down shirt, khakis, and boots—odd dress before a black-tie dinner. I made my way over to him.

"Rental shop run out of tuxes?" I said. John had jokingly vowed to teach me how to tie a bow tie—he, of course, never wore a clip-on—and I couldn't resist a little revenge.

"I know, I know," John said. He was so late, he explained, he thought he should just show up as is, then quickly change before the dinner.

"What happened?" I asked.

"I flew my plane down," John said. "Carolyn was late, so she wound up taking the shuttle, but I had waited for her, so I was late taking off. And there was a fire on the ground in Maryland. I had to fly around the smoke."

Tomorrow, John explained, he would fly back. Why didn't I fly with him?

"Sure," I said. "That'd be fun."

Dinner seemed endless. While John and Carolyn entertained the celebrities, I labored to enliven a table full of cosmetic company ad buyers. They were nice people, but politics was not their forte; it was easier for them to talk about fashion, movies, *Sex in the City*—that kind of thing. My only respite came when Sean Penn and I happened to head to the bathroom at the same time, and photographers chased him to the bathroom door. Standing two urinals over, I nodded to Penn and said, "At least they didn't follow you in."

"They better not," he said.

In years past, John had always skipped the celebrity-laden after-party thrown by *Vanity Fair*. No point in helping a competitor. Penn, however, wanted to go. So some fifteen of us walked across Wisconsin Avenue to the old Russian consulate, a castlelike mansion situated at the avenue's crest looking south toward the White House. At the gates, *Vanity Fair*'s hired help—prim, officious women toting clip-boards and head-set microphones—were willing to admit only John,

Carolyn, and our celebrity guests, but John insisted that it was all or none. Without further ado, we were ushered in.

Moving quickly through the hubbub, we set up station on the lawn, as far away from the rest of the crowd as we could get, a little circle of *George* folks sheltering John and Carolyn. I chatted with Claire Danes about her freshman year at Yale, and asked Sean Penn, who stood smoking and rocking back and forth on his feet, his impressions of Washington. They were very funny, quite astute, and not particularly printable.

"By the way, you should talk with John about *The Game*," I said. "I think he liked that movie."

I looked over toward John and Carolyn then. I'm glad I did, because I treasure that memory. Carolyn was sitting on John's lap, staring happily into his eyes. Wearing a long black dress that separated into a clamshell-like top that tied around her neck, she looked lovely. Her eyes were bright, her smile full of love. As usual, she wore no jewelry. On Carolyn, jewelry would have been a distraction.

John too was laughing. His worries momentarily forgotten, he appeared optimistic and carefree.

The next day I had some business in Washington and John had to leave early, so I never did get to fly home with him.

· · ·

I remember that image of John and Carolyn so vividly because of my own emotions at the time. Their happiness contrasted sharply with my own pain, for suddenly Nyssa and I were falling apart.

One April Saturday night, after we had come home from a dinner with friends full of wedding chitchat, Nyssa had touched me softly on the arm and said, "There's something I have to talk to you about."

She had a look on her face that I'd never seen before.

"I've been having doubts," she said.

"Doubts?"

"About the wedding. About us."

My stomach performed a slow roll and my legs felt weak. I low-ered myself into an armchair. Nyssa sat on the couch. "Go on," I said.

She'd been feeling this way for some time. She had hoped it was just premarital butterflies, but it wasn't. She could not look me in the eye as she said that things were not right between us.

"Tell me what's wrong," I said. "Tell me what we need to fix."

Nyssa shook her head slowly. "It's just . . . wrong," she said. Some-thing was missing that needed to be there.

She would not be more specific. Something had changed for her after I had proposed, and I, alternately insanely busy and deliriously happy, had failed to notice. I think she didn't want to say she didn't love me anymore.

Nyssa spent the next week at a friend's apartment and asked that we not talk during that time. Maybe, she said, the distance would help her figure things out.

Maybe. But the separation tore me apart. Even when the week ended and Nyssa returned, I couldn't eat, couldn't sleep. So I forced myself to work. I remembered how my colleagues and I had suspected that Biz's divorce was sapping her energy; I vowed no one would think that of me. It would not help to fall apart at the office. I couldn't help but wonder, though, if work had precipitated the downfall of my rela-tionship. If I hadn't been so busy, might I have seen something loom-ing, some cloud on Nyssa's horizon? If I hadn't been so caught up with my new job at *George,* would I have noticed that she looked a little thin? That she wasn't sleeping well?

Too late now. I threw myself into work like a man with nothing else to lose, and when my colleagues asked how the wedding plans were going, I gritted out smiles and said fine, fine. And kept working. Because if I had stopped, I could not have started again.

.   .   .

The negotiations between John and David Pecker over *George*'s future continued that spring, with the *Post*'s Keith Kelly issuing bulletins—"D-Day for George!"—like a one-man Greek chorus. It was assumed that John wanted to sign a new contract with Hachette; few magazines could survive the turmoil of being jettisoned by one publisher and rescued by another. If another publisher even wanted *George*.

It didn't help that our advertising situation remained dire. Frustrated, John had forced out our third publisher, Stephen McEvoy, in April, but that only stretched the rest of us thinner. I was jetting to Los Angeles, to San Francisco, to Italy, to plead *George*'s case before car makers, e-businesses, and fashion houses. With a new presidential election on the horizon, I insisted, the next year would be *George*'s best. They appreciated the attention, but remained skeptical.

Then came news that complicated matters even further: David Pecker was quitting Hachette. He was part of an investor group taking over American Media, which owns the *National Enquirer*, the *Star*, and the *Globe*.

"That's just great," John said to me, rolling his eyes. "The *National Enquirer* . . ."

But whatever he thought of Pecker, at least John knew the man. He wasn't particularly fond of him, but he did respect his business skills. He'd never met Pecker's replacement, fifty-one-year-old Jack Kliger, the head of a media company called Parade Publications. Would Kliger try to make a success of *George* where his predecessor had failed? Or would he decide that the money-losing magazine and its high-profile cofounder were too much trouble?

"Maybe we should just turn *George* into a web site," John said to me one day. If we abolished the printed magazine, we would save on paper, printing, trucking, and mail costs.

"I don't know, John," I said. "*George* as a web site? I don't see it."

"It would solve a lot of our problems," John said.

"Do you really want to be the editor of a political web site?" I asked.

John sighed. "No. Not really."

· · ·

One Saturday in late May, Nyssa moved out of our apartment.

I had suggested counseling, but she rejected the idea. "It won't change anything," she told me. "Then what were we doing the last five years?" I answered.

She had found a new place to live, a small one-bedroom apartment just a few blocks away on 81st Street, very close to Central Park. Most New Yorkers spend weeks, if not months, searching for a home. Nyssa found one her first day looking. She wanted out fast.

I could not bear to watch the parade of memories leaving the apartment, half of my life toted away in garbage bags and cardboard boxes like crumbs on ants' backs, so I fled to the office. I brought a suit, because I was to attend the wedding of an old friend that night. Nyssa was supposed to be there, of course, but I had told my friend that she had been called away on a business trip. To confess the truth might have put a damper on his day, so I lied. She was in China, I said. No one could think I was making that up.

I was sitting at my desk staring at a blank computer screen when, at about three o'clock, John walked past my door. We looked at each other in mutual surprise—I, that John would be coming in on a weekend, when he could be outside; John, that *anyone* would be in on a weekend, when he could be outside.

"What are you doing here?" John asked.

"Catching up," I lied. "What are you doing here?"

He needed a reference book for a commencement speech he was giving the next day at Washington College in Chester, Maryland. He wanted to throw in some George Washington quotes.

While John searched for his book, I changed out of my jeans and T-shirt. He walked back into my office just as I was trying to choose between the two ties I'd brought to match my black suit and blue shirt.

"What do you think?" I said, holding them up for his inspection. One tie was a bright red pattern, the other a loud blue and orange stripe. He looked at them; I looked at them again. I realized that in my haste to leave, I had chosen two ghastly pieces of neckwear.

"I think maybe something a little . . . quieter," John said. "C'mere a second."

I followed him into his office as he opened its closet door and disappeared inside. There followed the sound of John throwing things around, like a kid rustling through his toy chest, and then he emerged holding a white tie box. "Try this," he said.

Inside the box was a silk tie by an Italian designer so exclusive I'd never even heard of him. Wrapped in crisp plastic, the tie was a deep, rich midnight blue, with a subtle robin's-egg streak. It matched my outfit perfectly. I slid the tie out of its cover and fumbled as I draped the cool soft cloth around my neck and started to make a knot. Without a mirror, it was hard.

"Here," John said. He reached out and took hold of the tie, smoothing out the creases. Then, his strong hands working the material expertly but gently, he slid the knot up so that it was snug in the center of my shirt collar.

He stepped back and sized up his handiwork. "That's better," he said.

Sometimes people do a kind thing that you barely notice, and sometimes, when your life is hard, the very same thing opens you right up.

"Thanks," I said. "Thanks a lot."

My voice must have given something away, because John looked at me and said, "You okay, Rich?"

For a second I wanted more than anything in the world to stop pretending, stop lying, and say, no, actually, nothing is okay. Somehow I believed that John could make me feel better. Who knew loss better than he?

But in the next second I thought, I can't do that. If I do, the next time I show up late in the morning or linger late at night, John will think he knows why—and wonder if it was a mistake to promote me. If I was yet another *George* employee who paid a heavy price for getting close to John.

"I'm just a little tired," I said.

That night, my friends were married at a beautiful estate on the east bank of the Hudson River as the sun set behind them. I forced myself to smile every time someone pointed to the happy couple and said to me, "You're next!" There would be a time to tell the truth, but this wasn't it.

The following day, a radiant spring morning, John flew himself down to Washington College and delivered his thoughts on life after graduation. "You have accomplished something the great man George never did," he congratulated the class of 1999. "You are college graduates. And believe it or not, he went on to do great things in politics without ever having to become a lawyer.

"But don't be constrained by the seeming perfection of his example. He was a human, and was afflicted by many of the miseries that afflict those who choose a life in politics. He was publicly spurned by a woman he courted, Betsy Fauntleroy, who thought that he wasn't rich enough. His opponents circulated rumors about his illegitimate children. He was plagued by an embarrassing presidential relative. . . . And he was on occasion excoriated by his opponents for padding his expense account.

"But enough about him," John said. "Today is your day."

·   ·   ·

On May 25 John and Carolyn took a commercial flight to San Francisco, where John was to address the San Francisco Advertising Council. We desperately needed high-tech advertising, but selling a political magazine to Silicon Valley wasn't easy. Computer geeks didn't think much of political dweebs. And thanks to the Microsoft antitrust case, Washington state didn't think much of Washington, D.C.

That night, John and Carolyn had dinner with Steve Jobs, the head of Apple Computer, and his wife. While they were dining, I arrived in San Francisco with Michael Voss, our new marketing director, a warm, enthusiastic man whom we had hastily pressed into service. Ordinarily this would be a publisher's trip. But we didn't have a publisher.

Meetings of the Ad Council usually attracted about fifty people. Seven hundred came to see John at lunch on May 26, and he was funny, warm, and personable. Asked about the 2000 races, John said, "The big question is whether Hillary will run for the Senate and if it is unacceptable for someone born in Illinois who lived in Arkansas to run in New York. . . . Sort of as acceptable as someone who was born in Washington, D.C., coming to San Francisco to get you to buy an ad in a New York magazine."

Would John ever run for office? someone asked.

He admitted that he had thought about it. "Something is wrong that needs to be right, and a magazine is a start."

From San Francisco John, Carolyn, Michael, and I headed north to Seattle, where we were pitching Microsoft. John wanted the software giant to partner with *George* in a series of online chats with the 2000 presidential candidates. Moderated by John, the chats would be hosted at Harvard's Kennedy School of Government. Microsoft would provide the technology, pay for them, and, of course, advertise in *George*.

Taking different cars to the airport, we planned to meet at the gate. But when Michael and I arrived along with Michael Klein, our West Coast sales representative, we didn't see John and Carolyn there. Then, as we sat down in the hard plastic chairs by the boarding ramp, a tall, elegantly dressed woman wearing sunglasses and a scarf over her hair approached us.

"We're over there," Carolyn whispered, nodding toward the most remote corner of the waiting area. "You walked right by us."

Though we had seats in business class, we waited until everyone else had boarded first. It wouldn't do to have every other passenger filing by John and Carolyn. I was glad to see that the Boeing 737 we were flying had only two rows of business-class seats. We would have at least a little privacy.

Without discussing it, John and Carolyn took two window seats in the same row, while I took the aisle seat next to John, across from Michael Voss. At first, I thought it odd that John and Carolyn sat divided by an aisle. They must both really want windows, I reasoned.

Certainly for John, that was true. As the plane lifted off the runway and banked north, gliding over the Pacific and along the rocky coastline, John put his right hand against the skin of the plane and pressed his nose against the window, watching silently until the ground was hidden by clouds. As he pulled his head back from the window, he looked like he was lifting his head from prayer.

Turning to speak to Michael Voss, I realized that the seating arrangement wasn't just about the view. On the aisle, John and Carolyn would be vulnerable. Michael and I formed a human barrier. Other passengers were less likely to chat up John or Carolyn if even the slightest obstacle blocked their way.

"How was dinner last night?" I asked John.

Excellent, he said. Jobs was intense, thoughtful, and charismatic. John was sure the visit would lead to Apple ads for *George*. The only problem was that Jobs was a vegetarian, and there was nothing to eat.

"Nothing?"

"You know—roots," John said. "Beans. Grains. We weren't really sure what it was. Carolyn was starving."

Meanwhile, Carolyn and Michael were talking about relationships. Over dinner, Jobs' wife had voiced the theory that relationships were like horticulture. In both instances you had gardeners and flowers, people who nurtured and people who needed nurture. Relationships between two gardeners could blossom; so could relationships between a gardener and a flower. But a relationship between two flowers would never last.

In her relationship with John, Carolyn said, she was the gardener. She had to take care of her husband, because he needed all the love and attention that she could give him.

Somehow Michael and she then got on the topic of feminine beauty. Truly beautiful women have something otherworldly about them, Carolyn said. Like, say, Uma Thurman? Michael suggested. Exactly, Carolyn said. Now, Gwyneth Paltrow, she was pretty. But her mother, Blythe Danner—*she* was beautiful.

"It's how I feel about John," Carolyn added. "Sometimes I look at him while he's sleeping and he's so beautiful, I can't believe he's really human."

John needed to talk business with Michael, so I switched to Carolyn's side. Instantly she switched to the topic of the wedding.

I couldn't lie to Carolyn. Those piercing blue eyes would see through me before I could finish a sentence. "Actually," I said, "things aren't so good."

Slowly at first, then with a growing sense of relief, I told her everything. She listened intently, her gaze never breaking from my face. When I was done, she said without a second's hesitation, "Well, you have to fight for Nyssa. You can't just let her go."

She knew that behavior in a woman, Carolyn explained. She'd been that way herself. Why, she had refused John's proposal of marriage for almost a year. She had done everything she could to run away from him, but he had refused to let her. No matter how many times she broke down in tears and told John she couldn't be with him, she was too scared, he wouldn't take no for an answer. He was the only man she'd ever known who was so strong, so patient, so sure of what he wanted. She hadn't realized how much she needed that until John provided it.

"There's a beast within Nyssa, and it's strong," Carolyn said. "You have to give up your ego. You have to sacrifice your self. She needs you to be strong. She needs you to fight for her. I know why she's running away. No one's ever fought for her before."

I was too needy to evaluate her advice at the time, but I wondered about it later. Carolyn didn't know Nyssa particularly well, certainly not well enough to diagnose her with such conviction. Was she really even talking about Nyssa? Or just as John had in his commencement speech, was she merely projecting her own experience? Maybe this was the inevitable result of *not* being able to talk about yourself, because your private life is a commodity, and you have to do everything you can to protect it. Inevitably those feelings, fears, and revelations force their way to the surface—unintentionally clouding your ability to see other people's problems clearly.

Carolyn continued for the next hour, the words shooting out of her like water from a firehose. Buffeted and barely able to get a word in, I kept dwelling on three thoughts. The first was, My God, where does she get the energy? The second was, Maybe she's right, maybe what worked for John will work for me. And the third was, Should she be so loud? There were passengers in the row in front of us, and Carolyn wasn't exactly whispering. I couldn't help remembering a gossip report that passengers on a 1997 flight to Martha's Vineyard had overheard John and Carolyn arguing.

But she didn't seem to care who heard her, and after a while I stopped worrying about protecting John and allowed myself to bask in the solace of this woman, who offered something I hadn't been feeling—hope.

The airport was blessedly free of photographers when we landed, so John, Carolyn, Michael Klein, and I walked to pick up the bags while Michael Voss headed to the rental car desk. As we headed toward the luggage carousel, John nodded in my direction and said to Carolyn, "So, sweetie, did you give Rich any wedding tips?"

Carolyn shot him a warning look and shook her head.

"What?" John said, looking puzzled. "I'm always the last to know."

"I'll tell you later," I said.

We waited on the sidewalk for Michael Voss to pick us up in our rental car, and finally I disclosed to John that my marriage was off. His face grew sad.

"Well, maybe Nyssa just needs time," he said. "Carolyn did."

"She told me," I said.

"Yeah, she did her best to run away," John said, laughing a little at the memory.

Just then an African-American boy walked up to Michael Klein holding a piece of paper in one hand. He was maybe five or six years old. "Are you John-John?" he asked shyly.

I stifled a laugh. Michael Klein was about 5′ 8″ tall and looked nothing like John. "No, I'm not," he said.

"Oh." The little boy looked crestfallen. "Because my momma asked if I could have your autograph." He pointed down the sidewalk. A hundred feet away, a woman standing behind the glass of an information booth smiled and waved at us.

Carolyn smiled gently at the child and nodded at John. "That's John Kennedy," she said. "He'll sign it for you."

"Oh, c'mon, baby," John said.

"John . . ." Carolyn warned, like a wife reminding her husband to take out the trash.

John accepted the piece of paper from the boy's outstretched hand and signed it. The child promptly scooted back to his mother.

About twenty seconds later, the boy reappeared. He held another piece of paper in his hand, and this time he knew where to go. "Could I have another one?" he said.

John shot Carolyn an I-told-you-so look and bent down to look the boy in the eye. "One's enough, okay?" he said. "Tell your mother that one's enough."

Michael Voss pulled up at the curb. We threw the luggage in the trunk, and then the five of us crammed into the car, a Volvo sedan. Carolyn insisted that I take the front seat, while she sat in the back with John and Michael Klein.

As John was putting the last bags in the trunk, a pretty, brown-haired teenage girl spotted him. "Mr. Kennedy, Mr. Kennedy," she squealed. "Could I just take your picture?"

"No," John said flatly. "I don't do that."

The girl's face fell. John got in the car and we pulled away from the curb. The girl stood on the pavement, watching us go, until we rounded a curve and I couldn't see her anymore.

When we turned into the driveway of Seattle's Four Seasons, it was Carolyn's turn to be anxious. "Don't stop the car in front," she said to Michael. "It'll be a zoo." But apparently Pacific Northwest paparazzi were less voracious than their East Coast counterparts, because no one harassed John and Carolyn as we unloaded our bags.

At the desk, the clerk informed John that the hotel had upgraded him and Carolyn to a deluxe suite.

"Really?" John frowned. He didn't need any special treatment. A standard double would be fine.

The clerk raised his eyebrows. "A standard double?"

Sure, John said. That would be fine.

"Very well, Mr. Kennedy," the man said, and handed John a key.

Half an hour later, John, Michael Voss, and I met at the top of the hotel, in its business center. The cluttered room, outfitted with several desks, computers, and faxes, was actually the hotel's administrative office, and it was off-limits to guests. But when John told the concierge we needed a place to work, the man had quickly instructed a bellman to unlock the office for us. He did, then brought us some sodas and glasses with ice. We hadn't even asked.

The three of us compared accommodations while I booted up a computer. "They gave us a room with two single beds," John complained.

"That's what you asked for," Michael said.

"I did?"

"John, that's what a standard double is," Michael said. "Two beds."

"Oh, God," John groaned. "I can just see the headlines. 'Marriage on the Rocks! John-John Demands Separate Beds!'"

For the next hour, I sat in front of the computer while John and Michael rewrote our sales presentation. To make this pitch, John had to be comfortable with its voice, and at the moment he wasn't. So John would read a line, then we would all suggest changes, and I would type in the corrections.

There, in that little room, working on our magazine, we were having fun. No one was watching, making us self-conscious. Michael and I could forget that our boss was who he was and the three of us could simply enjoy the pleasure we took in our work, the satisfaction that comes from being good at what you do, the camaraderie of three men, too tired to be guarded, all with different but interlocking skills, working together.

As the minutes ticked away and the sun set, we got punchy, and we cracked bad jokes, and we were comfortable knowing that although our upstart young magazine had its back to the wall, we were doing what we could to improve its chances of survival. I felt again that devil-may-care sensation from the summer of 1995, when no one expected *George* to last more than a year, maybe two if we got really lucky. I might have lost my fiancée, but there was refuge in this work, the company of these men, and that wasn't a perfect salve, but it helped.

When we were done we joined Carolyn, who was waiting for us at a nearby restaurant with an old friend of John's named Dan Samson. Dan was a big guy with a kind face and a booming laugh. He made you feel as if you'd been friends for years. With Dan were his parents, his wife, and their new baby girl.

It was late for Seattle dinner-goers, and we were the only customers in the darkened restaurant. John sat next to Dan's father, a doctor and Holocaust survivor whose wisdom had been carved by the years into his peaceful face. Dr. Samson and John spoke quietly for much of the meal, John listening carefully whenever Dr. Samson spoke, Dr. Samson nodding and chuckling when John said something. It wasn't quite like the bond between a father and a son, more like the relationship between a godfather and godson, an old man and a young one, the young one thirsty for the knowledge of the elder, the old man delighted in the progress his charge is making.

While the rest of us ate, Carolyn stood and held the Samsons' tiny baby against her chest, rocking it softly, whispering reassuring words. Her usual intensity was replaced by a sense of calm. Usually, Dan said to Carolyn with a laugh, she's a big crier. She must like you. Carolyn held that baby as if it were her own, and every once in a while, John would look up from his conversation and peek at the two of them, and the love on his face was a thing to see.

.   .   .

The next morning Carolyn stayed at the hotel while John, the two Michaels, and I drove to Redmond. Michael Voss was behind the wheel. John sat in the passenger seat.

Once we were on the highway, John lowered the window and stuck his head out to feel the breeze. "John, you're going to get your head ripped off," Michael Voss warned. John pulled his head back in. "Michael, hasn't anyone turned you on to the joys of dog-driving?" he said. Then he put his head back out.

In a small auditorium tucked away somewhere on Microsoft's sprawling campus, John made his pitch before about a dozen slightly nerdy but scarily smart division heads. He was even more articulate than in San Francisco, and when he was done, the Microsofties drilled him with questions, like hotshot students in a graduate seminar. Their queries were more thoughtful than anything I'd heard the press ask John, and I could tell he was enjoying the back-and-forth, because he started asking them questions back. How will the Internet change politics? How come you can't vote online?

John headed back to the hotel to pick up Carolyn and fly east. The two Michaels and I stayed to meet with a smaller group. It went well: The Microsoft reps got the idea. When they started talking money, Michael and I threw out a figure twice what we would have accepted. The Microsoft people didn't blink.

I flew home exhausted but encouraged. It felt as if the momentum was turning. With John at the top of his game, we just might make it after all.

Shortly after John returned, he met with Jack Kliger, Hachette's new CEO, for the first time. That meeting did not go well. Kliger was not inclined to sign a new contract with *George*. Nothing personal, he told John. Just business. He had assumed his new job to discover that Hachette's profitable magazines were suffering from declining circulation and falling rates of subscription renewals. Kliger had only so much time. He needed to focus on magazines that made money.

Shortly afterward, John started drafting a press release. It read: "For immediate release. June—, 1999. George Publishing Co. & [Hachette Filipacchi Magazines] have mutually agreed to dissolve their partnership." Hachette would sell its 50 percent stake in *George* by the end of 1999.

If we were going to survive, it wouldn't be at Hachette.

Fourteen

The first weekend of May 1999, John crashed his ultralight plane.

He'd been flying the contraption, which was officially called a Buckeye Dream Machine, since shortly after *George*'s founding. It provided an escape from the pressure, the next best thing to flying a real plane. And you didn't need a license to fly the Buckeye. All it required was a few hours of training.

Looking like something an inventor might cook up in his garage, the ultralight was basically a three-wheeled go-cart with a propeller on the back. Protected by a steel frame, the pilot would strap himself into a small seat bolted onto the chassis. To take off, he accelerated along the ground, inflating a large parachute dragging behind and giving the craft lift. If the engine failed, the parachute would lower him to safety. That, at least, was the idea.

John loved that Dream Machine. He would take off from the beach near the Kennedy compound at Hyannis Port, flying up and over the water, often silhouetted against the sunset. Once he descended so near some power lines that neighbors feared he was going to collide with them. When he returned to the office afterward, he laughed off the incident, saying that he'd been nowhere near crashing.

Carolyn may have enjoyed flying with John in his plane, but she didn't love the idea of him perched on a motorized chair high above the earth. She couldn't talk him out of it, though. John was addicted to the open air, the invigorating rush he got from cruising thousands of feet aboveground with nothing but the wind and the sky to keep him company. The only reason not to love it was the risk—but that, John enjoyed. In a life where so much came easily to him, he seemed to need to generate his own challenges.

On the evening he crashed the Buckeye, the sun was nearing the horizon. It was one of the first beautiful weekends of the summer, and John worried that dark would have fallen by the time he hauled the Buckeye to the water's edge. So he decided to try something he'd never done before—take off from the compound's rolling lawn.

It was a bad idea. As John started his ascent, he saw a tree looming in front of him that he had thought he would clear. He quickly veered to one side, but he wasn't fast enough. The Buckeye slammed into the tree and plummeted earthward, landing in a crumpled heap like a bird shot from the sky. The collision bent John's left foot backward, tearing ligaments in his ankle. It hurt like hell, but he was lucky. It could have been much worse.

When he returned to the office, hobbling on crutches with his lower left leg encased in a cast, John was in a foul mood. His ankle sent shooting pains up his leg, and the painkillers he took were making him woozy. To keep his leg elevated, John had to recline in a long black lounge chair, inches off the ground, his head about knee-high, which made conversation challenging. He was embarrassed by the accident and quickly tired of people asking what happened. He even gave different versions, telling some people that he had hit a stone wall while landing and others that he had hurt himself rollerblading.

The timing of John's injury could hardly have been worse, for that summer's work would determine *George*'s fate and we needed every bit of John we could get. On June 10 we threw a cocktail party at Bloomingdale's to promote the release of a *George* book called *250 Ways to Make America Better*. (More planks in John's political platform.) John and I took a car to the event, and as I opened the door for him at the entrance on Third Avenue, I felt like I was tossing a wounded seal into a pool of sharks. I tried to block the photographers long enough for John to at least get out of the car. But once he was up on his crutches, I could only hold open the door to the department store and hope for the best.

Inside, things were better, but not a lot; John looked pale and drawn, and wasn't up to giving the short speech he would have normally delivered. I have a picture of us from that event, standing side by side. John is leaning on his crutches. He looks exhausted and vulnerable.

The timing of the accident was lousy for another reason. With summer in full swing, John was forbidden by his doctor to engage in athletics—no frisbee, no rollerblading, no biking, no swimming. This was a man who grew cranky if he missed a single workout. "I feel sorry for you, having to put up with him," Michael Voss joked to Carolyn when she visited the office one day.

"I feel sorry for you," Carolyn joked back. "I only see him at night and in the morning. You guys have to put up with him all day long."

John was more frustrated than anyone else that his injury was hampering his work. But he took some consolation when *People* ran a photo of him crutch-walking down the street. He happened to be wearing one of our white, baseball-style T-shirts with "George" emblazoned in bright blue on the left arm, fully extended along his crutch.

He hopped into my office, sans crutches, holding out the issue of *People*. Grabbing my desk for balance and holding up the photo, he grinned and said, "Now, *that's* branding."

Meanwhile, our more deliberate efforts to get *George* in the news continued, fueled by a simmering sense of urgency. If John was pitching the magazine to other publishers, we needed every drop of good ink we could hustle. On the weekend of June 11, *USA Today* published an op-ed that John had written to promote the *250 Ways to Make America Better* book. He called for legalized voting over the Web to boost voter turnout, especially among young people. Like the editor's letter about John McCain and Russ Feingold, John's op-ed was substantive and patriotic—good for *George*'s image, good for John's.

Then Lisa Dallos, our in-house publicist, informed me that the *New York Times Magazine* wanted to photograph *George* staffers for a fashion layout in its "Styles of the Times" issue. Their hook was our columnist and New York bon vivant Al D'Amato. The *Times* had decided that *George* was hot, and though we certainly weren't more au courant than we had been in 1995, we would do nothing to disabuse the Old Gray Lady. Sure, posing for a fashion shoot was shallow and superficial and the editors of *Harper's* or *The Atlantic* would never do such a thing. We, however, would happily participate. We needed the publicity. After December, for all we knew, we might not even have a publishing company.

On a Monday morning in early June, I headed downtown with four colleagues to meet D'Amato and the *Times* photographer at Bowery Bar. (John would not be participating.) We wandered around the courtyard of the closed restaurant, chatting with celebrity photographer Timothy Greenfield-Sanders and sipping cranberry juice out of oversized martini glasses. Two fashion editors selected my wardrobe. In the midst of restaurant tables and chairs, I changed out of my suit into a $700 Hugo Boss sweater, $500 Canali pants, and $400 Armani shoes. Then I was plunked down on a stool in front of a makeup mirror, where a young woman with a nose stud and black nail polish dusted my forehead with powder and filled the air with hair spray.

D'Amato squeezed into a booth with the rest of us. Feeling slightly ridiculous, we laughed and clowned while Greenfield-Sanders snapped away. We threw our arms around each other, feigned air kisses, and raised our glasses high. "Great! Beautiful! Perrr-fect!" Greenfield-Sanders exclaimed, his shutter *clickety-clicking,* the film *whir-whirring.*

In the midst of all the fun, I suddenly remembered that night four years earlier, when Nyssa and I and John and Carolyn had come to this very restaurant, and John had fled before an onslaught of paparazzi. That evening seemed distant and surreal now. Back then I had felt painfully out of place, a wide-eyed supplicant in a king's court, surrounded by the better-dressed and better-looking and more sophisticated courtiers who knew all the rules of the kingdom.

Life had changed. Now I was the executive editor of a national magazine, appearing on television shows and speaking at press conferences. People looked impressed when I told them of my job. Dressed in clothing that cost twice my monthly rent in Washington, I was posing for a fashion layout in a national magazine. So what if the clothes were borrowed and the smile a prop? I had seen things I had never expected to see, met people I never thought I'd meet, and grown in ways I could not possibly have anticipated.

And yet I had paid a price. Somehow, in all the excitement, I had lost the person who meant more to me than all the glamour. Was what I had gained worth what I had lost? I tried not to dwell on that, because the question was moot. I had made my choices, until the only option I had left was to keep pushing. If that meant faking a smile to promote *George,* that was what I would do.

Part of me wished I could go back to the life I'd led before, back to a simpler time in my career. Part of me wished I had never met John Kennedy.

The rest of me hoped that this time would never end.

· · ·

In the weeks after his accident, John could not fly. On a plane, he couldn't keep his leg elevated.

Which was why we wound up riding the Amtrak Metroliner to Washington for our June 15 evening with BMW. The German car company was one of our most loyal advertisers, sticking with *George* long after competitors like Saab and Mercedes had abandoned the magazine. But we could take no client for granted, and so we'd created for BMW an event we called the "Politicians versus Pundits" auto races. Members of Congress such as Jesse Jackson, Jr., and Mary Bono would race spiffy new BMWs against television pundits such as Laura Ingraham and Ann Coulter (who also wrote a column for *George*). The races would take place in the parking lot of the US Air Arena, a little-used stadium in rural Maryland forty minutes from Washington. Congressmen seeking campaign contributions from BMW's American subsidiaries would schmooze company executives. BMW bigwigs would get to press the flesh with members of Congress. And we'd get publicity for *George*, develop sources on Capitol Hill, and land more ads. In these races, everybody won.

John's ankle was killing him, and until the last minute he considered skipping the event. But we desperately needed that business, and if John didn't show, BMW would not be pleased. So John and I decided to take the train. It was faster and roomier than the backseat of a Lincoln.

I knew John had to go, but the trip worried me. John Kennedy with a bad leg, in the middle of Penn Station, one of New York's most crowded and turbulent public spaces. . . .

My anxiety increased when I couldn't get John to leave the office. We were to take a car to Penn Station, and though I hovered outside his door, John wasn't ready until fifteen minutes before our early afternoon train left. Even when he did gather up his crutches and get moving, he proceeded with an excruciating slowness. Having seen him bang his foot against doorways and curse in pain, I could understand why. But if we were going to catch this train, we had to hurry.

We didn't, but we got lucky. Broadway was free of traffic and we reached the subterranean terminal with about six minutes to spare. While I carried our bags, John donned sunglasses and a cap. We rode the escalator into the dingy, fluorescent-lit station, like some sort of Soviet bomb shelter, and . . . nothing happened. John F. Kennedy, Jr., stood underneath the massive Departures/Arrivals board in the middle of Penn Station and not a soul recognized him.

One reason was the disguise. A hat and sunglasses can hide just enough. But I suspect the real explanation was a phenomenon whose flip side I'd always seen with John. New Yorkers pay endless attention to the rich and famous, but very little to the weak and vulnerable. To them, a man on crutches is just a man in their way.

The all-aboard was called about a minute after our arrival, and we rode the federally mandated handicapped elevator down to the track. "Thank God for big government," John joked.

Resting in the Metroliner's otherwise empty business-class car, we didn't talk much during that train ride. We both needed a little downtime. John rested his wounded leg on the seat in front of him, staring at the countryside rolling by and looking strangely shrunken in his seat.

"I wish you could open these windows," he said. "I wish they made convertible trains."

That evening we ate salad and shrimp and pasta in a huge tent set up in the arena parking lot. There was no booze—it wouldn't do to have a congressman crash.

After dinner a BMW staffer rolled up in a golf cart and putt-putted John over to the race course, swooping lanes of orange cones laid out on the tarmac. Propping himself on his crutches, John posed for pictures and watched in frustration as Ann Coulter, Al D'Amato, and numerous others zipped around the track. It looked like fun.

Instead Mary Bono buttonholed him, standing inches away from John and speaking softly. One of our writers had just finished a profile of congressman Sonny Bono's widow. Even though she had cut her long hair into an androgynous Washington bob, Bono, who had been voted into her husband's seat, was strikingly attractive. She had high cheekbones, sparkling eyes, and a sexy mouth. Our art department had unearthed a photo from her modeling days that featured her wearing a spiky black wig, a fur bra, and a tattered leather loincloth. If she knew we were running that picture, John was going to hear about it.

When the races finally ended, John and I piled into a chauffered BMW for the ride back to our Washington hotel. He sat in back, to prop up his leg. I turned around in my seat and said, "What did Mary Bono want?"

"She wanted to talk about the story," John said. Bono thought our reporter's questions had been overly personal.

I could tell from his voice that John liked Bono, and I knew that he felt a certain sympathy for a political widow.

"What'd you say?" I asked.

"I told her not to worry," John answered. He had been through much worse than whatever *George* would say about her, he told Bono, and you get used to it. In the end, the press isn't so bad.

I started to laugh.

"What's so funny?" John said.

"John Kennedy defending the press," I said.

· · ·

I was working at my desk one afternoon a few days later when John strode into my office and shut the door. His face bore an expression of deep irritation. "Have you seen this?" he said, thrusting a piece of paper toward me. "Someone left it in the printer."

I scanned the sheet and felt the color draining from my face. The document was an internal e-mail. Its recipients included every woman on the *George* edit staff—and none of the men. It detailed a litany of office incidents that the women considered sexually inappropriate. There were a dozen or so complaints, ranging from a lesbian joke made by one male editor to another man's suggestion that a female editor should wear skirts rather than pants because she had "terrific legs." The women had been forwarding this e-mail so they could all contribute any gripes they had—put one in and pass it along. They called themselves "Marthas," as in George and Martha Washington. There was something annoyingly clever about that.

Nothing on the sheet involved John. Still, he was fuming as I finished reading and gave a little whistle. "Never a dull moment," I said.

"What do you think?" John asked.

A couple of the incidents were sexist, I admitted. Others were just part of the objectification required for the production of any glossy magazine, especially one trying valiantly to make politics sexy. The truth was, if anyone at *George* was sexually objectified, it was John.

"Of course," I said, "I can't believe that someone actually wrote this down. If the *Post* got a hold of it . . ."

Neither one of us said anything, because the prospect was too grim. The headline was easy to imagine: "JFK JR. SLAPPED WITH SEX HARASS CHARGES!" Page One in huge type. The results would be instantaneous: finding a new publishing company for *George* would suddenly get a lot more difficult. Not to mention the personal consequences for John. Inevitably, it would be said that John had engaged in the same misbehavior for which he'd ostensibly criticized his cousins. And John's own staff—the very people supposed to protect him— would have furnished the evidence.

"This is insane," John said. He had done everything he could to make this office enjoy a casual, family atmosphere. This was his reward? He couldn't believe that the women hadn't talked to him before preparing this indictment. It read like a prosecutor's opening remarks.

"I'm going to talk to the women," he said. "Right now."

Within minutes Rose had called every woman on the edit staff into John's office. Afterward, John filled me in on what had happened. With hardly an introductory word, he had demanded to know what was going on.

There was a silence, for John was barely containing his anger and most of these women hadn't worked at *George* long enough to witness John's temper. Then, gradually, a few spoke up. This wasn't an epidemic of sexual harassment, they said. It wasn't as if they were going to file a lawsuit. But they wanted to sensitize the men in the office. Some things needed to change.

Fine, John said. We'll have a meeting of the entire office. And I want you to talk. If I'm going to bring this up, I don't want to hear silence when I do.

Maybe half an hour later we gathered in the forty-first-floor conference room. With the door firmly shut and no one making small talk, John bluntly explained that a situation had come up that needed to be addressed and he wanted people to talk about it.

Slowly at first, we did, with hesitant honesty but genuine respect. The women raised their concerns, and the men admitted some culpability and offered apologies. We sounded like a family resolving a problem in a way that usually happens only on after-school television. John's approach—making us sit down and talk about the conflict openly and immediately—had defused a very volatile situation.

John himself said next to nothing during the meeting. I don't think he trusted his ability to quell his anger. The stakes were so high right now, the pressure so great.

·   ·   ·

On June 22, I left on a trip to Florence to court advertisers at the men's fall fashion shows. When I returned, there was more travel, television and radio interviews in Washington for *250 Ways to Make America Better*. The constant motion was draining, but I preferred it to the empty apartment that awaited me after work.

John busied himself with the hunt for a new publishing company—another media giant, perhaps, or a wealthy private investor. He was getting input from Gary Ginsberg, who'd landed a prominent position at Rupert Murdoch's News Corporation, as well as from other outside financial advisers. In early July he began drafting a memo to some of those consultants about how to explain *George*'s apparently imminent departure from Hachette. We needed to present, he wrote, the positive version of the breakup.

We had just received advance copies of our August issue. August is never a good month for magazines; people don't shop, they hit the highways and beaches, so advertisers hold off until September. But even by August standards our issue was slim. Hopping around the office, John held the magazine high, joking, "Look, Ma! No ads!"

His joking wasn't much of a morale-builder, but it was understandable. A little dark humor seemed justified.

·   ·   ·

On the afternoon of Wednesday, July 14, I was working at my desk when I heard John's raised voice. The wall between our offices was thin, but not that thin. In startling, staccato bursts of rage, John was yelling. His yells would be followed by silences, then John's fury would resume.

At first I could not make out the words. Then, after a particularly long pause, I heard John shout, "Well, goddammit, Carolyn, you're the reason I was up at three o'clock last night!"

The shouting lasted maybe five minutes, but John's office door stayed shut for some time.

The next day, Jack Kliger held a lunch at the Palm steakhouse on 50th Street, just across the street. He wanted to introduce himself to the editors and publishers who now worked for him. Kliger had rented the entire dining room, a bustling space full of wooden booths and waiters with thick New York accents. Painted on the walls were color portraits of local celebrities—Donald Trump, Susan Lucci, Rudy Giuliani.

At his invitation, I sat at Kliger's table, watching the man whose signature would be on my paycheck—for the next few months, anyway. A big man, with a wrestler's barrel torso and a square head with thick gray hair, the new CEO was a good host. He knew his wines, and he used his imposing physical presence to anchor the conversation. A steakhouse was the perfect arena for him.

Just one thing about the meal was awkward: John was having lunch elsewhere. He had asked me to send his regrets to Kliger, but his absence was a poorly hidden sign that John had other priorities. He wasn't entirely missing from the lunch, however. On a wall plainly visible from our table were the Palm's newest etchings, flattering portraits of John and Carolyn.

It was a tricky way to begin my relationship with Hachette's new boss. The situation was loaded enough already. Just that morning the

Post had run yet another story saying that Kliger would probably jettison *George*. Though neither of us were at liberty to say so, Kliger and I both knew that the situation had progressed beyond "probably."

Back at the office later that afternoon, John called the edit staff into the conference room for a meeting.

He had some things to talk about, he announced. First, he wanted to apologize if he had seemed a little withdrawn lately. (The apology was strange, because he hadn't.) He said he'd been distracted by a personal issue, "a family problem." It had taken up a lot of his time. But, he said, that problem "will be resolved soon."

Second, he wanted to assure us that no matter what we read in the papers, *George*'s situation was not so bleak. Talk of the magazine closing was bunk. Whether with Hachette or somewhere else, *George* would continue. "Don't worry," John said. "We will all have our jobs at Christmas."

Later in the afternoon, John met with the business staff. I wasn't there, but I was told by several people who were that John offered the same assurances. "As long as I'm alive," John said, "this magazine will continue to publish."

One other thing happened that day. A doctor cut the cast off John's foot.

That night John went to a Yankees game with Gary Ginsberg. Gary had invited along Lachlan and James Murdoch, the sons of media magnate Rupert Murdoch. *George* might be a fit at News Corporation. Rupert Murdoch already owned one political magazine, the conservative *Weekly Standard*. Hiring a Kennedy would balance his media portfolio.

Besides, Murdoch might grasp what Hachette didn't seem to: that having John Kennedy in his stable would be worth millions in publicity and connections, more than whatever the magazine might cost him. *George* may have lost money, but relatively speaking, the amount was small—almost certainly less than $5 million a year. Many flagship magazines, such as *The New Yorker,* lost comparable amounts, and they had much stronger business infrastructures pushing them than *George* did. Anyway, John was a long-term investment. If he went into politics . . . well, it couldn't hurt the Murdochs to have rescued the business of a man who might one day be president.

The Yankees lost to the Atlanta Braves that night, 6–2, and after the game John and Gary shared a car home. Driving through the Bronx toward the east side of Central Park, Gary told me later, they spoke about John's dealings with Jack Kliger. John confessed that after Kliger said he was cutting *George* loose, John had felt both depressed and liberated—depressed because he hadn't expected Kliger's decision, liberated because now the worst had happened and he knew he would survive it.

He had felt uncomfortable with Kliger, John admitted. He had a problem with male authority figures.

Gary pointed out that that was understandable, given that John's father was a national hero.

John also admitted that he'd been thinking about death a lot lately. Anthony Radziwill's sickness was weighing on him.

Gary wasn't surprised: Carolyn had already told him that she didn't know how John was going to handle Anthony's approaching death. I don't know how you do it, Gary said to John. You were so strong when your mother died.

His mother was an older generation, John explained. He'd had time to brace himself for her loss. But Michael Kennedy's death had changed him. After Michael, each new death just seemed closer and closer. Harder to keep at a distance. And now Anthony was so close. . . .

John instructed the driver to head south on Fifth Avenue. He would be staying at the Stanhope Hotel, at 81st and Fifth. He told Gary that he had lost his keys.

Later, it would be written that John had gone to the hotel to work on business plans for *George*. The sources for this story were unnamed "friends," anxious to disprove rumors of a split between John and Carolyn. Others repeated the story that John had lost his keys and did not want to wake his wife.

But those stories were false. The truth was, John had fought with Carolyn. That didn't mean they were headed for divorce, as would be reported in the tabloids, just that the two had had a fight hurtful enough for John to sleep elsewhere. If you'd ever seen John's temper or Carolyn's determination, you knew that wasn't so unthinkable. And if you'd ever seen John and Carolyn make up after a fight, you also knew how temporary those rifts could be.

John told Gary one other thing that night—that he was ready to fly again.

. . .

I got to work a little late the next morning, just past nine on Friday, July 16. The week had tired me out. It was a small pleasure not to wear a suit on casual Friday; I always felt overdressed editing while wearing a tie. John came in sometime after that—around ten, I'd guess.

Phone calls filled the morning. We were busy landing a September cover with Rob Lowe, star of a new fall TV program about the White House called *West Wing*. The show was perfect *George* fodder, a pop culture fantasy of a Kennedy-esque president played by Martin Sheen. And Lowe himself was an ideal *George* story. A politically involved actor, Lowe had seen his career tank after he was videotaped enjoying a ménage à trois at the 1988 Democratic National Convention. Now he was making a comeback on a TV drama where he played a White House aide. Perfect.

For October we were planning a cover with Harrison Ford and Kristin Scott Thomas, stars of a fall movie called *Random Hearts*. He played a D.C. cop, she a congresswoman. They meet and become lovers after their spouses die when their plane plummets into Miami harbor.

Around one o'clock I poked my head into John's office and asked if he wanted to grab a bite. "Sure," he said. "I'm starved." He reached for his crutches, which he still needed even though his cast was gone, and we inched down the hallway toward the elevator. With every step, John looked like he was assessing how much pain his ankle felt.

Before we got very far, a little furball came scampering down the corridor; Jennifer Miller, our photo editor, had sneaked her new puppy past the building guards. Friday was too big to fit in a knapsack now and John rarely brought him in anymore, but other staffers with puppies kept the tradition alive.

With measured, careful movements, John knelt down and called to the animal. It ran to him instantly. John closed his eyes and stuck his tongue out, and the dog promptly licked John's cheeks. Grinning, John levered himself upright. "You have to get the kiss," he said, and we started walking again.

"What do you think, New World Grill?" I asked, referring to a restaurant on the next block. New World Grill had patio seating, and John ate outside whenever possible, wraparounds hiding his eyes, hungrily soaking up the sun.

"It's gonna have to be Trionfo," he said, nodding apologetically toward his crutches. The food in the Italian restaurant at the base of our building was only so-so, but Trionfo had the virtue of proximity. Anyway, it wasn't the best weather for eating outside. The day was hot and hazy, one of those New York summer days where the heat is something to push out of your way as you walk down the street.

The maître d' beamed when I opened the door and John hobbled in. They loved John at Trionfo, and whenever he came for lunch they ushered him into a private back room where he could eat undisturbed. Just past the bar, it was a square space about twelve by twelve with maybe four tables, one wall a long glass window covered by a gauzy white curtain. The maître d' always made sure to keep the other tables empty.

John sat first in a chair facing the entrance, and then realized he'd made a mistake. With the window to his left, there was no room to prop up his leg, and with his face to the door, he might be spotted. So we switched seats. Much better.

After gently easing off the shoe on his bad foot and pulling up a third chair to rest his leg, he ordered a salad, chicken in white wine sauce, and peppermint tea. I ordered a Diet Coke, a salad, and a chicken breast stuffed with salmon, which made John raise an eyebrow. We both laughed when it arrived looking like a misconceived TV dinner.

John was in a contemplative mood. We spoke about the magazine's future, and he sounded confident and upbeat. He didn't know where *George* would go, but he knew it was going somewhere, and there were more possibilities than he had realized before he'd started looking around. That morning Lachlan Murdoch had called Gary asking more about *George*—the size of its circulation, how involved John was.

"What about that television show you told me about?" I asked. "Maybe if we started developing that, it'd make us more attractive to another media company."

John shook his head. They'd be more intrigued by the possibility, he said. The real thing was never as exciting as what someone could imagine. And they'd have a greater commitment to the show if they helped create it themselves.

The irony, John said, was that Michael Berman had always wanted to make a television deal, but even if *George* stayed at Hachette, Michael wouldn't be around to see it. Jack Kliger had bought out Michael's contract. Today was his last day.

I could tell that was another good omen for John. Four years after starting the first time, John was getting a chance to start over, having learned from his mistakes. Losing Michael's energy and acumen had cost John, but he was stronger now, ready to go it alone.

We spoke about whether we'd need to make staff changes when the magazine changed publishers. John thought the answer was yes. "You know," he admitted, "for a while I hired people because I found them entertaining." That had made the office fun, but it hadn't always helped the magazine. No more, John said. When we moved, not everyone would move with us.

Changing the subject, he kidded me about a woman I'd gone on a date with, a young, beautiful ad buyer for Gucci. We'd met at the Council of Fashion Designers Awards banquet a couple weeks earlier; John was supposed to go, but wasn't feeling up to it. I hosted the table in his stead, but not very well. I spent most of the night talking to the woman next to me. Her name was Kate. She had straight, dark hair and wore a long, sleeveless black dress. She had once worked at Calvin Klein, and she had the clean, angular looks of one of their models.

"Taking one for the team, huh, Rich?" John said.

"Anything for an ad," I joked back.

It was silly, false machismo. I couldn't tell John that my heart wasn't in it—he seemed relieved that I was dating. I'd gone out with the woman because she was lovely and warm, and I hoped that those things would bring my heart back to life. But inside, I knew I wasn't ready.

"Hey, John," I said as he was paying the bill with his American Express corporate card, "that personal problem you were talking about in the meeting yesterday—you okay?"

"I am," John said, and there wasn't a hint of tension or denial in his voice. "It's resolved."

I nodded and left it at that. If John wanted to say more, he would. We slowly headed back to the lobby and rode the elevator to the forty-first floor. Walking down the hallway, I asked John about his plans for the weekend.

"I'm flying to Hyannis Port for my cousin's wedding," he said.

I glanced down at John's foot—even the short distance back from the restaurant had tired him—then gave him a skeptical look.

"Don't worry," he said. "I'm flying with an instructor."

"Just don't crash, okay?" I said. "Because if you do, that speech about all of us having jobs at Christmas goes right out the window."

It was a guy thing to say, a way to express my concern without embarrassing both of us. It was a language we spoke to each other easily and often.

"Not to worry," John said. "I'll be fine."

We arrived at our doors. "Well, thanks for lunch," I said, and I went into my office and John went into his.

Fired up by the conversation, I had a productive afternoon. For the first time in months, I felt certain that everything was going to be all right. John was on the mend. I would get over Nyssa. *George* would find a new home. The year could be salvaged after all.

At around 4:00, John came into my office with a question. He had been sent a previously unpublished Jack Kerouac poem about Washington. Should we publish it? Neither of us thought the poem was much good, and we decided against it. John returned to his office to write the rejection letter.

I left early, around 5:30 in the afternoon. The office was quiet. Most of my colleagues had departed for their weekends away on Long Island, Martha's Vineyard, Connecticut. For some reason I don't remember, I didn't say good-bye to John. Maybe he was on the phone—as I say, I don't remember. I just remember that I didn't say good-bye, because that was unusual.

At about 6:30, Michael Berman rode the elevator down to the

lobby and left the Hachette building for the last time. Maybe ten minutes later, John also left 1633 Broadway. He had to meet his sister-in-law Lauren Bessette, who worked for the investment bank Morgan Stanley. They would drive to the airport in Teterboro, New Jersey, where John kept his plane and Carolyn would be waiting.

The traffic out of Manhattan was unusually heavy that evening. The haze overhead was getting thicker.

That night, I rented a movie and watched it by myself. The next morning, the phone woke me up.

It was six-something on a Saturday. Too early for the phone to ring. I'd been dreaming, about what I don't remember, but I forced myself awake and fumbled for the phone. The space next to me, the half of the bed that should have been occupied, was empty. I picked up the receiver. Maybe it was Nyssa. Maybe she'd had a revelation. A change of heart.

"Hello?" My voice was husky with sleep.

"Rich? It's Claire."

It took me a second to realize that it was Claire Shipman, *George's* White House columnist. Her voice sounded funny.

I sat up in bed.

"Claire . . . what's going on?"

"Rich . . . ," she said. "John's plane is missing."

Fifteen

I hung up the phone and swung my feet out of bed. Numbly, I shuffled to the kitchen, brewed some coffee, and clicked on the television.

Pundits were suggesting that maybe John had made an emergency landing somewhere and hadn't notified anyone.

That seemed highly unlikely. John attracted so much attention when he traveled—the idea that he was kicking back in a Rhode Island beach house that happened to be near a landing strip didn't make any sense.

Maybe, others speculated, they were alive and in the water, clinging to life preservers.

But the Atlantic is cold, low sixties even in July. You start to shiver after about ten minutes in that water. Half an hour and your teeth won't stop chattering. By nine in the morning, John and Carolyn and Lauren would have been immersed for almost twelve hours.

It was time to wake up.

·   ·   ·

About forty minutes later, I sat in my office with the TV on and answered the phone until too many of the calls were from reporters.

Then I had our interns, who had also rushed to work, take over. Many of the reporters had written for *George*. "I'm so sorry," they said. "My boss knew I'd worked for you . . . I had to call. Can you tell me anything? Anything at all?"

I understood their dilemma, but the answer was no. First, I didn't know anything more than anyone else. Second, Rose had called to inform me that John's sister Caroline had asked that no one from *George* speak to the press. All of us understood and respected that request; Caroline must have been suffering immensely. Besides, the Kennedys knew how to act in such situations. We were just learning.

Andrew Sullivan called. We'd barely spoken since our fight years before, when he'd published "Why *George* Sucks." Yet when I heard the concern in his voice, I broke down. I tried to get a hold of myself, but the effort made me sound as though I were choking. Andrew was surprised by my display of emotion. He still thought John was just our boss.

By noon virtually the entire staff had returned from their weekend destinations. People hugged, held hands, and cried. Moving as if drugged, they clustered around desks and switched on their computers and perched in front of televisions, flipping channels between ABC and CBS and NBC and MSNBC, the same channels that we had hungrily turned to for news about O. J. Simpson and Princess Diana and Monica Lewinsky. All showed the same endless, cryptic ocean. For hours, we watched the blue sea, waiting, but it revealed nothing.

· · ·

I decided that the staff shouldn't see me crying. I was *George*'s most senior employee, and at age thirty-four, just about its oldest. It was my job to be strong; it was my responsibility.

But the pain was too much to contain. So every half an hour or so, I slipped out of my office and walked down the corridor to an out-of-the-way cubby once used by a secretary at *Road & Track*. I would release my breath and the tears would flow. After a couple of minutes, I'd collect myself and return to my station.

A little while later, I'd see another image of that flat blue ocean on television, or a picture of John, or hear a recording of his father saying that we all return to the water, we are all made up of it, and I'd have to leave my office again, to cry in an empty cubicle.

·   ·   ·

Late that morning Matt Drudge sent me an e-mail. "Hang in there," he wrote. "The press is going to be brutal."

Fifteen minutes later, I checked his web site. "Thirty years to the weekend after Chappaquidick!" it screamed. "Family and friends worried about JFK flying that plane!"

·   ·   ·

At about noon, a Hachette employee named John Kaiser appeared in my doorway. That was odd. A taciturn middle-aged man with dark hair and glasses, Kaiser didn't have much interaction with *George*. He worked on newsstand circulation, and we rarely saw him. Once a month or so he would meander into the art department and examine the covers to see how *George* could better lure passersby.

"John?" I said.

For a few seconds he said nothing. Then he seemed to be talking to himself. "I found myself on the subway," he said. "I didn't really know why I was coming."

He gave me a look that contained bewilderment and hurt and fear. He threw his hands up slightly, then lowered them back down.

"I don't know why I'm here," he said.

. . .

Matt Berman came into my office some time after that and sat for a few minutes without speaking. It was nice to have another person in the room. Then Matt said, "Rich, I think he's gone," and got up and walked out.

. . .

That night, while Rose manned the phones at John's loft, I invited the staff to gather at my apartment. No one wanted to admit that the day was over, because if we woke up on Sunday and they were still lost, then surely they were dead.

I picked up some chips and salsa, and Inigo Thomas brought half a dozen bottles of red wine and some scotch.

No one ate. Everyone drank. Once in a while people would venture outside to smoke. People must have talked, but I can't remember a word of conversation. I heard only the labored hum of the air conditioner, churning away against the suffocating summer heat, and the white noise of the TV commentators, droning on like the politicians on C-Span.

Eventually it grew late, and my colleagues drifted off to their lonely homes.

. . .

On Sunday morning Barbara Walters called. It was about nine o'clock. I was awake, had been all night.

She introduced herself and asked if I would agree to be interviewed on television. I didn't wonder how she had gotten my unlisted phone number. She was Barbara Walters.

"Ms. Walters," I said, "I can't do that."

It won't be sensational, she assured me. It will be sensitive.

I remembered John's moan when Barbara Walters had asked Monica Lewinsky about the stain on her dress.

"You don't understand," I said. "I don't think I'd be able to speak. I'm pretty emotional right now. I'm afraid I would cry."

I didn't say that going on television was the last thing in the world I wanted to do.

Walters promised that anything I was uncomfortable with could be edited out. But I was still a journalist, and I knew how the game was played. Once you're interviewed, you have no control. And that's how it should be.

"I'm sorry," I said. "I just can't."

She could not have been more gracious. She said that she understood, and hoped that we could talk again.

Only after I hung up the phone did it occur to me that I wasn't thinking clearly. I had told Barbara Walters that I shouldn't go on her show because I might cry. As if that would discourage her.

. . .

Later that day, the news confirmed earlier reports that Lauren Bessette's luggage had washed up, her business card tucked inside a leather tag with a plastic window. And Carolyn's orange bottle of prescription medicine had been found as well.

How symbolic the smallest things can be, the flotsam and jetsam of lives.

. . .

Some things are washed ashore. Others are swept out to sea.

I started to feel something that I couldn't quite put my finger on—as if I were losing not just John, but the authenticity of his memory. There was the man I knew and the one that was now being broadcast out to the world. The first had grown almost unbearable to think about. The second had grown huge. Like a float in New York's Thanksgiving Day Parade, this John drifted over the heads of thousands, millions of transfixed onlookers.

I tried to think of something small and specific, something to keep my memory grounded; I tried to remember John's laugh. But instead I felt as though I were standing on a beach and John was offshore in a raft. The tide was sucking him out to sea and there was nothing I could do to stop it.

. . .

At eleven on Monday morning, Jack Kliger convened the staff of *George* in the forty-first-floor conference room. It was the first time most of my colleagues had met Kliger, but already they mistrusted him. They had been reading the papers, and they knew that John had felt his back was against the wall.

Kliger tried to be businesslike. He had worked at Hachette for six weeks. He would not pretend that he knew what we were going through. It was admirable, I thought, that he did not try.

You may be wondering what will happen to *George*, he said.

We were—the papers were already declaring that *George* was on life support. "Will a magazine die with its editor?" the *New York Times* asked.

Try not to worry, Kliger said. Hachette is contractually obligated to publish the next two issues, so nothing's going to happen right away. After that, we just don't know. We have to talk to the Kennedy family, and they have other things on their minds right now.

That sounded reasonable to me, but I was in the minority. After the meeting, people were furious. Kliger hardly mentioned John, they said. How could he talk business at such a time?

Their feelings were understandable, but unfair. If Kliger had tried to empathize, the staff would have been equally mad. He barely knew John, they would have said. Where does he get off?

No, something else was going on. My colleagues wanted Jack Kliger to tell them that things were going to be all right. They hoped he would share some reassuring secret information that authority figures are supposed to possess. But there was no such knowledge, no secrets being withheld, and we had to accept that.

That afternoon Kliger dispatched a team of grief counselors to the forty-first floor, half a dozen earnest professionals who gathered expectantly in Michael Berman's old office. It was his way of saying, I can't talk to you about your loss, here are some people who can.

Except they couldn't. We'd spent four years not discussing John with strangers; we weren't about to start now. At such a time, our instinct was to say less, not more.

After they had sat by themselves for about an hour, I walked in. They perked right up. A customer!

"I'm sorry," I said, "but no one's going to talk to you. I think you should go."

"Maybe we should wait a little longer," one man, the leader, said. "Just in case."

"No," I said. "No one's going to talk to you."

The counselors looked both confused and disappointed. As they filed out, one of them pressed some business cards into my hand. "Someone might change their mind," he said.

When they were gone, I tossed the cards into the garbage.

*   *   *

On Tuesday morning, I bolted out of a shallow sleep with the thought that maybe they never knew what hit them. Maybe the plane had descended gradually, so that no one suspected anything was wrong. And then, boom, they crashed into the ocean. Instant obliteration. No pain. No fear.

Clinging to that small hope, a tiny handhold in a sheer cliff wall, I climbed out of bed, brewed some coffee, showered, and shaved. Then I began reading the papers.

The news reported that radar showed that John's plane had plunged at about 100 feet a second. Over a mile a minute. Seventy-plus miles an hour pointed, more or less, straight down.

There was to be no consolation.

That afternoon, divers found the bodies.

*   *   *

At some point around midweek—things were happening very quickly now—we learned that John had left his 50 percent ownership of *George* to his sister. The news was worrisome. Even though the tabloids were running stories like "Caroline's Battle to Save JFK's Legacy," I'd been told by people who knew her that Caroline was not a big fan of the magazine. *George* was John's baby, not hers. She did not seem to share the part of her brother that loved the idea of *George*.

That worried me. One quiet statement from John's sister—"I think John would not have wanted the magazine to continue"—and

George was doomed. Hachette could not deny this survivor's edict, no matter how softly it was whispered.

But I believed that John would have wanted *George* to endure. I kept thinking about how proud he was when people started calling the magazine *George,* as opposed to "John Kennedy's *George.*" I imagined how ticked off he would have been if we bailed out now. I could picture the disappointment in his face, hear the words he would say. "Jesus Christ, Rich, is that the only reason you worked here? Because of me?"

.   .   .

David Remnick, editor of *The New Yorker,* sent an e-mail. Would I write about John for his magazine?

I had dreamed of writing for *The New Yorker* since I was a boy, sitting at home by myself after school, poking through my parents' magazine rack.

It would have been easiest simply to inform Remnick of Caroline Kennedy's request for silence, but that didn't seem appropriate. In any case, I couldn't imagine writing about John just then. I e-mailed Remnick back. "I'm sorry. I don't think I could write anything coherent now."

He responded gracefully that he understood, and sent his sympathies.

.   .   .

New York was compiling an oral history of John's life, and one of our staff writers wanted to be a part of it. I asked her not to participate. Where's the harm? she said angrily. I have only good things about John to say. It's my right to talk. That's what writers do—talk.

No, I wanted to say, writers write.

But Caroline doesn't want us to talk, I answered. Caroline owns half the magazine now, and we have reason to believe that Caroline has no great affection for the magazine. So if you talk, you hurt *George*.

But other people are talking, she said. And that was true. Douglas Brinkley, a telegenic young historian who had written for *George,* was busily informing the world that he and John were both vegetarians— although John wasn't. John Perry Barlow, on whose ranch John had worked as a teenager, spoke of being a father figure to John and warning him not to fly.

And there was newspaper columnist Mike Barnicle, his grumpy mug all over the screen. He seemed to have forgotten that he'd once called John a "thin-lipped, dim-witted, bad-backed polo player" with "an empty head."

Historian Doris Kearns Goodwin was similarly inescapable. How many times did John ask you to write for his magazine? I thought. And how many times did you reject him? But you're happy to sprinkle dirt over his grave.

Some people who knew John had to talk because it was their job. MSNBC pundit Paul Begala was such a person, as was Claire Shipman. Christiane Amanpour, an old friend of John's from college days, spoke up on *60 Minutes*. "We, his friends, owe him to tell what we know about him from an accurate and honest perspective," she said.

True enough. But we at *George* had to stay silent. We had to accept that now was not the time for us to talk about John. That's what I tried to tell the writer who wanted to be interviewed by *New York*.

She talked anyway, which led to a falling-out between us. Some months down the road, it would be reported that I fired her for doing so, but that wasn't true. Still furious over the argument, she had balked at turning in her next story before the year was out, so

I bought out her contract. I wasn't pleased with her decision, but I understood. It was a hard time, and none of us knew just what to do.

•   •   •

I picked up the *New York Post* one morning and read a blind item on Page Six. "Which editor of a magazine—who may lose his job soon as those in the know continue to predict the magazine's demise— is deeply troubled because his longtime girlfriend just told him to beat it?"

Minutes later, Nyssa was on the phone. She sounded distraught. "I'm so sorry," she kept saying. "I'm so sorry they did this to you."

I tried to laugh. "It's okay," I said. "It's just the *Post*. Don't take it too seriously. It must have been a slow day for gossip."

I was trying to be stoic. I didn't want to tell her that the item stung like a slap across the face. It wasn't as if her apology would change anything. She was sorry, but not sorry enough to come back.

•   •   •

Rosemarie Terenzio and the Kennedys planned a funeral for Friday, July 23. You had to have an invitation to get in. There was a page-long phone script to be read to the invited. "If you do not receive your ticket or misplace your ticket, you will need to go to the Robert F. Kennedy Elementary School at 110 East 88th Street between Park and Lexington to pick up another one." Tickets to a Kennedy funeral being handed out at a Kennedy school.

I kept my invitation in my jacket pocket, to make sure I couldn't possibly lose it.

•   •   •

John's office had been locked all week because we were concerned that someone from outside the magazine might try to steal things from it. One day a friend from law school arrived to pack up John's stuff. He brought cardboard boxes and masking tape, and shut the door behind him. He did that to protect himself, which was understandable, but I wished he hadn't. Though it would have been difficult for the staff to watch, for some people it might have been healthy. Too much about John was being packed away too quickly.

When he was done, there was nothing left but a desk, a bookshelf, the round table, and some chairs. And that view—west across the Hudson, and south, toward the Statue of Liberty. Four years, gone in an hour or so. A small space, a huge emptiness.

. . .

Someone broke into our office storage closet and stole our remaining copies of the first issue, the one with Cindy Crawford on the cover. Copies of *George* were popping up on eBay, the Internet auction site. Hundreds of dollars for Cindy. Same for the September 1997 magazine, the poster boys issue.

I thought back to September 1995, when Gary and I joked that Hachette paid us so poorly, we should go hawk Cindy Crawford in Times Square for twice the cover price. Six bucks.

Meanwhile, *George* was flying off the newsstands. In terms of circulation, we were on our way to our best year ever.

. . .

On Friday, at 8:30, the staff, maybe thirty in all, met at Sarabeth's, a restaurant on 92nd and Madison, for coffee before the funeral at St.

Thomas More cathedral. It was a bright, cloudless day. Blocked off by police barricades, the streets were eerily quiet. Though the service would not start until 11:00, already people were lining up behind the gates.

We left Sarabeth's about 10:15. I asked my assistant, Tsalem Mueller, to lead us. A barrel-chested bodybuilder from North Carolina with a heart as big as his torso, Tsalem walked us through the checkpoint on Park Avenue, where well-dressed guards gave our invitations the once-over. They looked like Secret Service men, protecting John as they had when he was a boy. For all I know, they *were* Secret Service men.

As I walked up the church steps, I looked down the block toward Madison Avenue. First there was a wall of cameras, then bystanders three, four, five deep. It was like our convention party in Chicago—only this time, everything was quiet.

The silence was unnatural; the city was never this silent. It felt wrong, like a movie without sound, a flower without color.

So this is how New York feels without John, I thought.

. . .

Inside the church, a somber temple of stone and wood and glass, the *George* contingent sat on the far right, toward the back. We were surrounded by famous faces. Muhammad Ali, frail from brain damage, was being helped to a seat; he had visited John in our office just a couple weeks before, and posed for pictures with some of the maintenance guys, who were big Ali fans.

Mike Nichols and Diane Sawyer were there, as were Arnold Schwarzenegger, Maria Shriver, Christiane Amanpour, and Maurice Tempelsman. Bill, Hillary, and Chelsea Clinton arrived at the last possible moment. And everywhere you turned, there were Kennedys, Radziwills, and Lawfords.

Those were the famous people, whose pictures made the papers the next morning. But as I looked around, I saw that they were outnumbered by people of a different type. Not celebrities, but they looked successful. Not beautiful, but handsome. Not famous, but they looked as if you should know them. Here was the support network behind the Kennedy family, emerging from out of the woodwork, and somehow their presence felt reassuring.

The service started. I remember these things . . .

Caroline Kennedy Schlossberg, standing upright, read from *The Tempest* in a determinedly steady voice: "Our revels now are ended. These our actors, as I foretold you, were all spirits, and are melted into air. . . ."

In the funeral program, she was listed as Caroline Kennedy, which was also how she identified herself at her mother's funeral.

Anthony Radziwill shuffled to the podium to read Psalm 23: "The Lord is my shepherd; I shall not want. He maketh me to lie down in green pastures. . . ." Radziwill was so thin, his suit flopped loose around his shoulders. Healthy, vigorous John was dead, while Anthony, whose death John had both expected and feared, was eulogizing him.

Wyclef Jean, from the hip-hop band the Fugees, a favorite of John's, sang "Many Rivers to Cross"—"but I can't seem to find my way over"—his gentle, soulful voice lofting toward the cathedral ceiling.

Many rivers to cross

Well it seems that I found my way over . . .

A gospel choir sang "Swing Low, Sweet Chariot," and I walked up to the altar and accepted the wine and the bread and whispered a prayer for John.

After communion Ted Kennedy spoke. Teddy, John called him.

This battle-scarred patriarch had doted upon his orphaned nephew and was revered by him. No matter what he had done in the past, no matter how tragic his failures, Ted Kennedy became a hero for me on that day as he said farewell to his nephew.

John "was a boy who grew into a man," Teddy said in that distinctive Massachusetts accent, so heavy it sounded like a crackly recording from another age. "He was a pied piper who brought us all along. . . . He had amazing grace. He accepted who he was, but he cared more about what he could and should become. . . .

"We dared to think . . . that this John Kennedy would live to comb gray hair, with his beloved Carolyn by his side. But like his father, he had every gift but length of years."

It was a beautiful, plainspoken, honest eulogy. How Ted Kennedy managed to find the strength to deliver it, I could not imagine. From where I sat, his eyes looked dry, the only dry eyes in the house. Maybe he had run out of tears decades before.

· · ·

I used to think that it was tacky to wear sunglasses when leaving a funeral, but I was grateful to have a pair to hide my reddened eyes as I walked down the church steps into that oppressive silence, broken only by the clicking of cameras and the soft murmur of comforting words.

The reception would be at the Convent of the Sacred Heart, three blocks away on East 91st Street, just off Central Park. I walked by myself, summoning my concentration just to put one foot in front of the other. Overhead I heard the *thup-thup-thup* of helicopters. I felt the sun beat down and the gaze of the crowds.

I noticed an elderly couple trudging slowly a few steps ahead—the historian Arthur M. Schlesinger, Jr., and his wife. Forty years before, he'd been an adviser to John's father. When JFK died, Schlesinger wrote a book about him called *A Thousand Days*. Now he was attending the funeral of the murdered president's only son.

The convent was a subtle building, one of those New York gems you can easily walk by without noticing how truly majestic it is. We entered from the side and walked up long, twisting flights of marble stairs to the top floor. The gathering was taking place in a large rectangular chamber with expansive windows overlooking 91st Street. It looked like a good room for a wedding reception. I was standing in line waiting to get in when an elderly man with a familiar face turned toward me. He put out his hand. I took it.

"Hello," he said. "Bob McNamara."

I said hello and that I thought John would have appreciated his coming.

"I'm sorry," he said. "Do I know you?"

"No," I answered. "I worked with John."

.   .   .

Next to the windowed wall facing south were a number of round, cloth-covered tables. Sun poured in through the windows. Against the western wall, long tables offered an almost unseemly array of food: slabs of salmon, steaming cauldrons of pasta, hunks of beef, heaping bowls of salad. For dessert, there were cakes and cookies and brownies. A veritable banquet.

Across the room senior editor Jeffrey Podolsky was chatting up Arnold Schwarzenegger. John had asked Arnold to appear on the cover of our November issue; his movie *End of Days* was coming out that month. The politically minded Schwarzenegger was a natural *George* story, and the only reason we hadn't featured him on the cover before was because John hadn't previously felt comfortable asking.

"I hope we can still count on you for that cover," I heard Jeffrey say, and Arnold responded, "Of course."

Maybe I should have been irritated—talk about putting someone on the spot—but instead I was grateful. To help *George*, Jeffrey was doing his job, and that seemed to me more important than ever.

I heard the sound of singing and followed it into a small, sparsely decorated anteroom where the gospel choir from the church, a clean-cut, racially diverse group, stood in a circle. Holding hands with a singer on each side was Ted Kennedy, who was leading the group in an Irish ballad. I'd never heard it, but I got the feeling that if you were Irish, you'd have known it by heart.

When that song was done, the choir launched into a slow, mournful hymn. Teddy didn't seem to know this one, so, still holding hands and rocking back and forth a little bit, he listened and waited until they finished. By now, a crowd had gathered, watching as much as listening, knowing that this was a scene we would not forget.

"We can't end with a sad song," Teddy declared. He launched into another Irish sing-along—faster, cheerier. Teddy's voice was strong. It wasn't polished, and it certainly wasn't smooth like the voices of the singers around him. But it was resilient, the voice of a man who knew death, and so realized that the rest of us needed someone to offer hope.

Tears came to my eyes again, as I watched Senator Kennedy muster his strength to lift the spirits of others. This is courage, I thought. Ted Kennedy, standing in a circle of black and white, singing for his lost nephew, his brother's son.

•   •   •

A few minutes later, I noticed Caroline Kennedy standing alone. I approached her and reintroduced myself. "We've met before," I said. "A few years back."

"Yes. Of course," Caroline answered. Her voice was firm, but her eyes were weary.

"I just wanted to say—if there's anything we at *George* can do for you . . ."

"Yes," she said. "Thank you."

There was something definitive in the way she said it. There would never be anything we could do for her.

I nodded. "Just let us know," I said, and left her alone. A few minutes later, I left the convent to make my way home.

Sixteen

We decided to make our October issue a tribute to John. Putting it together wasn't easy. To accompany a photo essay on the people in politics John most admired, we combed through all of John's writing for excerpts. Some of it, such as John's introduction to his interview with the Dalai Lama, seemed eerily prescient.

"At the precise moment that our allotted time was up," John wrote, "we said our good-byes and then he hustled out the door and ducked under an umbrella to escape the late-monsoon rain that had just begun. I watched until the small entourage disappeared down the hill, and I smiled at the few aides who were still in the room. We were oddly deflated. It was as if we were all in a dark room and the man with the lantern had just left."

I scrapped the planned *Random Hearts* cover, of course, and we chose an iconic shot of an American flag instead. The picture had come from a photo shoot featuring movie star Bruce Willis, and John had always liked it. Some outsiders speculated that we would put John on the cover, but we would never have done that. John would have hated the idea. He *did* hate the idea. He used to joke that the issue he was on the cover of would be the last issue of *George*.

.   .   .

I wanted so much to hold the magazine together, but as the summer turned into fall, I realized that I could not. We were losing all the clout and access that John had provided, and there was nothing I could do to stop it.

For the past two years, a group of distinguished Americans had served as judges of the Newman's Own–*George* Awards, the prize Paul Newman and John had started to honor the most philanthropic corporations in America. The judges included Colin Powell, Maya Angelou, and Phillipe de Montebello, the director of the Metropolitan Museum of Art. Heavyweights. Because I hoped that the awards would continue, I sent letters to the judges asking if they would serve once more.

About a week later, someone from Phillipe de Montebello's office called me. A young woman, she sounded as if she were about twenty years old—an intern, perhaps.

"I'm afraid Mr. de Montebello won't be able to participate in your competition," she said.

"I'm sorry to hear that," I said cautiously. "Do you mind if I ask why?"

"Well," she replied, "he doesn't know what it is."

This was maybe six weeks after John died.

Then an editor from the *Times* called to say that they would not be running the Bowery Bar fashion shoot. "We feel it would be morbid now," he said.

"I wish you'd reconsider," I responded. "We're trying to let people know that this magazine is still alive."

"I'm sorry," he said.

. . .

In late September, Caroline Kennedy sold her 50 percent of *George* to Hachette, which announced that it would continue publishing the magazine. Jack Kliger suggested that John's death had given *George* such an unprecedented blast of publicity—we had sold an average of about 300,000 newsstand copies of the July, August, and September issues—that the magazine was more viable than while John was alive. I suspect, too, that he did not want to be known as the man who shuttered John's magazine just weeks after John died.

Part of me found the news of Caroline's decision very sad, but I couldn't blame her for selling. She had her own life to live, and John wouldn't have wanted his sister to spend it as the caretaker of her sibling's legacy. He was the last person to think that somebody should be forever burdened by a tragic past.

. . .

Now that Hachette had publicly committed to continuing publication, I told Jack Kliger that I would not be staying at *George*. I was the last of the original editors, and those familiar hallways had become haunted for me. Staying without John was inconceivable. Besides, if you care about something, sometimes the best you can do for it is to stand aside. For *George* to survive, it would have to change, maintaining its strengths while evolving into something new. Only an editor unburdened by the past could make such changes. I was not that editor; I *was* the past. I took it to bed with me at night and it weighed on my chest in the morning when I woke.

I had no choice, but I did have a responsibility. So I made Kliger a promise. I would work until he found a new editor-in-chief. And until he did, I would not inform the staff of my intentions. They needed to make their own decisions in their own time.

. . .

Efgenio Pinheiro returned to his homeland of Portugal. He took Friday with him.

. . .

Jack Kliger began interviewing prospective editors-in-chief, none of whom felt right to me. They were inside-the-Beltway types, the kind of people who looked down at *George* while John was alive but still managed to give him lots of free advice. The papers were filled with rumors of candidates such as Jonathan Alter, a television pundit who also wrote for *Newsweek,* and George Stephanopoulos.

So I nominated the political satirist Al Franken. He was smart, hilarious, knew everyone in politics, and could get on TV whenever he wanted. And, though not an editor, he had written a bestseller about Rush Limbaugh. Someone else could do the nuts-and-bolts editing work—not me, but someone like me. The idea was a little bizarre, but it might have worked. You weren't going to save *George* playing it safe. The press would say that hiring Franken was either a stroke of genius or a mark of insanity. Either way, they would write about him, chronicle his tenure like a soap opera, and that was all right, that was good. At least they'd be talking about the magazine. You know you're in trouble when they stop talking about you.

Besides, I thought, these hallways could use some laughter. People needed to start smiling again.

I had lunch with Franken at Remi, an Italian restaurant on 53rd Street, and he was intrigued. About a week later, he and Kliger met and talked about the job. But they could not agree on money.

As it turned out, Al Franken may have been the only person Jack Kliger interviewed who did not subsequently share that information with the press. Most of the others had no real interest in trying to fill John's shoes. But they did want it known that they had been considered for the vacancy.

. . .

The *Today* show wanted to interview me about the tribute issue. Hachette thought that was a good idea, and I did too. If we were going to put out a magazine, might as well get people to buy it. What good was a tribute if no one read it?

So I rose at 5:30 on the morning of September 21 and headed to NBC's studios in Rockefeller Center. I had the flu, and my head felt as if it were stuffed with insulation. In the dressing room, I started to sweat from fever, and the makeup woman had to keep refreshing my powder. I barely noticed a brief commotion: Amy Fisher, who had become famous for shooting her lover's wife, had arrived. Apparently she was demanding a separate dressing room.

A few minutes later I was sitting across from Matt Lauer trying not to be distracted by the tourists staring through the window, holding up their signs of greeting. I'd gotten better on television over the past years. But that morning, I was miserable.

. . .

Though none said so to my face, some of my colleagues thought that we shouldn't publicize the tribute issue, that it would be more powerful to simply let the magazine speak for itself. A conspiracy theory began to take root among a few of the more disgruntled: I was in league with Jack Kliger. I had gone on television because I was gunning for John's job and I wanted to promote myself.

I understood how pain could spawn such paranoia, but the

accusations hurt nonetheless. Still, I could not tell my coworkers that I had already resigned.

It was increasingly clear that with our center removed, things in the office were not holding. If the weeks after John's death had brought out the best in us, now the pendulum of emotion was swinging the other way. As we finished working on the November issue—the one with Arnold Schwarzenegger on the cover—people grew testy and started bickering. No one wanted to work. A screaming fight broke out between two staffers in the art department. Jealousies and rivalries long checked by John's presence were breaking out like a disease escaping quarantine.

Somehow we did finish work on that issue, and we did a good job. But rising to the occasion had exhausted everyone, and I wondered how long it would be before people started to break.

. . .

Late in the morning of November 29, Jack Kliger summoned me to his corner office on the forty-fifth floor. I sat down on his leather couch and stared out the wall-to-wall windows.

"I want you to meet the new editor of *George*," he said.

In walked a diminutive fifty-eight-year-old man with black hair and a bushy mustache. His name was Frank Lalli and he had once edited a magazine called *Money*. It helped people make money.

I stood up, we shook hands, I sat back down.

"I want you to know," Lalli said to me, "that when Jack called me to talk about editing *George*, I read some back issues. And I have to admit, it's much better than people say."

I thought, John is somewhere watching this and laughing.

"We like to think so," I said, and knew that it was time to go.

A few days later, I called an edit meeting in the conference room. I did my best to look interested while we kicked around some story ideas.

"There's something I need to say," I told the group after the idea discussion was over.

By the time I was finished, I was fighting back tears. These people had been like a family to me, and I still couldn't tell them the whole truth about why I was leaving. They needed to figure out their futures without advice from me.

A few of my colleagues were also crying. I would like to think that some of those tears were for me, but they weren't, not really. My departure was just one more loss.

· · ·

I had agreed to stay a few weeks to help with the transition, so officially my last day was January 1, 2000. By the close of business on December 22, however, I knew that it was pointless to return. My presence was making everyone feel awkward.

Knowing that, I had cleared my desk, emptied my file cabinets, and purged my computer. I had packed the things that mattered. The calendar that John had signed for me after my engagement. The fountain pen he'd given me at Christmas the year before. A few snapshots of the two of us. The small scrap of paper with the Phil Simms adage, *You may not win them over, but if you hang around long enough, you'll wear them out.* It was also possible, I knew, to hang around too long.

Almost everyone else had left by the time I had sent off a few last letters and returned some final phone calls. The sky had turned black and I could see the bright lights of Christmas shining from the streets below, the crowds pouring into Times Square for shopping, theater, and holiday festivities. I decided to take one last walk through the office.

I stopped in the art room and remembered John there, checking out the galleys taped to the walls, looking over that month's issue with pride in his eyes.

I gazed out the windows west across the Hudson, north to the George Washington Bridge, south toward the World Trade Center and the Statue of Liberty.

I walked through the hallways and thought of John striding through them, rollerblades tossed over his shoulders, keys dangling from a belt loop, Friday trotting along beside him.

I stood in front of John's office. I remembered him there, smiling and laughing, his father gazing out from one wall, his wife smiling down from another, his mother an invisible but constant presence.

I whispered good-bye and thank you. John was a big one for thank-you notes. Maybe one day, I thought, I'll try to write you a proper one.

Then I walked down the long white hallway with the big soda-pop orange *George* sign. I rode the elevator down forty-one floors and walked through the lobby, out the revolving doors, and back into the ordinary world.

EPILOGUE

One year later, in January 2001, Hachette closed *George*. The company had given it the old college try. But the editors who had worked with John had all departed, the new editorial was uninspired, ad sales had plummeted, and the subscribers who signed up after John's death were drifting away. You could not blame the company for its decision.

Hachette published a final issue, another tribute to John. They put his picture on the cover of this one. Much as it pained me to see it, I couldn't blame them for that either. They'd lost a lot of money on *George*, they had a right to earn some of it back.

I tried to think positively—not about *George's* demise, but about its tenure. There was much for all who had worked at the magazine to take pride in. Despite abundant skepticism, we had created the most widely read political magazine in the country. In a time of irony and cynicism, we had shown that there was still an audience of Americans who wanted to be optimistic about and involved with politics. We might even have persuaded a few people who didn't feel that way to change their minds. Though we had lost our leader, maybe we had planted a few seeds of idealism in young people who would one day become leaders themselves.

George's failure, after all, was not caused by an inadequacy of vision, but by chaos. The magazine that needed John to get its start could not survive his death. Not, at least, in physical form. But there had been an idea behind *George*—a belief that, as John had often said, "Politics is too important to be left to the politicians"—and that idea was stronger because *George* had existed.

· · ·

Grief takes time to fade, and some of it never does. But when any bit of it leaves, its departure liberates space in one's soul for brighter thoughts. Some time after his death, here are some thoughts I carry about John F. Kennedy, Jr.

He loved his wife, and he would have been a wonderful father.

He was not a perfect man, but he aimed to be a better one.

Even if he weren't famous, you would have liked to know him.

He was proof that you can be rich and famous and beautiful and still treat ordinary people as if the United States is a democracy rather than a oligarchy of wealth, power, and celebrity. John mattered not just because he was born a president's son, but because, though a retreat into isolation would have been understandable, he tried to lead a good and public life. Skeptical about the merit of his own wealth, power, and celebrity, he remained endlessly optimistic about America's ideals, government, and people. In a quiet and modest way, John F. Kennedy, Jr., reminded Americans of what is important in our country.

It's not a thought, however, but an image that sticks with me most, the image of John kayaking on the Hudson River. It is night, and he is surrounded by things he loved—the sparkling lights of Manhattan, the tugboats chugging along, a warm summer breeze, the soft splash of his paddle, and the gentle lapping of the waves. He is headed south, toward the Statue of Liberty, and then east, toward the Atlantic. He is on the water, and he is free.

AUTHOR'S NOTE

The writing of any book is a journey, and this one is no exception.

When I left *George*, I was physically and emotionally depleted. The idea of another magazine job felt anticlimactic, if not pointless. During the previous four years, I'd devoted myself to a publication whose mission I had passionately embraced, and I'd worked with one of the most fascinating people I would ever meet. I could not think of a job to compare with the one I had had to leave. Maybe I was just exhausted, but even the thought of looking for such a job felt somehow inappropriate.

So I did something wholly out of character—I flew to Australia and learned to scuba dive. Down under, trying to breathe while surrounded by the curious fish and shy sea turtles and jittery sharks of the Great Barrier Reef, I pondered my next move.

But instead of envisioning the future, I found myself thinking back to *George* and John. I kept remembering a letter that one teenage girl from Los Angeles had written to us after John's death. Her name was Tessa. "I am only 14 years old," she wrote, "but I will miss him more than words can express, and my heart goes out to anyone who got the pleasure of knowing him as a person and not only as the icon the rest of us were so used to."

She was right; John was more than an icon. He was a man—often misunderstood, usually underestimated—about whom much had been said. Complimentary though most of it was, it still felt oddly inadequate, almost trivializing, to me.

Sometime during that Australian journey, I decided to write this book. It was a personal decision, and maybe a selfish one. I wanted to try to remember John as clearly and vividly as I could, to preserve for myself a remarkable experience. I also wanted to try to show just how different a "public figure" can be from the people we read about in the papers.

Perhaps because that decision was so personal, it was inevitably misunderstood. Back in the States, several of my former colleagues reacted angrily to the news that I was writing a book. They lashed out, accusing me of greed, opportunism, and various other bad intentions. And since anything about John still made great copy, several reporters printed those charges. One day I walked out of my apartment and was chased by a tabloid camera crew. As I sprinted down my block I thought, Well, isn't this ironic?

In one way, the attacks on my character actually helped me. I understood that they flowed from the depth of feeling people had for John, and they reminded me of the responsibility I had taken on. Intentionally or not, the people who criticized this book before it was written only bolstered my conviction that John deserved serious consideration.

As it happened, a large percentage of the staff of *George* supported my decision, for which I'm grateful. I especially want to thank those who confirmed facts or shared reminiscences with me. *George*, after all, was a team effort. Everyone who worked there contributed to the magazine and had a unique relationship with John. I wrote from my experience because it would have been presumptuous to try to record that of others, and I am solely responsible for the perceptions offered here of both John and his magazine.

. . .

So many people helped in the writing of this book that I could not possibly thank them all, but I would be remiss if I did not mention some in particular. Art Alexakis, Bernard Bailyn, and John Tyler led by example. Joe Armstrong, Steven Gillon, and Ramsey Walker offered unflinching support. Neal Gabler talked through some of the ideas in this book with me, and his own writing provided some of its theoretical foundation. Kerry Lauerman helped me retain perspective on the foibles of journalism. I benefited immensely from the counsel of Andrew Auchincloss, Glenn Kurtz, and Robert Raskopf at the law firm of White & Case. Lauren Field was a close reader and Martha Sutro helped make sure that everything was factually correct; if there are mistakes in this book, I made them. Kate Macaluso stuck with me through my lowest moments. Cristina Roratto gave me inspiration. Townsend Davis and Lauren McCollester were loyal and wise friends—one couldn't ask for better. My family was supportive, patient, and understanding.

I learned during the writing of this book that the world of publishing can be as bizarre as the world of journalism. So I feel particularly grateful for having worked with a number of deeply talented professionals. I want to thank everyone at Henry Holt, and particularly Christine Ball, Elizabeth Shreve, George Hodgman, Jennifer Barth, and John Sterling. Their expertise has improved this book immeasurably, and their passion is inspiring.

I also appreciate the help of Jennifer Sherwood, Tracy Fisher, Eric Zohn, Andy McNicol, and everyone at the William Morris Agency. Above all, I want to thank my agent, Joni Evans. During the writing of this book, Joni was more than an agent. She was an editor, a friend, and a steady hand who kept me from going too far astray. I couldn't have done it without her.

Finally, I want to thank John Kennedy, who is always missed.

About the Author

RICHARD BLOW was editor of *Regardie's* magazine in Washington, D.C., from 1993 to 1995. He joined the staff of *George* several months before publication of its first issue and worked there until 2000. His work has appeared in the *New York Times*, the *Washington Post, George, The New Republic, Rolling Stone,* and *Mother Jones.* He lives in New York City.